TV CREAM'S ANATOMY OF CINEMA

TV CREAM'S
ANATOMY OF CINEMA

THE FILMS THAT CRITICISM FORGOT

Phil Norman

Chris Diamond

First published in Great Britain in 2007 by Friday Books
An imprint of The Friday Project Limited
83 Victoria Street, London SW1H 0HW

www.thefridayproject.co.uk
www.fridaybooks.co.uk

ISBN – 13 978-1-905548-46-0

British Library Cataloguing in Publication Data

A catalogue record for this book is available from the British Library

Cover design by Craig Ward
www.wordsarepictures.co.uk

Cover illustration by Matt Buck
www.mattbuck.com

Illustrations by Phil Norman

Internal design by Jason Taylor
www.liquorice-creative.co.uk

Printed by MPG Books Ltd

The Publisher's policy is to use paper manufactured from sustainable sources

For Suzy

CONTENTS LIST

ACKNOWLEDGEMENTS

Thanks and praise to the following, without whom this book would be gathering dust on the cutting room floor of life: Suzanne '*Wings of Desire*' Norman, TJ '*Mrs Brown, You've Got A Lovely Daughter*' Worthington, Ken '*Billion Dollar Brain*' Shinn, Graham '*Condorman*' Kibble-White, Jack '*Animal Crackers*' Kibble-White, Jon '*The Bad Seed*' Peake, Steve '*Billy Liar*' Berry, Jane '*Harlequin*' Redfern, Rose '*The Red Shoes*' Ruane, Peter and Judith '*Ten Tall Men*' Norman, Larry and Margaret '*Kelly's Heroes*' Diamond, Jean and Ian '*Carry On Abroad*' MacLeod, Emma '*Trading Places*' Diamond, Chris '*Galaxina*' McKeag, Peter '*Where's That Fire?*' Gordon and all at Kettering magazine. Plus apologies to the late Willie '*The Bed-Sitting Room*' Donaldson for shamelessly ripping him off for the Auteurs section.

INTRODUCTION

This book is brought to you by the letter 'b'. The world of film is rank-obsessed. Over a hundred years' worth of multifarious cinema is huffily sorted into two boxes: the good stuff, a handful of designated top-drawer classics whose status is beyond dispute, and the rest. The B-list. B-movies made with second-grade talent – fine for a wry glance now and again, but ultimately largely worthless. Curiosities, not classics. Best to leave them be.

In 1959, Warwick Films made *Idle on Parade*, a light-hearted film about the tribulations of a British rock star 'doing an Elvis' and joining the army. As was the style at the time, the film's cast toured the regions, attending various cinemas for the local premieres. Anthony Newley, fledgling actor and pop star, future King of Broadway and Mr Joan Collins, was the lead, bolstered by Bernard Bresslaw, yet to become a household name on the back of the *Carry On* films, and David Lodge, still at the start of a long film career. None of this meant anything, however, to the snotty manager of a cinema they wound up in one evening, who introduced them thus: 'Ladies and gentlemen, before the film starts we've got a few of the stars here tonight. You've probably never heard of 'em, but here's Anthony Newlyns, Bernard Braden, and Danny Hodges!'

Naturally, if that cinema manager were introducing, say, John Mills, James Mason and Ingrid Bergman, he'd have made damn sure he got their names right. That kind of boorish snobbery lives on, lazily dusting off a hand-me-down hymn sheet of acknowledged classic films and notable stars, blithely taking the wisdom of previous critical judgements as read. This is how *Citizen Kane*, a film that is impossible not to admire but incredibly hard to like, becomes not merely a technical *tour de force* from a young film pioneer, but definitively *the* best film that has ever been, or ever shall be, made. Anyone questioning this latter status is either stirring up trouble or being hopelessly naive. That's the way things are. Someone or other said so once, and who are we to argue?

Recently, the old school canon of classics – *Kane, Casablanca, High Noon, Psycho* – has been usurped by a brace of slightly newer films. Where Welles once reigned supreme, *Apocalypse Now* rules the roost, or sometimes it's *Goodfellas*, or *Pulp Fiction* – maybe even *Star Wars*. It's a breezier, more modern, definitely more laddish selection. The only problem is, it's just as predictable as the old canon, and even narrower in scope. If it has not got a gun or a spaceship in it, then it is not coming in. One dreary prescription has been swapped for another, and the inevitable Top 100 lists are once more set in stone. Not that there aren't plenty of reasons to celebrate all the above films, but they're dragged out so often that everything else is forgotten, which is a shame, as that abandoned box is where the really interesting stuff lies.

Why this is still happening is something of a mystery. At the same time that critical opinion shrinks the whole of filmdom down into an ever-decreasing nucleus of films it is OK to like, Cable TV, DVD reissues and all manner of legally dubious internet witchcraft

1

are combining to make the contents of that big old B-list box ever more readily accessible, and ripe for re-evaluation. Films are returning from obscurity with a vengeance. Where once the proposition 'The original *Casino Royale* is a load of old rubbish' could only be tested when the film made its way onto ITV on a wet Bank holiday afternoon, now, with the deployment of a few quid and a couple of clicks, anyone can judge that wayward film's various charms for themselves.

This book is just such a dip into that box of preterite productions. It is not an all-encompassing directory that reduces every film to two largely sniffy sentences for reasons of space and still manages to leave out the very one you were looking for; neither is it yet another list of 'The Greatest Films Ever Made I Think You'll Find, And No Returns'. Few of the films here would be considered classics in the conventional tightly scripted, passionately acted and slickly shot sense. A big old sprawling mess can be just as great as a disciplined slice of craftsmanship. Indeed, some of the films herein are – whisper it – not actually much cop at all. However, there will be a glimmer of something unique and fascinating in them, or a story behind them, that makes them as worthy of consideration as any auteured classic. This is not an ironic exercise in slumming among the funny little folk of trash cinema. This is genuinely worthwhile stuff.

Since there is so much of it, this is a cross-section at best, a toe in the water, a glimpse of the sort of mad and nourishing stuff that's been kept locked in the attic by opinion formers for so long, lest it run amok and embarrass polite society. Here you will find comedy, music, drama, gore, action, poetry, elegance, gaucheness, fine wit and crass stupidity (and that's just *Theatre of Blood*). From Hollywood to Cricklewood, New Zealand to Newton Abbot, here are films taken from beneath the critical radar and thrust into the limelight at last; stars that time forgot given a fitting remembrance. It may barely scratch the surface of the mass of film product that is increasing on a daily basis as yet another lost gem finds its way onto a shiny silver disc, but it's a start.

That cinema audience knew exactly who Tony Newley and Bernard Bresslaw were, and cheered them to the rafters. If there's a point to this book (and that's admittedly a big 'if'), it's to side with that audience, who know there's far more fun and variety to be had in the world of film than that dour kid in the sunglasses and the *Clockwork Orange* T shirt keeps telling them. It's for people who go to a cinema to look at the film, rather than over their shoulder to make sure the right people are sat behind them. People who are not at home with that most posturingly pointless of words, 'cult'. People, in short, who like films for what they are, not for what Brownie points they'll gain by standing next to them in a rather fetching hat. Folk who can tell a Bresslaw from a Braden when they see one. Let prattle commence.

TEN GREAT BRITISH SILENT FILM TITLES

The British silent film industry is one of the great unsung endeavours of international cinema. Everyone assumes Hollywood was first past the post, but from Yorkshire to Walton-On-Thames, plucky British pioneers were churning out silent innovations by the mile while Chaplin was still doing the music halls. Sadly, most of it, being printed on notoriously combustible old nitrate stock, has long since mouldered away to sludgy nothingness in sheds and attics across the land. What do survive are the titles, lovingly preserved in dog-eared catalogues and company records, and often these alone are enough to provide entertainment aplenty, evoking as they do a tantalising world of hijinks, drug abuse and, well, sausage. Here are ten of the most intriguing:

1. *The Flapper's Elopement* (Fitz Films, 1912)
2. *The Sanctimonious Spinsters' Society*
   (British and Colonial Kinematograph Company, 1913)
3. *Winky and the Gorgonzola Cheese* (Bamforth Films, 1914)
4. *Lieutenant Lilly and the Splodge of Opium* (Hepworth, 1913)
5. *Too Much Sausage* (Kineto Films, 1916)
6. *Scroggins Gets the Socialist Craze* (Cricks and Martin Films, 1911)
7. *The Runaway Knock and the Suffering Milkman* (Bamforth Films, 1898)
8. *Two Naughty Boys Upsetting the Spoons*
   (Williamson Kinematograph Company, 1898)
9. *Jack Spratt's Parrot Gets His Own Back* (Clarendon, 1916)
10. *Diddums and the Haddock* (Clarendon, 1911).

CARRY ON FILMS

The 'Carry Ons' have had a strange ride. In their time they have been seen as cheap programme fillers, successful comedies, reviled bastions of an age best forgotten, ironic slices of knowing camp, and properly reclaimed classics of British humour. Which is the true spirit of *Carry On*? Well, they all are, to varying extents, depending on which ingredients in the largely unchanged recipe were thrown into producer Peter Rogers' and director Gerald Thomas' great big melting pot.

The main ingredient is the *Carry On* gang itself. Although they arrived in dribs and drabs over the first few years, it was not long before the mainstays slipped into their archetypes like battered but comfortable old boots. Kenneth Williams began as a laidback, slightly supercilious know-all, but soon stepped up a gear as the full cinematic impact of the 'Nostrils of Indignation' became apparent. Sid James, once a straight actor of parts small and seedy, found the leading role hitherto denied him as the pork pie-sporting, catarrh-gargling letch with one eye on the 3.15 from Chepstow and the other on a freshly-soaped backside. Charles Hawtrey practically fell into his otherworldly dipsomaniac boy-scout character, while Joan Sims only needed a few films' worth of fine tuning to perfect her 'respectable' persona – with that rough-hewn Essex coarseness perennially showing through the thin veneer of airs.

It's very much a case of old friends dropping round for tea when *Behind* or *Doctor* crop up on a Sunday afternoon. It's an old joke that the films are rarely watched all the way through. This state of affairs is reinforced by assorted TV compilations chopping them up into bite-size bits of business on perpetual random shuffle – Jim Dale on a hospital trolley, Terry Scott drawing a willy in the sand, Babs wobbling up the hospital steps, 'Fakir! Off!', and on, and on, and on. At their best they are proper full-length entertainments and while you'll never be on the edge of your seat rooting for Bernard Bresslaw to nick that consignment of contraceptives from under Hattie Jacques' nose, you certainly can go the distance. And when you do go, always put plenty of paper down first.

CARRY ON SERGEANT (1958)
The first in the series is hardly recognisable as a harbinger of what was to come, being a rather cosy tale of a ramshackle platoon of National Service misfits setting out to make Sergeant William Hartnell proud of them, while romantic lead Bob Monkhouse pines for Shirley Eaton. It's jolly good though, and many characters are already taking shape: Kenny's arch, bookish intellectual, Hawtrey's frail 'elderly boy' no-hoper and Kenneth Connor's neurotic twitcher are all present and incorrect. There's even Hattie in putative Matron mode. All they needed to do was pick up the pace, phone Sid's agent, buy a rhyming slang dictionary and they were away.

CARRY ON FILMS

CARRY ON CABBY (1963)
Talbot Rothwell took over from Norman Hudis on scripting duties here, and would provide the bulk of the badinage for the next twelve years. Here he's just finding his feet, but there's something undeniably heartwarming about this tale of Sid's no-nonsense cab firm being usurped by his neglected wife's rival, all-girl 'Glamcabs' concern. Playing that vengeful spouse is the wonderful Hattie Jacques, who delivers what must be the most fully-rounded, sensitive character portrayal in a *Carry On* film (these things are relative, you understand). Spurned by a thoughtless Sid one minute, then in charge of a cab firm as sultry alter ego Miss Glam the next, she even has pangs of conscience about her revenge scheme. Conscience! In a *Carry On*! Give that woman a medal.

CARRY ON CLEO (1964)
A momentous point in the series' history, as not only do the team get something approaching a budget to work with, they also hit upon the film pastiche angle that would serve them so well for so long. Here Liz Taylor's Egyptian bore-in is dragged through the double entendre mill (as are some of its sets and costumes), and though the most famous line – Kenny's 'Infamy!' gag – was unashamedly nicked from an old Frank Muir and Denis Norden radio show, there's a hogload of fun to be had with Hawtrey's ditzy father-in-law to Ken's uppity Caesar, Jon Pertwee's oddball soothsayer and a fed-up Joan Sims stuffing her face with grapes as the boys counterplot endlessly on.

CARRY ON SCREAMING! (1966)
'Frying tonight!' The *Carry On* Rep company may have been firmly established by now, but here's proof a few substitutions needn't hurt the franchise. Kenny's old chum Fenella Fielding makes Joan Collins sound like Hylda Baker as the vampiric *femme fatale* in this spot-on Hammer pastiche, and Sid James' absence is barely registered when Harry H Corbett's there to deputise effortlessly as the bewildered Sergeant Bung. It's like he's been doing them all his life! As with *Cleo*, there's real attention to detail in the technical department too. Costumes, sets, lighting – someone's made an effort here, and it all adds to the glorious whole. On release, this film was augmented with a tie-in range of themed horror toys, an idea which sadly wasn't 'Carried On' with subsequent releases, thus denying the world's eBayers the opportunity of bidding silly money for a poseable Gladstone Screwer.

CARRY ON – DON'T LOSE YOUR HEAD (1966)
As the series grew in popularity, there came the first of two films with a detachable '*Carry On*' prefix with an opportunistic view to flogging overseas (it didn't sell, and neither did the limp *Follow that Camel* with Phil Silvers). This Scarlet Pimpernel romp is great value for Ken and Peter Butterworth as the bungling French duo of Citizens Camembert and Bidet, Sid's dual role as the periwigged Sir Rodney Ffing and the covert Black Fingernail, and perhaps best of all Charles Hawtrey's giggly, oblivious aristo, sauntering to the scaffold with all the light-headed abandon of a tipsy maiden aunt stumbling to the lav on Christmas afternoon. A true kinky runner, if ever there was one.

CARRY ON UP THE KHYBER (1968)

While lacking in some departments (Roy Castle was a wonderful bloke, but a convincing guardsman he was not) this solid tale of the last days of the Raj in deepest Wales... sorry, India, does boast Kenneth Williams' best performance as the imperious Khazi of Kalabar, forever undercutting his regal demeanour with that time-honoured trick of dropping out of character to deliver a choice line in his trademark nasal 'Snide' voice, which not only ends the film on that magnificent 'Oooh, I dunno, though!' but transforms the following timeless exchange with daughter Angela Douglas:
'They will die the death of a thousand cuts!'
'That's horrible!'
'Nonsense, child... the British are used to cuts!'

CARRY ON CAMPING (1969)

For better or worse, this entry, neither great nor especially terrible in the scheme of things, has come to define the 'essence' of *Carry On*. Well, one scene in particular. The average Briton will spend an estimated two and a half hours of their life watching clips of Kenneth Williams saying 'Matron, take them away!' Babs Windsor will spend approximately two and a half years of hers talking about it on chat shows. Who decides these things?

CARRY ON AT YOUR CONVENIENCE (1971)

That it took the team thirteen years to get round to setting a film in a toilet factory might be considered unconscionable dallying, but this fine entry, eschewing the threadbare period trappings for a firmly contemporary world of striking shop stewards, filthy front rooms, bookie's shops and spotted underpants, was worth the wait. While moustachioed socialist Kenneth Cope leads his brothers and sisters reluctantly to the picket lines (no prizes for guessing where the producers' political sympathies lay at the time) Sid and Hattie's loveless marriage is spiced up by a budgie that predicts race winners, Charles Hawtrey revolutionises the bidet ('Hot... cold... down the hole!') and the gang put aside industrial relations for a joyous works outing with Hawtrey, Williams, Sims *et al.* romping half-cut (probably literally, in a few cases) down the pier – a lovely sight to silence even the most hardened 'it's all just knockers and swanee whistles' critic.

CARRY ON ABROAD (1972)

This fun package holiday jaunt to the half-built Hotel Elsbels is many things, but mainly it's a wonderful showcase for the talents of the unsung star of the *Carry Ons*, Peter Butterworth. Habitually given the dim sidekick role while Kenny and Sid are upfront grabbing the glory, Pete transforms an underwritten part with a facial ballet of furrowed brows, quizzical grimaces and uncomprehending tics. Here he's perfect as the owner-cum-manager-cum-bellboy-cum-waiter of the ramshackle hotel, unknowingly insulting guests ('Ah, Mr Farkyharse!') going red in the face when the switchboard explodes and finally collapsing in despair as the building falls down around his ears. A *Carry On* without a Butterworth role is rather like a butter-less roll – dry, bland and somehow just not naughty enough.

CARRY ON FILMS

CARRY ON ENGLAND (1976)

Strange how the *Carry Ons* are so closely associated with the 1970s, as after 1972 there really was not much going on at all. Misfit addenda *Emmannuelle* and *Columbus* aside, this sorry saucing up of the original *Sergeant* is the death knell of the series. Pretty much everyone of note had legged it long before, and Butterworth notwithstanding, it's hopeless. Windsor Davies is just about stomachable, but Patrick Mower, with the best will in the world, can sod right off; and Peter Jones looks positively pained. So tatty is the whole affair you have to remind yourself it's supposed to be set during WWII. A profoundly unpleasant experience all round. Don't remember them this way.

PETER BUTTERWORTH

VIRTUOSO FIDDLER

The discovery of one's true calling in life often comes at the least expected times, but even allowing for that, a Dutch PoW camp in 1940 must rank among the least likely. That's how it happened for Fleet Air Arm lieutenant Butterworth, who became fast friends with co-captive Talbot Rothwell, future scriptwriter for the 'Carry On' films. Among the many heroic escape attempts –one of which was dramatised in *The Wooden Horse* (1950), for which Butterworth himself later auditioned and was rejected on the grounds that he did not convince as an escapee – were raucous concert parties in the camp, held mainly to detract from the noise of tunnelling beneath. As the war ended, Butterworth left the navy and pursued his new career with gusto.

Small parts in Val Guest's second Richmal Crompton adaptation *William at the Circus* (1948) and as a drunk in a post-war version of the inexplicably ever-popular *Jane* comic strip *The Adventures of Jane* (1949) led to a slightly meatier turn in another Guest production, *Murder at the Windmill* (1949), the first manifestation of the 'dogsbody' role he would later inhabit, as constable to Jon Pertwee's sergeant. Further lightweight guest action alternated with tiny parts in more serious fare such as Jules Dassin's masterful film noir *Night and the City* (1950) but the big time for Pete came via television as Terry-Thomas's car-less chauffeur in *How Do You View?* (1949) alongside wife Janet Brown, and then in children's programmes such as *Whirligig* and the temptingly titled *Butterworth Time*.

However, in cinema, the road to stardom was longer and harder. Roles in *Mr Drake's Duck* (1951), *The Gay Dog* (1954), *Fun at St Fanny's* (1956) and the like mingled with unnamed soldiers in tuppenny war films. A starring role finally came as a brass band conductor in early Children's Film Foundation production *Blow Your Own Trumpet* (1958), but otherwise his fledgling CV was still dominated by inspectors who turn up right at the end of murder mysteries and sundry parts with a number in their description.

Finally, in 1965, Butterworth reunited with Rothwell for the first time since *How Do You View?* for Rothwell's fifth *Carry On* entry, *Carry On Cowboy*. A new inductee to the gang along with Bernard Bresslaw, Butterworth went in with all guns blazing, employing all the means at his disposal to steal screen time from the manic giants around him, ranging from outright tumbling into a water trough to the famous 'Butterworth Fidget'.

The Fidget looks simple but, unlike *Carry On* semi-regular Jack Douglas's baffling epileptic turn, it's subtler than it seems. The celebrated scene in ...*Up the Khyber* (1968) where the oblivious Raj take dinner as cannon fire pounds their palace is topped off beautifully by the slowly-boiling pressure cooker of facial tics and ruddy-cheeked panic demonstrated by the one guest not possessed of a preternaturally stiff upper lip – Butterworth's cowardly, amoral Brother Belcher. It's a masterclass in close-up clowning that's repeated in all sixteen of Peter's entries in the series, and while it's not quite as iconic as the James Leer, the Windsor Giggle or the Williams Nostrils, it's just as sound a territorial marking in the fierce upstaging war that constitutes any good *Carry On*. Butterworth may only get a mention in dispatches as far as most critics are concerned, but if he was not there, you'd miss him.

The loyal Butterworth stayed with the franchise to the (very) bitter end, interspersing it with fun turns as an accident-prone wedding wrecker in silent comedy short *Ouch!* (1968), in the film of *Bless This House* (1972) as Sid James' rhubarb brandy-brewing chum, Richard Lester's great Sherwood-com *Robin and Marian* (1976) – though sadly not as Friar Tuck, a role he proved he was born to play in a *Carry On Christmas* TV special – and Lester's considerably less great adaptation of 'gay hotel' Broadway farce *The Ritz* (1976), in a rather... er, fetching pair of chaps. Butterworth signed off from the silver screen with a minor role in sturdy Sean Connery/Wayne Sleep caper film *The First Great Train Robbery* (1979), leaving behind one of the most distinctive character comedy careers of British cinema.

THE ESSENTIAL SILLY ADVENTURE FILM

FLASH GORDON (1980)

What's not to like about *Flash Gordon*? Never mind high-falutin' theories of film and cinema, of narrative thrust and story arc, of the essential cosmic qualities of timeless themes married to a modern medium. What matters here is big, silly, daft, adventurous fun, qualities the average filmgoer is rather more concerned with. Rockets! Hawkmen! Big jaggy collars! Velvet catsuits! Goodies who are all good! Baddies who are all bad! Sometimes cinema really can be this simple and still be as good as anything as portentous as the avant garde can churn out.

Who do we thank for this piece of knowing yet pleasingly non-ironic retro-kitsch? First of all, producer Dino de Laurentiis. The legendary Italian producer of such varied work as *Hurricane* (1979), *Mafioso* (1962), *Crazy Joe* (1974) on one hand, and *Conan the Barbarian* (1982), *Manhunter* (1985) and *U-571* (2000) on the other, de Laurentiis is a man for whom the word 'small' is not familiar. When Dino makes a film he makes it big. So when he chose to create a big screen feature version of the old comic book and Universal serial character he went straight for quality and landed Mike Hodges. Well, actually he didn't. Hodges, the director of seminal British gangster picture *Get Carter* (1971), is said to have been Dino's eighth choice as director, with one of his predecessors in the chair having been for a period laughing Nicolas Roeg. The thought of Roeg at the helm of a comic book adaptation is certainly a sobering thought. The preponderance of midgets in *Flash Gordon* may have something to do with a hangover from Roeg's initial input. Thankfully, none of them appear to have made it through space and time with red duffel coats on.

Dino pulled together an art department that managed to make buckets full of coloured water look eerily like an alien stratosphere, and costumes that perfectly captured the essence of the old black and white serial. This may have backfired on him however, as his next big sci-si venture was the stupendously inept *Dune* (1984) a film so shoddily produced, yet at the same time so clearly expensive, it beggars belief.

Hodges also turned up trumps. He described *Flash Gordon* as 'the only improvised $27 million movie ever made', but it was probably this laissez-faire attitude that contributed to the success of the venture. Certainly none of the leading actors are over-directed. Brian Blessed remains resolutely Brian Blessed all the way through, and reinforces his own legend as a man who could drown out the sound of a nuclear test should he ever stub his toe on a door. Topol as boffin Dr Zarkov is similarly over the top, though in his particular case calling him a ham is probably a little inappropriate. Melody Anderson and Sam J. Jones (who had his dialogue dubbed for him by someone who could inflect something akin to actual feeling in his voice) do what they are required to do, which is to drive the plot

10

forward, then get out of the way so the people we really want to see get on with it… and the people we really want to see are Max von Sydow and Peter Wyngarde.

Emperor Ming the Merciless and his odious masked sidekick Klytus are, regardless of whatever else may be going down plot-wise, what everyone wants to see. When they're not on screen, the audience waits patiently for the next moment they are, and they are rewarded for their patience by two great performances. Wyngarde has the harder job as he is behind a mask, but still manages to convey with his eyes and, especially, his extraordinary voice all of the evil, malice and perversion that is required of his excellent character. He purrs and burrs like a man who has spent five years at a How to Be George Sanders night class and passed at the top of his year, so malevolently silky is his delivery. When he comes out with threats in a straightforward way, such as condemning Prince Barin to death when he lands in the Hawkman Kingdom to set things right; he almost shrugs the lines off as they offer no chance to inflect some choice oily sarcasm into the lines. But when mask to face with Gordon in his cell, Wyngarde plays Klytus like a cosmic Abanazar: sarcastic, evil and funny in equal measure. It's only a shame he wasn't able to capitalise on it, since most people didn't realise it was him behind the tin.

If Wyngarde's the Prince of Darkness, the king of all he surveys is von Sydow as Ming the Merciless. Clearly modelled on Charles Middleton, the Ming of the original serials, von Sydow gives one of the greatest performances of any film. He inhabits the role of Ming so completely he probably did himself no favours for many years to come, since it became almost impossible to separate Ming from Max for long enough, if ever at all. Smirking, snarling, ironic, vindictive, sadistic, self-obsessed and supremely arrogant – even with a spaceship stuck in his back – von Sydow's portrayal of the ultimate intergalactic baddie is a triumph. His is the first voice heard in the film, in voiceover for the famous, 'Klytus, I'm bored...' introduction, setting hairs on the back of the head on end. When the list of great film villains is compiled, Max von Sydow's Ming the Merciless will be up there with the best of them. Don Corleone may have more credibility, but it didn't take a spaceship to bring him down.

The other best-loved element is the extraordinary score by *Queen*. It's a frightening thought that Hodges at one stage considered *Pink Floyd* for the gig. As it is, Brian May's titanic guitar lines and Freddie Mercury's properly hysterical vocals (the other two probably did something as well) provide a spine for the film as a whole; not just a tremendous theme but a superlative score altogether, with the incidental themes just as suited to the material as the more famous opening number.

Perhaps, as Hodges suggests, the film's success is something of a happy coincidence. He says a film shouldn't be over-directed, with the senior staff coming to a project with a fixed idea of how everything should turn out. If that's the case then who knows how *Flash Gordon* may have turned out under some other hand. Perhaps if Roeg had stayed the distance it would have been photographed a little better and acted a lot worse. Who can say? But as it is, the multifarious strands that either come together to make a great film, or unravel in a stringy mess to leave a disastrous shuddering lump of cinematic phlegm, happily converge to leave to posterity one of the bawdiest, most garish, silly and overwrought films ever made. Bless them all!

KENNETH GRIFFITH

NOT NICE ON PURPOSE

There can hardly be a character actor who played disagreeable parts as often as Kenneth Griffith. Lots of actors specialise in baddies (Julian Glover for example – nasty across both space and time) and some can't help but be cast as the evil villain, even when they're supposed to be playing it for laughs (please stand up, Donald Pleasence). Very rarely will actors allow themselves to play straight up and down horrid people. At least, not for very long. If a player's too closely connected with a certain type of role they inevitably come to be thought of as like that themselves. The cheerful thing about the proudly Welsh Griffith was if such a thing happened, he wouldn't have given a toss.

In Peter Sellers' comedy *Only Two Can Play* (1962) his role as the oily Jenkins, errant companion of Sellers' librarian character, is a little essay in how to make such a seemingly small part bristle with life. Perennially damp in the vertical water feature that passes for Welsh weather, Griffith uses his harsh and slightly sinister features to suggest snide outrage at almost everything that passes into his vision, and at the same time imbue them with a look of searing jealousy, most of it without a single word.

Other choice creeps include the odious Dai in *I'm All Right, Jack* (1959), helping to cause trouble for Terry-Thomas and the management at the Missiles factory from the safety of the shadow of Fred Griffith's overalls, and the less offensive but fantastically dim yokel Charlie (so named simply because Terry-Thomas, who plays his boss, liked the sound of himself shouting 'Charlie!') in first and best sequel to the original nightmarish girls' school chronicle *Blue Murder at St Trinian's* (1957). There was a severe choirmaster in *Tiger Bay* (1959) and a part in superior big screen version of gritty spy series *Callan* (1974). Before all of those was his portrayal of patron saint of bastards Adolf Hitler in *Two-Headed Spy* (1958). Though, just to be awkward he may well have picked that for the sympathy vote.

Griffith became ever more radical in his political views, and was soon causing a bit of trouble by voicing his support for a plethora of causes and making denouncements of a whole range of groups, though his consistent bugbear was British colonialism. Indeed, his support for the IRA gained him special membership of that rather energetic organisation (he couldn't be a full member as he wasn't Irish, apparently) and a documentary he made on the subject wasn't broadcast for nearly thirty years. The roles he started to take began to reflect this somewhat, including the part of Bishop Crick in *Who Dares Wins* (1982) and especially Witty the medical orderly who comes a cropper protecting President Limbani and his sidekicks in *The Wild Geese* (1978).

Along the way there was involvement in plenty of big screen forth too, including mediaeval charmer *The Lion In Winter* (1968), rubbish spy spoof *S*P*Y*S* (1974) and swinging spycom *The Assassination Bureau* (1969). Towards the end of his life, Griffith found himself embroiled in the sort of whimsy he probably hoped he had left behind in the 1950s. Small parts in *Four Weddings and A Funeral* (1994) and *The Englishman Who Went Up a Hill But Came Down a Mountain* (1995) were, unfortunately, all that were mentioned in his obituaries, as if he had never appeared in anything more substantial, or indeed spent years being vilified by the very press who were determined to castrate his legacy by attaching the dread label of 'harmless eccentric' to him.

His very last film role was fittingly set in Wales, and afforded him a last chance to be a bit objectionable. *Very Annie Mary* (2001) saw him play the part of an opinionated, bad tempered and foul-mouthed evangelical minister, which might well be seen as a metaphor for his whole character and career. On Griffith's death, little mention was made of his support of controversial groups, or of his documentary work on subjects such as Napoleon or his expert knowledge of the Boer War. Instead he was made out to be some old national institution, or even worse, national treasure. It has to be hoped that he was offered a knighthood or similar, if only for the looks on the official faces when he told them to shove their 'honour' up their collective Establishment arse.

CINEMATIC TOGAS

Why are films about the Romans so popular? Is it the sheer scale of the stories described in the Classics? The timelessness of their eternal themes? A cultural resonance that reverberates in the popular subconscious through language and custom? Men in skirts? Possibly it's all of these, but mostly it's the men in skirts or, more precisely, togas. Chaps draped in half a yard of bar towel with the stripe down the side have populated the screens of the West since films began. A version of *Julius Caesar* was made as far back as 1911, for example. But quite why the linen and legionnaires continue to endure so well is a bit of a mystery. However, just because the central theme or time-period is essentially the same, the genre is very much a mixed bag.

QUO VADIS (1951)

As befits an MGM production put together under the powerful hands of old school director Mervyn Leroy, this is a big film and arguably the most quintessential Roman epic ever made. As usual with these things the lead players, Robert Taylor and Deborah Kerr, are the least interesting persons on screen, dwarfed by the likes of Peter Ustinov as a demented Emperor Nero and Finlay Currie as Paul (who hadn't yet achieved the headline billing of Saint Paul). In turn, those great talents struggled to avoid being themselves dwarfed by the epic sets constructed to recreate a Rome that existed primarily in the minds of excitable production designers. The usual technical difficulties associated with large-scale film production took place, of course. Professional heavyweight boxer Buddy Baer, playing Ursus the particularly hefty convert to Christianity, was required at one stage to wrestle with a bull in the gladiatorial ring. Realising this might not be such a good idea safety wise, a heavily sedated cow with udders strategically hidden was drafted in to take the fall, despite the inevitable detrimental consequences to any aspirations to realism – a lesson the producers of *The Robe* (1953) would have done well to keep in mind when arranging for Victor Mature to tussle with giant cuddly lions. Sadly, the look of a pathetically mooing creature being set about by a veritable giant of a man merely made Baer look a right sod. Exit sympathy for the nascent Christian cause, enter much unwelcome hilarity. Elsewhere, Ustinov's performance as Nero really is astonishing and the Oscar nominatination that came from it was well deserved. All throughout it is easy to see in Pete's swivelling eyes and maniacal chanting that Mervyn Leroy's motivational description of Nero as 'A man who plays with himself nights' was never far from his mind. But others among the cast are worth looking at too, especially the great Felix Aylmer and the wonderfully stiff D.A. Clarke-Smith as toga-bound supporting players Plautius and Phaon. Long before their involvement here these two old pros, formerly great friends, had fallen out over a misunderstanding to do with Clarke-Smith's wife and Aylmer's cottage. Until they began to cooperate indirectly on set over *The Times* crossword, using Ustinov as a sort of peacekeeping lexicographical cipher, they hadn't spoken for years. Never were the intrigues and politicking of ancient Rome so faithfully recreated as in *Quo Vadis*.

A FUNNY THING HAPPENED ON THE WAY TO THE FORUM (1966)

Of a slightly different bent but still a genuinely massive picture, this adaptation of the smash hit musical farce is a truly epic endeavour. Under the art direction of Syd Cain and the photography of laughing Nicolas Roeg it looks far more like the old town probably did than in any other Romanesque romp. That is, it's manky. The cast list is no less impressive, including the immortal talents of Zero Mostel, Jack Gilford, Phil Silvers in his best ever big-screen role, Peter Butterworth, Jack May, Michael Crawford in full on Frank Spencer mode alas, Roy Kinnear, John Bluthal, Alfie Bass, John Pertwee, Ingrid Pitt and Henry Hall on the piano. Best in show is Michael Hordern as the incredibly tatty Senex, master to slave Zero and neighbour of procurer Silvers. Indeed, the whole magnificent if slight canon of Michael Hordern In A Toga ought to be a genre of its own. Henpecked, run down and as exhausted looking as the eternal city itself, Hordern is a joy to watch. His song and dance number with Zero and Silvers, *Everybody Ought To Have a Maid*, is the high point of the film. Whoever decided the English theatrical knight would work well with two American Jewish clowns deserves some sort of special recognition. That would be director Richard Lester, already notable for his nack for top-flight incongruous casting having previously employed Wilfred Bramble of *Steptoe and Son* television fame to be John Lennon's Grandad in *A Hard Day's Night*. He even has the audacity to feature a chariot race at the end that is much more fun than that other one in the less interesting *Ben-Hur* (1959)… and *Ben-Hur* doesn't have Buster Keaton in it, either, though it should have done.

THE FALL OF THE ROMAN EMPIRE (1964)

Remarkable for spending the greater part of its first hour or so in places other than Rome, and then not actually featuring its Fall when it finally does lead us there, this is better known nowadays as, 'that film with the same plot as *Gladiator* (2000) but without the tigers'. Alec Guinness is Emperor Marcus Aurelius in this one, mithering over his learning difficulty-imbued son Commodus (Christopher Plummer) taking over the old firm when the old lad shoves off to the Hades Riviera. What he really wants is for upright but crashingly dull soldier Livius (Stephen Boyd) to run things instead. What Marcus fears is that Commodus will go off the deep end once in charge and bring about the, well, Fall of the Roman Empire. The empire does indeed fall to bits once Commodus gets his mits on it. Or at least the audience are told that's what happens by a voiceover. Even after more than three hours into the 'action' Commodus does finally make an exit, but the empire seems to be bumping along just fine. Plummer wears a purple toga to let us know he's the boss, but there's not much else on show other than the admirable sets. Unfortunately, Sophia Loren gets in the way of them a good deal. Even usually dependable supporting players such as Omar Sharif and James Mason can't detract from the feeling the whole exercise is a race to see whether it will be either Rome or the audience which falls into disrepair by the closing credits. Matters are not helped by the bizarre casting of English stuffed bodkin Anthony Quayle as a supposedly hard-bitten and gnarled soldier, rather akin to casting Russ Abbott as Batman's dad. Once described by John Gielguid as having a face 'like two tins of condemned veal', Quayle does not convince, though throughout the marathon escapade he does at least have the decency to look bored.

UP POMPEII (1971)

The triumph of both the telly series and its spin-off can probably be traced to the massive success of A Funny Thing...(see above) which apparently generated a searing and lasting desire in the breasts of the audience for funny togas as opposed to protracted and pointless ones. The British run of A Funny Thing... starred Frankie Howerd as slave Pseudolus at the Strand Theatre (as well as Crazy Gang members Charlie Naughton and Monsewer Eddie Gray). Francis recreates his similar televison role of Lurcio the slave here to similarly brilliant effect making him probably the most successful actor to have ever pulled on the toga. Michael Hordern puts in another of his majestic turns as Lurcio's master Ludicrus Sextus, shambling about the place with all the dignity he can muster, which isn't much. Also of note is the great Bill Fraser as Prosperus Maximus, villain of the piece, grumbling, muttering, threatening and cajoling all and sundry in the sinister breathy-but-funny way that only he was able to master. The ladies make most of the running plot-wise (plot?) with former Miss Norway Julie Ege as Voluptua, Barbara Murray as Ludicrus' wife Ammonia and Madeline Smith as their daughter Erotica, between them constituting the Lays of Ancient Rome. Gloriously silly, the whole is really a vehicle for Howerd. It's often said to fail because Francis is unable to carry the whole thing on his own for the length of a feature – well, that's just cobblers. Some of writer Talbot Rothwell's gags for this are as good as any he ever conjured up for his Carry On... stamping ground. When constipated by the regular rota of Roman rumination on film, take a dose of the pomp of Up Pompeii and relax.

SPARTACUS (1960)

Peter Ustinov once testified that the making of Spartacus took so long that although his daughter Andrea had only just been born at the outset of filming, by the time the film was completed she was responding to queries at school as to what her father's job was with the answer, 'Spartacus'. When one considers that the eventual director was none other than goggle-eyed Stan Kubrick, never to garner for himself the nickname 'One Take Stan', this seems less than surprising. The first director was Anthony Mann, soon to take his revenge for being bumped from this epic by being responsible for the age-spanning The Fall Of The Roman Empire. To be fair to Kubrick, he did have to contend with some of the most monstrous egos ever to have occupied the planet, some of them, like Charles Laughton's, visible from space. Laurence Olivier did his bit on the self-obsession front too, and doubtless Tony Curtis would have been attempting to claim his place amongst the big apes as well. The biggest ape of them all was principal star Kirk Douglas, magnificent as the title character, though Laughton, managing to be petulant, oily and sympathetic with the same character and often all at the same time, is also superb. One of the more entertaining of the woolly blanket genre, this is notable for the excellent cast, workable story and last gasp of Kubrick as a watchable director, before he got too involved with monkeys eating their dinner.

BRITISH HORROR GIMMICKS

The drive-ins of 1950s and 1960s America were riddled with publicity-drumming novelties, from 'Hypnovision' to flying plastic skeletons to life insurance forms for the easily scared-to-death. The more staid British fright-mongers had no truck with such tawdry trappings, of course. Well, up to a point…

GHOULISH GIVEAWAYS

It's a rule as old as the sprocket hole: if in doubt, punt free crap out. Perhaps surprisingly, Hammer, the more 'respectable' horror house, were the culprits here. A double bill of *Rasputin: the Mad Monk* and *Plague of the Zombies* (both 1966) was augmented with stick-on beards and 'zombie eyes'. Boxes of 'vampire dust' (i.e. loose glitter) accompanied kung-fu romp *Legend of the 7 Golden Vampires* (1974). 'Danger of reincarnation if contents are recombined!' warned the box, thrillingly, alongside the more prosaic 'Not to be taken internally'. Perhaps best of all, audiences for the grisly *Demons of the Mind* (1972) were thoughtfully provided with specially made 'stomach distress bags'.

3D REDUX

Those old red and green sweet wrappers were so 1956, so when Milton Subotsky decided to take Amicus' Jekyll and Hyde project *I, Monster* (1971) into the third dimension, he opted for a stereoscopic method purloined from the pages of *New Scientist* which didn't quite work and unfortunately relied upon everything in frame to be constantly moving to maintain the illusion of depth. Cue more queasy camera pans than a 1990s bank ad and one very annoyed director. The plan was scrapped before the premiere, to the relief of young retinas nationwide.

THE WEREWOLF BREAK

Amicus' supremely jerrybuilt blaxploitation horror *The Beast Must Die* (1974) had one thing going for it in this heavily-signposted pre-denouement interval, in which the action (such as it was - the mansion-bound lycanthropic whodunit was never going to leave anyone breathless in the upper circle) stopped, and the sepulchral tones of Valentine Dyall demanded the audience pause to decide for themselves which of the motley cast really was the titular beast. Or nip smartly to the lav; it's a free country.

MADELINE SMITH

MORE THAN MEETS THE EYE

If you're planning on being a British screen siren of the 1970s, spending the mid-1960s working as a shop girl in Biba is very possibly the ideal place to start. According to legend, Madeline Smith was plucked from the modish Kensington boutique by star-spotters unnamed, for a career in late-1960s films such as the Italian generation gap sexcom *Escalation* (1968) and the thoroughly British mess *The Mini-Affair* (1967), as one of a troupe of deranged groupies kidnapping pop stars and politicians with matrimonial intent.

A brush with one-man raunchy film industry Donovan Winter for the 1969 *Alfie* clone *Come Back Peter* was a signal of things to come, though she managed to retain all her clothes for her role. A dire remake of *What's New, Pussycat?* (1965) – called, imaginatively, *Pussycat, Pussycat, I Love You* (1970) – saw Maddy bear witness to the madness that says Ian McShane can do comedy.

After you've experienced that horror, you're well prepared for the Hammer variety, and Maddy went hotfoot to the House of Carreras for a small role in *Taste the Blood of Dracula*, and a rather larger one in *The Vampire Lovers* (1970). The latter, with Maddy falling under the spell of Ingrid Pitt's bisexual vampire Carmilla, gave the ailing Hammer a temporary boost, and her career a longer-lasting one, even if typecasting seemed to be tagging doggedly along with it.

Sure enough, disrobing started to become a feature. *Up Pompeii* films, *Carry Ons*, yet more lusty horrors – sauce with everything. So ingrained did this become that one review of Lionel Jeffries' delightful children's ghost story *The Amazing Mr Blunden* (1972), observed she 'for once is cast not for her breasts', a lazy slur which said less about Maddy (then completing an English degree at Goldsmith's College) than it did about attitudes in the film industry.

Some choice roles were there among *Percy's Progress* and *Anyone for Sex?* But still, whether fluttering eyelashes as a doe-eyed seductress in *Theatre of Blood* (1973), or having Roger Moore unzip you with a magnetised watch in *Live and Let Die* (1973), there was still a sense of déjà vu. Despite being bigger than ever before, Smith moved more into television work, before retiring to start a family in 1984.

Though she has no regrets about her film career, it's still a mighty shame she wasn't granted a full walk of the counter with the roles she was offered. Proof of her undoubted talent and versatility can be found in something she did shortly before retiring: BBC children's programme *Eureka!* in which she plays a member of a wisecracking fictional repertory company, who take it upon themselves to act out the history of great inventions, taking multiple parts and generally throwing gags about with joyous abandon. Sounds a bit juvenile, but there's a comic vitality and subtlety there to leave the likes of Roger Moore, to say nothing of Ian McShane, standing.

PORTMANTEAU HORROR

The portmanteau, or anthology film – a feature-length flick comprising three or more self-contained stories, linked together by fair means or foul – is a much underrated form. It's been practised in just about any genre you care to mention: drama (*Trio, Train of Events*), comedy (*The Magnificent Seven Deadly Sins*), sex comedy (*Everything You Always Wanted to Know About Sex*), sci-fi (*The Illustrated Man*), fantasy (*The Wonderful World of the Brothers Grimm*), even opera (*Aria*). Perhaps because the the short story is the superior form of the genre, horror has benefited more then any from the portmanteau's grab-bag charms.

Perhaps it's the thrill of the best of them containing finely-honed little gems of stories, with none of the flabby filler of their feature length counterparts. Maybe it's the 'keeping score' element that tides the viewer over even when the entertainment is several notches below top – 'Oh, that one didn't quite work... ah, that one was a bit better'. Or maybe it's the joy at the many contrived ways the makers try and weave the different strands together, linking narration or framing story. Whatever the reason, there's nothing in any other film genre that is quite like a good horror anthology, and, perhaps thankfully, nothing quite like a bad one.

DOCTOR TERROR'S HOUSE OF HORRORS/FLESH AND FANTASY (1943)

The horror anthology is almost as old as cinema itself, originating in Germany with silent expressionist fare such as *Tales of Terror* (1919) (paintings in old curiosity shop come to life and narrate their stories) and *Waxworks* (1924) (poet concocts tales about exhibits in the titular museum). However, the genre was pioneered in English with the American offerings in the title. The first is really a cheat, being an opportunistic (and legally dodgy) compilation of heavily abridged versions of half a dozen 1930s horror classics including *White Zombie* (1932), introduced by the titular Doctor in the portentously fruity tones that would serve this genre well. The Universal Studios hit *Flesh and Fantasy*, meanwhile, weaves three original tales of clairvoyance around Robert Benchley's preoccupation with prognostication, wherein Edward G. Robinson talks to his own reflection, and trapeze artist Charles Boyer gets spooked by Barbara Stanwyck.

DEAD OF NIGHT (1945)

Ealing Studios assembled four of their finest directors to film five tales of supernatural creepiness, and in the process created what remains the finest horror portmanteau of them all. Architect Mervyn Johns, haunted by a recurring nightmare, visits a country house, the inhabitants of which regale him with stories of their own nightmarish experiences: a premonition of death, a child from the past, a possessed mirror and a ventriloquist (Michael Redgrave) possessed by the malevolent spirit of his dummy. Sounds like a lot of supernatural baloney, but the execution is flawless, and even after sixty-plus years this film retains the power to frighten. The various directors work wonders; that old dark house is a den of claustrophobia, and a simple slow track into a closed hospital ward curtain is imbued with unnameable dread. So effortlessly brilliant was this film, it unwittingly laid down several ground rules most subsequent horror anthologies have followed (or tried to) ever since. There's the excellent linking narration, which not only provides a segue from one story to another, but allows various characters featured in the stories to talk to each other, even quibble over the likelihood of the tales, and gives a shape to the episodic structure by building to a brilliantly gothic climax in itself ('Oh doctor, why did you have to break your glasses?'). Second, it injects some pace into the rigid framework, starting off with a five-minute palate-cleanser featuring an ominous hearse driver ('Room for one more inside, sir!') and building up to the longer Michael Redgrave segment at the end. Sadly, it also introduced the concept of the mid-film 'comic relief' story, with a pair of Charters and Caldicott-like golfing duffers getting mixed up with wagers, hauntings and supernatural hand gestures. It's not a bad story really and effectively lightens the mood before that ventriloquist's dummy brings it crashing down again – but it set a dangerous precedent.

THREE CASES OF MURDER (1955)
This accomplished Wessex Film Productions trilogy comes close to *Dead of Night* in terms of multipart brilliance. The stories are linked, excitingly, by Eamonn Andrews as himself. (In a similar celeb-narrated vein, see also Danziger Productions' 1954 effort *Gilbert Harding Speaking of Murder*.) The final segment stars Orson Welles, having a whale of a time as a blustering politician tormented by a wily Welsh rival who enters his dreams. The best segment, though, is the first, in which Alan Badel walks into a painting and gets up to various nightmarish antics in a German Expressionist-type house. Doesn't sound like much, but the atmosphere of lingering unease is right up there with *Dead of Night*'s dummy segment.

TALES OF TERROR (1962)
A three-piece portmanteau woven from Edgar Allen Poe stories by Roger Corman, and decorously worn by Vincent Price, who in the first fights with Maggie Pierce over his wife's demise, then gets bricked in by a wine-bibbing Peter Lorre, and finally hypnotises Basil Rathbone to cheat death. Oddly enough, the middle comedy segment is the most fun, thus reversing the *Dead of Night* Rule.

TWICE-TOLD TALES (1963)
Vinny returns under new management for a trio of chillers inspired by Nathaniel 'The Scarlet Letter' Hawthorne, involving crushed bodies under slabs, a daughter with a weird blood disease that makes everything she touches give off purple smoke and die, and a really rather good proto-*Poltergeist* imploding model house. Best of all, each story is introduced by a big, illuminated ancient book, the pages of which are turned by a skeleton!

TV CREAM'S ANATOMY OF CINEMA

DOCTOR TERROR'S HOUSE OF HORRORS (1965)

Things really took off here, as Milton Subotsky and Max J. Rosenberg, trading under the name of Amicus Productions, moved away from pop 'n' roll showcases like *It's Trad, Dad* into the Hammer-baiting realms of multistory horror. This film is an exemplar of the transitional period between the old Gothic school of Hammer (vampires, castles and dry ice) and the more gory and raunchy contemporary 1970s style (whisky tumblers, cravats and breasts). In the linking scenes Peter Cushing, as the sinister doctor with the tarot cards, mugs conspiratorially to camera as his foolish train-bound companions dismiss his prognosticatory powers. Taking a lead from Vincent and pals, the stories eschew *Dead of Night's* subtlety for all-out Grand Guignol: Donald Sutherland suspects his wife of nocturnal bloodsucking; critic Christopher Lee is terrorised by the severed hand of a slagged-off artist; Roy Castle steals voodoo jazz riffs with disastrous results, and a Brylcreemed Alan 'Fluff' Freeman defeats a strangling vine with the smoke from the pipe his friend lights in order to ponder over the solution. A precendent is thus established.

DR TERROR'S GALLERY OF HORRORS (1966)

Nothing to do with the previous title, this is nothing but a rotten American assemblage of tenth-rate corn (most of which, such as the story of a supposedly cursed clock in the basement of a New England mansion, doesn't even make sense) joined up with a slumming John Carradine, and featuring an end-of-the-line Lon Chaney Junior as a cut-price Frankenstein.

TORTURE GARDEN (1967)

A poor second bite of the portmanteau cherry for Amicus, with Burgess Meredith as Dr Diabolo, a carnival showman with a rather easily guessed secret, introduces tales varying from a rather good story of obsessive Edgar Allen Poe collectors Peter Cushing and Jack Palance, to a belief-beggaring ineterlude featuring a mobile, murderous piano called Euterpe.

THE HOUSE THAT DRIPPED BLOOD (1970)

Amicus commenced their anthological heyday with this four-piece affair in which over half the male cast wear cravats. The first story is the most effective, with Denholm Elliot stalked by his own literary creation – it genuinely makes you want to board up all your windows. Jon Pertwee hams things up tremendously in the final segment as a horror actor with a magic cloak (a vampiric Ingrid Pitt flapping up to Pertwee instead of using the stairs is unforgettable). In between, Christopher Lee fumbles with a witchy daughter in a well-shot tale, but Peter Cushing, alas, is frittered away in a rather dull waxworks affair that is most notable for its fish-eye dream sequences.

TALES FROM THE CRYPT (1972)

Lurid EC Comics stories are the source material here. A cowled Ralph Richardson predicts the grisly demises of five visitors to his crypt. Joan Collins does her husband in under the mistletoe and is set upon by a maniacal Santa for her sins. Ian Hendry fails to notice his death from a car crash. A nasty property developer hounds widower Peter Cushing to the grave, and beyond. Richard 'Robin Hood' Greene revisits the old Monkey's Paw chestnut. Finally, the sadistic owner of a home for the blind sees his oppressed charges turn the tables via a razor blade-lined tunnel. Hammer veteran Freddie Francis calls the shots magnificently as the Amicus portmanteau charabanc finally hits full speed.

ASYLUM (1972)

Robert Powell is a trainee doctor at the titular establishment, asked by Patrick Magee to interview four patients in order to determine which is in fact the now-doolally former head doctor. From the opening scene of Powell getting out of a sports car to unfeasibly dramatic music, you know you're onto a winner, and so it proves, through the various tales with which the patients regale Powell. Richard Todd has an affair, and is terrorised by frozen chunks of his freshly-butchered voodoo-loving wife Sylvia Syms in the atmospheric 'Frozen Fear' (The menacing hum of the deep freeze! Sylvia's head breathing through the brown paper! The comedy kettle drum accompaniment to the waddling torso!). Then, in a rather old-fashioned piece, Barry Morse runs up a suspicious suit for Peter Cushing, both players overacting each other off the screen beautifully. Charlotte Rampling and Britt Ekland go head to head in yet another take on the old 'evil double – or is it?' chestnut (the obligatory rubbish segment), and finally Herbert Lom manufatures violent little toy robots with miniature human heads on top. In all segments the protagonists' actions pay not even lip-service to realism or logic, which is as it should be. Finally, Geoffrey Bayldon's demented giggling is worth umpteen Oscars.

VAULT OF HORROR (1973)

Bill Gaines, the EC Comics head honcho, hated this second Amicus version of his properties so much he huffily stomped off with the rights to any further productions, thus denying audiences the prospect of such tantalising Subotskiana as *More Tales From the Crypt, Haunt of Fear* and the 3-D *Tales of the Incredible*. But is it so bad? Well, the gambit of having five tales instead of the usual four is spreading the chills a little thin. For example, Michael Craig's tale wherein he fakes his own death, only to fall foul of gravedigger Arthur Mullard and cameoing medical students Robin '*Doctor*' Nedwell and Geoffrey '*Doctor*' Davies falls a bit flat, and the one where Curt Jurgens gets his via a load of old rope is money for precisely that. But three out of five is pretty good going. The marvellously titled vampiric 'Midnight Mess' sees Daniel Massey admitting that he's never been to a Horrific Harvester before, and impersonating a Grand Guignol version of a Stowell's of Chelsea wine box for his trouble. Then klutzy Glynis Johns reaches the end of her tether with fastidious Terry-Thomas, and sends him the way of a Hayward's pickled onion. Best of all is 'Drawn and Quartered', with Tom Baker in Bohemian beard and corduroy suit, getting his revenge on the art world (in the shape of Denholm Elliot and Terence Alexander) via a bit of voodoo painting hocus-pocus, until vanity and a clumsy decorator lead to his inevitable downfall. Granted, the bracketing story and its final revelation (a clumsy mixture of the punchlines from *Dead of Night* and *Doctor Terror...*) is no great shakes, but still, not bad going.

TV CREAM'S ANATOMY OF CINEMA

FROM BEYOND THE GRAVE (1973)
Dumped by EC, Amicus bought up the stories of esteemed horror scribe Ronald Chetwynd-Hayes, and created their masterpiece. Everything here is done right. Peter Cushing, as the sinister owner of the Temptations antique shop who sells the various cursed items that fuel the tales, has never been better, and the stories are all tip-top. David Warner buys a mirror which turns him into a serial killer, wronged ex-seviceman (sic) Donald Pleasence and daughter Angela team up to knock off children's parents (including Diana Dors), suburbanites Ian Carmichael and Nyree Dawn Porter are plagued by a shoulder-squatting demon from an old snuff box and Ian Ogilvy buys an old door which leads to a Regency sorceror in an eerie blue room. It's also the only film outside *Dead of Night* to make the comedy story (the snuff box) work on its own demented terms. Any derivative elements are more than compensated for by gorgeous atmospherics (Warner's seance and that blue room) and top-notch performances (a possessed Porter breaking the house up and the uber-sinister Pleasences). Sadly, this was more or less it from Amicus on the anthology front, as they moved director Kevin Connor onto *The Land That Time Forgot* (1975) and its moneyspinning sequels.

TALES THAT WITNESS MADNESS (1973)
Hammer veteran Freddie Francis oversaw the death throes of the British portmanteau's glory days with this frightfully silly effort for World Film Services, written by Donald Sutherland's vampiric wife from *Doctor Terror...*, no less! Donald Pleasence introduces Jack Hawkins to a series of loonies, who spin tales of an imaginary tiger, a haunted, time-travelling penny-farthing, and the notorious story wherein Michael Jayston dumps Joan Collins for a walking tree.

TRILOGY OF TERROR (1975)
This American TV movie consists of three stories all starring the great Karen Black in various guises. The first two tales are of the quality of a particularly weak *Tales of the Unexpected* entry, but the last segment, with a tiny, possessed African doll chasing Black around the house (and making bizarre Tasmanian Devil noises), seared itself into a thousand late-night telly memories. A belated sequel, *Trilogy of Terror II* (1996), followed, based this time around the talents of Lysette Anthony.

DEAD OF NIGHT (1977)
They like to recycle those titles, don't they? Nothing to do with the Ealing work, this threesome from the *Trilogy of Terror* pairing of director Dan Curtis and writer Richard 'Omega Man' Matheson is fairly solid stuff, with doctor Patrick Macnee up against vampires, and Ed Begley Junior buying a time-travelling car.

THE MONSTER CLUB (1980)
Subotsky wound up Amicus, completing its last unfinished film under the aegis of his newly-formed Sword and Sorcery Productions. Fittingly, it starred Vincent Price as the proprietor of the eponymous nightclub, giving horror writer R Chetwynd-Hayes (John

PORTMANTEAU HORROR

Carradine) a potted lesson in monster genealogy with three tales – two rather good (with lonely, even sympathetic monsters) and one immensely silly (Donald Pleasence, a vampire and a 'stake-proof vest') – punctuated by musical interludes from *The Pretty Things* and *B.A. Robertson*. This is possibly the only horror film with a reggae theme tune.

SCREAMTIME (1982)

Here the British portmanteau came to die… Sexploitation kingpin Stanley A Long tied up three supporting features penned by Michael *'Eskimo Nell'* Armstrong with a perfunctory linking device involving a bunch of Americans renting some 'British' horror videos and… er, watching them. First, a Punch and Judy man takes revenge on his puppetphobic family (including stepson Jonathan *'Bread'* Morris) by enacting the seaside entertainment for real. Then a young woman is haunted by housebound hallucinations with a rather effective supernatural twist. Finally, Dollar's David van Day has his petty cash thieving exploits undone by some possessed garden gnomes. An ignominious end. Rest in pieces.

NIGHT TRAIN TO TERROR (1985)

With British horror down and out, the Americans somehow kept going, producing average stuff such as *Cat's Eye* (1985) and the EC Comics-inspired *Creepshow* (1982). This entry, however, is indicative of the sorry state of disrepair things had fallen into. It goes back to those cobbled-together origins, in that it's little more than an excuse to release various remnants of aborted or left-on-the-shelf projects (including a story about a secret society who willingly wire themselves up to a killer computer) linked by a white-suited God and Brylcreemed Satan discussing various soul-selling cases in a train carriage as a *Kids From Fame*-style rock band rehearse in the next compartment.

THE ESSENTIAL URBAN HORROR

DEATH LINE (1972)

If you're going to make a horror film in a city, London's the city to pick. Lovingly sculpted by a generation of congenitally morbid Victorians into a maze of Gothically pointy spires and dark alleys, augmented in more recent times by forbidding concrete castles which terrify in an entirely different way, it's a ready-made film set no Hollywood designer could possibly beat. You don't have to go back to the nineteenth century world of pea-soupers and sinister tailcoated predators. That Victorian unease is there in the present, just under your feet, as *Death Line* amply demonstrates.

The premise: Russell Square tube station is playing host to a series of gruesome murders (including a show-stopping spade-through-head) uncovered by a token boring young couple (the man played with rainforest-strength woodenness by David Ladd, son of cowboy short-arse Alan and, more pertinently, brother of the film's producer Alan Junior) when they find respectable civil servant James Cossins face down on the stairs. This same station was the scene of a disaster in Victorian times, when the roof collapsed on a group of tunnel workers, trapping them underground. Could these two tragedies be linked? Well, it wouldn't be much of a film if they weren't, and fortunately they are – in a marvellously inventive way.

In a ten-minute tracking shot that would be called 'bravura' if it turned up in a big, grown-up arthouse flick, the source of the mayhem is revealed. To nothing more than a constant dripping noise, some ghostly echoes of the trapped workers and the odd sinister oboe stab, the wretched nest-cum-larder of the last two survivors of the tube disaster is slowly revealed as they huddle together among the corpses of their prey for inarticulate comfort. It's an eerie, gruesome, funny (the only dialogue is a repeatedly mumbled 'mind the doors') and ultimately, as 'The Man' tearfully realises his partner in entombment is dying, oddly touching scene.

In stark contrast to this silent catacomb is the office of the main detective on the case, Inspector Calhoun, played to the hilt by Donald Pleasence. Verbose, sarcastic and sporting a nasal sneer that would make Ken Livingstone's resemble Brian Blessed, Pleasence hits the ground running with a load of unimpressed backchat aimed at David Ladd, punctuated by the odd joyless wisecrack, grumpy old man-ism ('Get yer hair cut!') and howl against the minor irritations of modern coppering – paperwork and teabags, mostly. ('Teabags? And I've been blaming the Indians!') So intensive is all this, Pleasence comes over at first like some forgotten music hall turn finally given his star vehicle and furiously making up for verbal lost time.

But there's more to it than that, and as the bodies mount up along with pressure from

26

a supercilious MI5 man (Christopher Lee, turning in a fine day's work with a brief cameo played entirely down the nose), Calhoun looks less like a bluff cartoon know-all and more like an increasingly knackered copper desperately trying to get the job done. A fantastic scene in which Pleasence, along with his dogged sergeant played by the reliable Norman Rossington, get sloshed in a pub to alleviate the pain of the case, demonstrates this depth to perfection. As Rossington mans the pinball table, Pleasence harangues the time-calling publican with a stream of consciousness rant that veers from music hall comedy drunk turn to very real (and frightening) rage and back again, often within the same garbled sentence. It's an astonishing performance that would shame most critically acclaimed classic films, never mind a low-budget British horror.

Two worlds, then, but with more linking them than at first seems. The police station and various other London locations are all old Victorian spaces (the shoot is a hundred per cent location work), all echoey drabness, encroaching damp and gloss paint peeling off unplastered brickwork – a much more real 1970s London than the pile carpets and chrome tables of many a contemporary horror film. There's a bit of socialism at work here, too – very rare for a horror film. The theory that the underground bosses didn't try to rescue the trapped workers purely for cost-cutting reasons parallels Calhoun's defiant refusal to bow to the upper class civil servants who would tell him what to do 'on my patch'.

It's a film packed with witty dialogue and directed with bags of visual flair (the opening titles, with Cossins prowling among the blurred neon lights of Soho, as the electronic soundtrack burbles sinisterly in the background, is a budget-beating masterpiece in itself), so it's something of a surprise that neither director nor writer did much else. Gary Sherman (previous creative peak – that *New Seekers* Coke ad) went on to helm a few of the less rotten video nasties and little else, while writer Ceri Jones, art director Dennis Gordon-Orr and composer Will Malone similarly failed to set the world on fire with their demonstrably considerable talents. It's not so much a shame as a downright mystery. You don't think someone could be bumping them off?

DONALD PLEASENCE

CHILLING TO THE BONE... THE FUNNY BONE!

Some actors can be sinister, some can be funny, but not many can be sinister and funny at the same time. Donald Pleasence could. With the ability to chill the bone to the marrow just by staring, then inducing screams of hysteria by adding a slight smile to his round features, he was a truly unique character actor. Unique because he could use precisely the same technique for getting laughs yet never confused the two, managing to avoid the death knell of any horror scene, unintentional laughter.

Pleasence knew how to exploit his own strengths, too. When he was cast by John Carpenter as the US president in *Escape From New York* (1981), it was Donald who suggested that he be dressed up in female wig with lipstick and make up knowing how freakish he would look. Carpenter didn't argue, and the scene goes a long way to create the seedy, dangerous atmosphere of apocalyptic Manhattan that Harry Dean Stanton in a manky lab' coat wasn't going to be able achieve on his own. Casting Pleasence was one of Carpenter's infrequent but definite strokes of genius. When he stands atop the wall facing back into New York and machine-guns Isaac Hayes shouting at him, 'You are the Duke!' he establishes himself as the maddest, baddest mutha in the film. The Duke may have been the ruler of New York, but with his flashes of manic brilliance Pleasence let it be known that there was no one harder than the president. It's Donald's performance that makes the film.

Pleasence's first screen credit was in *The Beachcomber* (1954), playing a native in a far-flung colonial outpost in the Indian Ocean. No danger of being typecast as a result of that one, then. His taking the part of Parsons the nervous free-perspirer in *1984* (1954) gave him better scope for conveying his abilities. Then a fleeting appearance in *The Battle of the Sexes* came a bit later when he managed to convey the dread and terror he had of his former female boss by smiling at Robert Morley. After this, he managed to get himself involved in some of the best and most famous films of the 1960s, including the silly melodrama *Hell Is a City* (1960) with Stanley Baker, a weird plastic surgery frightener *Circus of Horrors* (1960) where he looked far more at home, and the Sid James and Kenny Connor froth *What a Carve Up!* (1961). Paydirt was well and truly hit with a run of top rate stuff, including the 'perfectly sighted' forger in *The Great Escape* (1963) and the creepy one in *Fantastic Voyage* (1966) before playing increasing degrees of bad as Ernst Stavro Blofeld in *You Only Live Twice* (1965), after the only slightly more disturbing Devil in *The Greatest Story Ever Told* (1967).

The 1970s highlights came just as thick and fast, as he provided the only thing worth hanging around for in the interminable *THX 1138* (1971) – George Lucas' study into how white you can make a screen without actually just pointing a camera at a piece of A4 – the Disney edition *Kidnapped*, playing against distinctly Cockernee Jacobite Michael Caine and then the dogged policeman trying to unravel the nasty mystery of the *Death Line* (1972). A slight change of tone was required as he assumed the mantle of Erich Count von Plasma in genteel period farce *Barry Mackenzie Holds His Own* (1974), then back to regular form as long-running German cabaret artiste Heinrich Himmler in *The Eagle Has Landed* (1976). Not everyone was a winner though. Along the way Pleasence got caught up in maniacal Peter Frampton musical *Sergeant Pepper's Lonely Heart's Club Band* (1978). It's a lasting testament to the esteem and general bafflement most held Pleasence in that it made not one tittle of difference to him that he'd taken part in a film that stank on ice. Viewers just chortle to themselves a bit about him being there then let him get on with it.

However, it was in *Hallowe'en* (1978) that he took his place among the stars as the dogged Dr Sam Loomis, the pursuer of eerie psychopath Michael Myers, though in time it becomes less clear who is the scarier one. A clutch of sequels cemented his position, with his presence in the proceedings lending an air of credibility. Each could only be considered 'a proper one' if he was involved. He took the name of Loomis once again in another Carpenter number, the pleasingly silly *Prince of Darkness* (1987) in which he vanquished Satan himself, that incarnation of all evil having the sense to back off when Pleasence got his dander up.

The rest of his CV runs up into the hundreds and is as varied as it is impressive, but all with the guarantee that, with him involved, there would be at least something worth watching in it – a feat for which the producers of *Cobra Mission* (1985) or *The Devonsville Terror* (1983) ought to be eternally grateful.

ROCK OPERAS

By the mid-1960s pop music was engulfing every mass medium in its path. Newspapers started making room among the births, deaths and marriages and court circulars for fruity tittle-tattle concerning the newly minted rock aristocracy. Television struggled to adapt its old school patrician façade to the happening beats of the post-skiffle coffee shop scene. Arguably more pliable than either of those top-heavy media, cinema seemed the most likely non-vinyl outlet for the burgeoning wave of turned-on youth.

The only problem was how to translate the three-minute attention span of pop into film's customary hour-and-a-half. Early solutions included the no-frills concert film, and the judicious slotting of 'beat groups' into traditional 'small town boy comes good' and 'stop the evil crooks!' formats. Before long, however, musicians fancied stretching their legs a tad, and so the uneasy and prolonged gestation of the rock opera took place.

From its oddball psychedelic beginnings to the elephants' graveyard of 1980s stadium prog, not forgetting such never-made wonders as *The Lamb Lies Down on Broadway* and *Captain Beefheart vs the Grunt People*, the rock opera is a genre as unwieldy as its perennially inaccurate moniker suggests, but that doesn't stop the best, and indeed the worst, of them holding a darn sight more fascination in their misshapen carcasses than *The Tommy Steele Story*. Here are some of the most notable of those ill-fitting suites.

MRS BROWN, YOU'VE GOT A LOVELY DAUGHTER (1968)
'A happy, tuneful comedy of today's groovy generation!' Herman's Hermits came far too late to the sub-*Hard Day's Night* film party, but threw themselves into it with gusto all the same (at least they did when the lads stopped setting fire to each other's arses and lobbing gooseberries about on set for long enough to do some filming). Peter Noone and the Hermits inherit the titular greyhound and have to form a band to get enough money together to go from Manchester to London (via psyched-up VW buses, jeeps and motorcycle combinations) to race it. (Wouldn't the more logical order involve them racing the greyhound to get enough money to form a band?). There's a rubbish pub fight (egged on by Rita Webb). Noone juggles two birds. The guard is changed at Buckingham Palace. Spaghetti is wolfed down. There's a daft fantasy wedding scene in glorious Metrocolour. Mona Washbourne plays the other Mrs Brown, Lance Percival is a bizarre spoon-playing tramp with airs and graces, and Stanley Holloway is the best thing in the film by a country yard as Washbourne's hubby, Cyril Fletcher-esque millionaire grocer George George Brown ('My old man 'ad a stutter!').

HEAD (1968)
After the Beatles revamped the old rags-to-riches rock 'n' roll movie cliché with a mixture of native scouse wit and Wilfrid Brambell, their manufactured counterparts went one

better (and two worse) by going to a motel with Jack Nicholson, talking cobblers into a tape recorder, then filming the result. And the result is a glorious mess, based loosely on a self-deprecating satire of the band themselves as artificial product, 'God's gift to the eight-year-olds', forever becoming trapped in a symbolic black box. Mix in pseudo-Yogic mysticism, Vietnam, an exploding Coke machine, Victor Mature, Frank Zappa, Mickey accepting the surrender of the entire Italian army, one of the largest suspended-arch bridges in the world, some really quite excellent songs and a glass of cold gravy with a hair in it, and you have the most majestic shambles ever to grace the silver screen in the name of rock. Sadly, audiences kept well out of it (though Nicholson claimed to have seen it 'like, 158 million times!' as if to compensate) and the lads' careers never recovered. 'No-one ever lends money to a man with a sense of humour!'

200 MOTELS (1971)
Fresh from his yak-toting cameo in *Head*, Zappa made this gorgy orgy of groupies, frogs and horses, and suddenly the *Monkees* film looks like *Chariots of Fire* in comparison. Filming at Pinewood (next door to *2001*) in little over a week, Zappa used video cameras to cut costs and flooded every frame with multiple Chromakeyed images, queasy colour saturations and restless fuzziness in general, in what starts out as a satire on a typical rock tour of America but quickly descends into a headache-inducing kaleidoscope soup. Keith Moon plays a nun. Ringo Starr plays Zappa. Ringo's chauffeur stands in for Wilfrid Brambell. A grand time is had by all.

GODSPELL (1973)
Jesus Christ Superstar (1973) may have got the ball rolling for the short-lived heyday of the all-in ecclesiastical wig-out, but for sheer warped bravado, this loved-up version of the Gospel of Matthew takes the prize. A bubble-permed Jesus in a *Superman* T-shirt and a distinctly Jerry Hayes-like John the Baptist join forces to gather up New York's disaffected youth for an orgy of praise, song and wagon painting. Only those with a desire to participate in that uneasy religious middle-ground between a drug-free 'be-in' and a themed school assembly need apply.

PHANTOM OF THE PARADISE (1974)
Brian De Palma comes good with a tempting blend of Lon Cheney and Goethe. Songwriter Paul '*Rainy Days and Mondays*' Williams plays Swan, the copyright-busting charlatan who nicks both the tunes and the girl from record press-deformed composer and serial De Palma mucker William Finley. The stage is set – literally – for some bloody revenge as the walled-up Phantom sabotages Swan's filched rock opera, with Williams' songs and Jack Fisk's gaudy sets smothering the Grand Guignol in queasy candystripe colours. (As *Kiss*-like singer Beef opines, 'The karma in here's so thick, you need an aqualung!'). De Palma's much-vaunted split screen obsession, so often an annoying bit of window dressing, is used brilliantly here in a scene following a ticking bomb from setting to detonation. A hit!

TV CREAM'S ANATOMY OF CINEMA

SON OF DRACULA (1974)

Considerably less of a hit, this is what happens when Ringo Starr, money a-burnin' a hole in his pocket, decides to make a horror musical with Harry Nilsson, Keith Moon and pals. Nilsson is the rock lovin' Count Downe, thirsty for mortality and, hey, love. The great Freddie Francis is wheeled in to direct, not that you would notice. Trumping even Macca's *Give My Regards to Broad Street* (1984) in terms of plotless folly, the final judgment is perhaps best left to Ringo himself: 'It's not the best film ever made, but I've seen worse'.

TOMMY (1975)

At the time, there was probably no-one better to film Pete Townsend's convoluted concept fable of a sensorially deprived serial victim who becomes the new messiah by hanging around amusement arcades than Ken Russell. The *grandpère terrible* of British arthouse had classical music lovers fishing monocles out of their gin after seeing his jazzed-up composer biopics for the best part of a decade, so his was always going to be a reliably unsteady hand on the tiller as the film ploughed through a sea of psychedelic effects, dodgy child-abuse gags and baked beans to do handsome business. The only losers were Southsea's South Parade Pier, which burned down during filming, and David Bowie, who discovered Tina Turner to be his 'if wet' replacement.

OZ (1976)

The Wizard of Oz (1939) was always ripe for a rock remake. In 1978 the all-black *The Wiz* flopped into cinemas, and iffy tweeness sadly triumphed over some rather grand production design and about two decent songs. Before that, this Australian road trip told the tale of a lost groupie catapulted into a fantasy Australia in search of Bowie-esque singer The Wizard, aided by a surfie, a mechanic and a biker (in place of the scarecrow, tin man and lion, respectively). With music provided by *Jo-Jo Zepp and the Falcons*, and Ross '*Sons of the Vegetal Mother*' Wilson, this was the campest thing to come out of the outback until *Priscilla: Queen of the Desert*.

JUBILEE (1977)

Arthouse takes on punk! Derek Jarman got endless stick from the likes of *Siouxsie Sioux* and Vivienne Westwood over this spit-drainingly pretentious homage to the anarchists of Callaghan's Britain. Jenny '*Final Programme*' Runacre, *Toyah, Little Nell* and *Adam Ant* are among the 'clammy slags' indulging in squalid polythene sex and dumping agents of The Man in the Thames while a time-hopping Elizabeth I (Runacre again) looks on aghast. Buckingham Palace becomes a recording studio, and Westminster Abbey a knocking shop, among various other bits of brick-subtle satirical business. Still, there's visual interest of a sort in the bombed-out Docklands locations and... er, *Toyah*'s orange body warmer.

SERGEANT PEPPER'S LONELY HEARTS CLUB BAND (1978)

In the town of Heartland, presided over by Mr Kite, Billy Shears, with a little help from his friends The Hendersons, reforms the titular mythical band in order to reclaim the magical brass instruments of peace, which have been stolen by evil estate agent Mean Mr

ROCK OPERAS

Mustard and plastic surgeon Maxwell Edison, who turns people into mannequins with his silver hammer… Sound familiar? Whether a young Ben Elton took time out during the height of punk to make copious notes during a showing of this monumental fantasy flop is unknown, but the West End trend for tiresomely literal musicals based on famous back catalogues began here. Record mogul Robert Stigwood is to blame, cynically deploying the Fab Four's greatest hits in a misbegotten mish-mash starring *The Bee Gees*, Peter Frampton, Frankie Howerd, George Burns and Steve Martin, who each get their chance to murder a classic Beatles tune. As opposed to Stiggy's previous ventures, *Saturday Night Fever* (1977) and *Tommy*, the good folk of 1978 took one look and wisely ran a mile. Of course, in these enlightened times, such bilge would be in its 'fifth fantastic year!' at the Dominion: so much for sophistication.

XANADU (1980)
Never let it be said these films don't aim high for their sources of inspiration. Greek mythology and Coleridge combine in this merry tale of Muses incarnated on Earth to help mankind strive for greater artistic triumphs – which in this case means Olivia Newton John getting Gene Kelly to open a roller disco. Lashings of *ELO* on the soundtrack and a bit of Don Bluth animation can't hide the fact this looks like they were making it up as they went along – which, indeed, they were. The year 1980 turned out to be the high summer of the disco movie – this fought for fleapit space with the delirious Village People 'biopic', *Can't Stop the Music*. Olivia was no stranger to the wacky world of rock opera – she'd been the singer in made-up band *Toomorrow*, promoted *Monkees*-style in the disastrous 1970 sci-fi musical of the same name.

THE APPLE (1980)
It gets little better. Hapless trashmasters Cannon Films fancied some disco musical action, and concocted a trite tale of a Canadian couple who enter the Worldvision Song Contest in the shiny future of 1994, only to be tempted into hell by devilish entrepreneur Vladek Sheybal. All very *Rocky Horror* in look and feel, though without the essential saving grace of that Richard O'Brien campy wit, and the endless gold lamé G-strings are less than easy on the eye. On the plus side, there's Joss Ackland in hippie tramp mode.

BREAKING GLASS (1980)
Hazel O'Connor, she of the Wagnerian post-punk school of apocalyptic bellowing, is the focus of what amounts to a bog-standard 'rocky rise to rock fame' story little different to the kind Tommy Steele used to appear in. Strikes, violence, Phil Daniels and smack are among the trimmings that mark it out as a film of its time, although not nearly as much as the climactic performance of portentous punk operetta *Eighth Day*, delivered by La O'Connor, clad in proto-*Tron* luminous techno-leotard, in front of a laser and dry ice arrangement that screams '1980' more loudly than any labour exchange queue or row of riot shields ever could.

SHOCK TREATMENT (1981)

Richard O'Brien's minimalist pseudo-sequel to *The Rocky Horror Picture Show* (1976) stuck Brad and Janet in a world of small town domestic strife, caught between quack psychologists (O'Brien, *Little Nell*) and a demented, blind game show host (a film-stealing Barry Humphries) in a luridly lit TV station-cum-asylum. The single set stylings (a giant maze of padded cells) lend a claustrophobic air to proceedings, and the songs are patchy (and allegedly written for a different, abandoned sequel which was to have resurrected Frank N. Furter himself), but there's great fun here in O'Brien's tricksy ruse of filming the whole thing in front of a studio audience, and the incongruous joy of watching Charles Gray, Ruby Wax, Rik Mayall and, er, *Sinitta* in full song.

PINK FLOYD: THE WALL (1981)

'The most expensive student film ever made' is director Alan Parker's considered opinion on this mightiest of mighty rock follies, and it's a pretty perceptive comment. In what must surely at some stage have borne the working title *Roger Waters Presents It's Hell Being Roger Waters (by Roger Waters)*, Bob Geldof portrays Pink, a virtually speechless waif who greets the various tribulations of his rise from lonely war orphan to stadium-stuffing rock lord with the same disaffected expression. High point: the excellent animation of Gerald Scarfe's spiky illustrations. Low point: a dalliance with real neo-Nazi extras who adopted Scarfe's goose-stepping hammer logo as their own, to the horror of all concerned. Leave the big statements to your bank manager, Rog.

UNDER THE CHERRY MOON (1986)

Witnessing Prince cock it all up is always a sad experience, like hearing that a well-loved family friend has joined the Territorial Army. Here he followed up his just-about-passable *Purple Rain* (1984) with a self-directed 1930s folly concerning two gigolos trawling the French Riviera for wealthy dames to exploit. It's a plot lifted from creaky Brando–Niven comedy *Bedtime Story* (1964), later remade as *Dirty Rotten Scoundrels* (1988) with more success than the Paisley One manages here. Still, the scrappy vanity project does at least have, in the *Parade* album, one stonker of a soundtrack.

THE ESSENTIAL
ROCK 'N' ROLL FILM

THE GIRL CAN'T HELP IT (1956)

The 1950s was probably the ultimate 'you had to be there' decade. What is left of it now with which to try and get a feel of the time when rock 'n' roll, in its lewd, ramshackle glory, turned up on America's doorstep and flicked gravel at Britain's bedroom window? The records of the time still speak for themselves, but visually, what is left? Those early telly pop jamborees are hindered by the awkwardness of the studio, the prudishness of the grey-suited makers and the five-fathoms-of-porridge murkiness of the pictures. Film is a brighter medium, but was even slower on the cultural uptake than the telly, and when they finally turned up it got it hopelessly wrong. *Rock Around the Clock* (1956) is historically interesting, but between those seat-ripping musical numbers there is an acre of plodding dramatisation to put up with. And as for Elvis's celluloid output… well, an hour-long compilation would be stretching things.

What was needed was a director with a background in the same kind of anarchy as the musicians, a film equivalent of rock 'n' roll. The nearest cinema got at that time was *Looney Tunes*. Frank Tashlin spent the 1930s and 1940s at Warner Brothers' animation complex Termite Terrace, turning out Bugs and co. classics such as *A Corny Concerto* and *Hare Remover*. Making the rare move to live-action, he piled on sight gags and snappy editing to comedies by Bob Hope – the magnificent western comedy *Son of Paleface* (1952) – and Jerry Lewis. So when Fox decided to rush out a *Rock Around the Clock* clone in time for the Christmas market, hitching their wagon to Tash was an inadvertently smart move indeed.

All early rock 'n' roll films should be comedies: the music lends itself to knockabout more than pathos, and any attempts to recreate an authentically gritty Teddy boys' picnic in studio are doomed to look historically laughable before the films at the chemist's. Tash penned a daffy script combining cartoon gags with a light but prescient satire of the barely four-year-old musical movement, eschewing the usual wooden leading man for Tom Ewell, eye-popping victim of Marilyn Monroe in *The Seven Year Itch* (1955), alongside pulchritudinous Monroe-esque bimbo Jayne Mansfield, as his romantic leads. A straightforward back-stiffener this was not going to be.

Setting the pair adrift on a wafer-thin story wherein gangster Fats (Edmond O'Brien) hires the drunken Ewell to make his non-singing moll (Mansfield) a rock 'n' roll star, Tash piles on the visuals (Jayne's décolletage causing milkman Phil Silvers' bottles to boil over) and some of the best rock numbers ever captured on celluloid. Quite sensibly just dropped in to the film with no warning, Gene Vincent scoots through *Be Bop A Lula*, Little Richard hammers fantastically away at *She's Got It* and Julie London brings the mood down a little for *Cry Me a River*. The quality varies, but unlike the high-gloss slapstick scenes, there's nothing starched or processed about these performances.

It all ends in stupidly happy ever after manner, with Fats going it alone in the music biz with galumphing novelty prison-yard hit *Rock Around the Rockpile*, and Ewell and Mansfield taking off together for an improbable afterlife of cosy domesticity and great big tureens of bouillon. The only thing missing is Elvis, who was slated to make an appearance until The Colonel upped the asking price and took Elvis off to make *Love Me Tender* (1956) instead, which went head-to-head with *Girl...* that Christmas, and blinked. The Colonel had the last laugh, stuffing Presley into a further thirty films, some OK, most rotten, but none with a tenth of *Girl*'s jukebox-trashing spirit of merrily goofy sassiness.

AS YOU'VE NEVER SEEN THEM BEFORE!

There's no entertainment law which states TV celebrities must at all times behave as they do on the box, but it's still a shock to come across an old light entertainment stalwart getting up to questionable hi-jinks on the silver screen. Cases in point:

Peter Sallis in *Taste the Blood of Dracula* (1970)
Clegg warmed up for *Summer Wine* by hanging about with the Bond films' Sir Frederick Gray and James Mason soundalike John Carson as part of a trio of cheerily debauched Victorian gentlemen nipping off to Limehouse to get their brothel-bound kicks from the likes of Madeline Smith.

Beryl Reid in *Psychomania* (1971)
She may have dented her wholesome front room image as a TV nurse with Susannah York on the side in *The Killing of Sister George* (1968), but Beryl's appearance in this undead folk-biker romp, as the Satanist mother of gang leader Nicky Henson who holds the secret to eternal life involving unnatural practices with a psychedelic toad kept in her swish modernist pad, gave her subsequent visits to children's telly, reading quaint tales of the adventures of a toy elephant called Mrs Pinkerton-Trunks, a whole extra dimension.

Brian Murphy in *The Devils* (1971)
It was only after *Man about the House* began that Murphy slipped into the 'hen-pecked' persona he'd bank on ever after, so perhaps it shouldn't come as too much of a surprise to find him relishing his role as a lank-haired torturer in Ken Russell's baroque medieval French witch-hunt while he can. Still, as he gamely helps out with the branding and sledge hammering during Oliver Reed's final 'interview', it's hard not to wonder what diabolical power Yootha Joyce must have used on the fellow in the intervening two years.

Barbara Streisand in *Up the Sandbox* (1972)
Babs took artistic control of her film career and fought against the terminal kookiness of her previous *What's Up, Doc?* (1972) as a pregnant New Yorker indulging in crypto-feminist reveries in her apartment: joining in an African fertility ceremony, bedding a transsexual Fidel Castro, blowing up the Statue of Liberty, that sort of thing. Result: a rare Streisand flop.

Irene Handl in *The Great Rock 'N' Roll Swindle* (1980)
Malcolm McLaren's revisionist 'it was all my idea, I think you'll find' mish-mash of bondage, Biggs and Branson digs roped in the hitherto wholesome likes of Dave Dee and Liz Fraser, but the image that sticks in the mind is of Handl as a run-down usherette in a run-down cinema looking glumly on as Eddie Tudor-Pole prances about with a Hoover singing wacky punk novelty 'Who Killed Bambi?' *Metal Mickey* must have seemed like Ustinov after that.

JOAN COLLINS

SHE'S LIKE A WICKED, WICKED WITCH

No daughter of showbiz agent Joe Collins would ever go on the stage. That was the impresario's plan anyway, but young Joan promptly enrolled at RADA, where the odd *Woman's Own* modelling stint compensated for her teachers' lament that she had to improve on her weak voice, 'otherwise it is "the Films" for her, and that would be such a pity'.

She promptly auditioned for the lead role in lightweight comedy *Lady Godiva Rides Again* (1951). On set, she discovered that, in film make-up, she resembled a young, albino Joan Crawford, and settled for a smaller part, shivering her arse off in a bathing suit in Folkestone town hall. A bit of proper career came when she hit on a seam of 'bad girl' (or 'pathetic little cockney tart') parts, with the likes of Lil in *Judgement Deferred* and Norma in *I Believe in You* (both 1952), during the filming of which she was taught to smoke and swear by Laurence Harvey.

She arrived too late for the glory days of the Rank Charm School, but the studio was still at full speed. *Cosh Boy* (1952), in which Joan played the lead mugger's girl, who falls pregnant and tries to commit suicide, became one of Britain's first X-rated films. This, and a role as one of three freshly released juvenile Holloway inmates in *Turn the Key Softly* (1953), cemented her status as 'Britain's best bad girl'.

The more familiar Collins glamour was finally given full vent when she appeared – on loan – in the shipwreck comedy *Our Girl Friday* (1953) at last appropriately cast as a scantily-attired rich girl fending off the clumsy advances of co-wreckees George Cole, Kenneth More and Robertson *'All Gas and Gaiters'* Hale. The exotic Majorca locations and Peter Sellers on comedy parrot noise duty helped ensure her first transatlantic success. The hasty attempt to cement this was an Egyptian princess turn in congealed epic *Land of the Pharaohs* (1955), where not even the most outlandish of Hollywood's pseudo-Nile costumery – a waist-length wig made of the hair of twelve Italian nuns, and a huge fake ruby concealing that cinematic no-no, the female navel – could upstage the sight of a big, shirtless James Robertson Justice wielding a bullwhip.

Undaunted, Joan signed a seven-year contract with Fox, in high-profile roles including the Walter Raleigh-shagging lady-in-waiting to Bette Davis' *The Virgin Queen* (1955) and as a socialite falling dangerously for architect Ray Milland (whose flat contains the titular saucy oscillating crimson contraption) in *The Girl in the Red Velvet Swing* (1955). The world's press was soon all over 'The Pouting Panther', though their Anglo-ignorant descriptions made Joan, in her opinion, come over as a cross between Rita Hayworth and Dame Edith Evans.

From then on, highs included *Island in the Sun* (1957), one of those dated, heart-in-right-place racial dramas with Harry Belafonte, and learning to striptease as the 'fluff' element in Rod Steiger's Monte Carlo heist gang for *Seven Thieves* (1960). Lows included the dismal *Stopover Tokyo* (1957) and burning in a bathful of detergent bubbles and being belted in the gob by June Allyson in *The Opposite Sex* (1956). Bing Crosby's constant hawking up of pipe tar onto the studio floor also somewhat took the shine off appearing in the last of the Bing 'n' Bob screwball capers, *Road to Hong Kong* (1962).

Then came marriage and family life with Anthony Newley, and Joan left the screen to raise the kids until the break-up nutfest of Newley's *Heironymus Merkin* (1969) dragged her rudely back to filmmaking. The following year's *Up in the Cellar* was marginally less bizarre, being a wayward student activist satire from Theodore J. *'President's Analyst'* Flicker, with Joan playing the wife of besieged college chief Larry Hagman, but nonetheless still a flop. Slightly firmer ground was sci-fi romance *Quest for Love* (1971), with Tom Bell zapping himself into a WWII-less alternative reality, and finding himself suddenly married to Joan, with the inevitable time paradox shenanigans stitched into the love story.

Things hotted up a tad with the advent of The Horror Years. She did two fine Amicus portmanteau pics, both playing victim roles. There was also *Dark Places* (1973), in which she and Robert Hardy broke into an old house after treasure, only to find it haunted by Christopher Lee. Hammer's *Fear in the Night* (1972) is probably the key text for Joan watchers. 'La Coll' was the wife of sinister one-handed boarding school head Peter Cushing, and as such got to strut around a lot and look 'icy' in endless 'atmospheric' scenes

– the first signs of that self-parodic high camp persona to come (the film's alternate title was *Dynasty of Fear*, meaningless coincidence fans). Of course, still she kept her oar in elsewhere, with *Star Trek* guest spots and more Euro efforts, such as Italian football/sex comedy *The Referee* (1974) and *Cry of the Wolf* (1975), the Spanish-produced Gold Rush wolf-attack thriller that Jack Palance doesn't like to talk about. The lady ended her horror phase with the worst of the lot, sadly, in the well-titled but otherwise useless cursed offspring potboiler *I Don't Want to Be Born!* (1975).

Then came 'The Sauce', as Joan plunged headfirst into *The Bawdy Adventures of Tom Jones* (1976) as randy highwaywoman Black Bess. It compared unfavourably with the 1960s version of the same tale, but then the only other work on offer included *Alfie Darling* (1975), the Caine-less *Alfie* sequel with Alan Price, *The Big Sleep* (1978 – Michael Winner edition!) and writhing about underneath the worst papier-mâché models you ever saw for *Empire of the Ants* (1977).

Small wonder Joan took the Brent Walker shilling for those shabby time capsules of aftershave disco glamour, sister Jackie's airport bonkbuster *The Stud* (1978) and its somewhat confused follow-up *The Bitch* (1979). The first, an unintentionally daft bit of hopeless shagpile-and-chrome anti-sophistication based on a book then already a decade old, did manage to cultivate a sort of forlorn grubby charm with its endless silk sheets, ornamental swimming pools and steamy scenes of Joan and leading man Oliver Tobias (Tom Jones was offered the part, but wisely kept well out of it) strutting their stuff on the disco floor. The sequel, despite the addition of an iconic chauffeur's cap and Quantum Jump's timeless classic *The Lone Ranger*, was less of the same all round.

Then in 1981 Aaron Spelling came knocking, and the rest is quarterback-shouldered history. However, despite the subsequent rise of her gold-digging Dynastic image, it's worth considering the amount of dementedly varied roles she took in order to get there – this is not the kind of career plan any ambitious young actress would consider for a moment these days. Whether that's 'star quality' or just some weird sixth sense for choosing the bizarrest projects on the trolley and running with them, who can tell?

THE ESSENTIAL VANITY PROJECT

CAN HEIRONYMUS MERKIN EVER FORGET MERCY HUMPPE AND FIND TRUE HAPPINESS? (1969)

Anthony Newley, ladies and gentlemen… Child film star, song-and-dance man, writer of high-concept musicals, tuppenny rice purchaser and inspiration for David Bowies the world over. Supremely talented, massively confident, willfully eccentric and randy as a vicar's dog to boot. Not one to follow the crowd, or do things by halves. So when Universal's bankers gave him carte blanche to make a film of his life, they can't say they weren't warned. And Tone certainly made sure they got what was coming to them.

The film is set, almost entirely, on a beach. We're in Malta, but it hardly matters – this is the beach of Anthony Newley's mind. Weston-Super-Mare at low tide would have done just as well. Federico Fellini did a film that started on a beach, *La Strada*. This is no mere coincidence. Tone loves Fellini almost as much as he loves Tone, and a hefty dollop of self-conscious Italianate artfulness, or rather a fusillade of half-cocked stabs at same, litters this odd-looking saga.

El Newley sets out his portentous stall from the off. 'Written in the sands of time… the magic quill of an Aristophanes…' It's Tone's fortieth birthday, and he's feeling a tad morose. He's about to embark on a lengthy bout of soul searching, we find, to establish 'the plain, bare-bottomed facts' about his life, loves and haircut, as his two young children look on, bored out of their tiny minds.

The great and good of showbusiness are called up to assist. George Jessel is The Presence, a sort of hazily-defined angel-cum-harbinger-of-death. Milton Berle is Goodtime Eddie Filth, some kind of embodiment of showbiz sleaze. Best of all is Bruce Forsyth as J. Poindexter Limelight, based on an old vaudevillian the young Tone found himself staying with during WWII, dressed in bashed stovepipe hat and enormous Union Jack-trimmed flares, belting out cockney songs on a battered upright. 'Forget the theatre! She's a strumpet! A harlot! A whore!' Brucie then stiltwalks while singing *On the Boards*, a breakneck paean to the roar of the greasepaint. 'I love the boards… those hordes of broads!' He accompanies himself with a soft-shoe shuffle, random conjuring tricks, custard pies, Groucho walks and a truly virtuoso rapid tap dance after which he promptly keels over and dies. The film never really recovers after that.

So much for the fellers. The women in Tone's life fare little better. The excellent Patricia Hayes is largely wasted as Gracie, Newley's doting, if rather confused, mum. Various wives, girlfriends and bits-on-the-side are given riotously punny nicknames like Filigree Fondle and Trampolina Whambang, and are played by a mixture of *Carry On* actresses and *Playboy* playmates of the month.

Then there's Joan Collins, gamely playing herself while her marriage falls apart in real life, albeit renamed as one Polyester Poontang (James Joyce takes rest of afternoon off). She falls for Newley at a performance of what seems to be Tone's hit show *Stop the World, I Want to Get Off*, and sings the tortuous ballad *Chalk and Cheese* ('How did you get into my horoscope, you funny, irascible, lovable dope?') while scantily clad dancers dressed as the signs of the zodiac strut their stuff to a cha-cha-cha beat and Tone shows off his bare arse. 'I don't mind chalk with my cheese.' The viewer suddenly feels as protective toward Joan as it's possible to be without physically becoming Christopher Biggins.

From then on, we get the potted version of Newley's life. He shags a long line of scantily-clad birds, along with 'the occasional exotic fruit' (cue bloke in cravat looking camply askance at the camera accompanied by comedy sound effect – he may be after the New Wave in cinematic terms, but the gags are firmly Old Hat). He cheats on Joan. He takes drugs and steam comes out of his ears. He sings to God in a towelling robe. He conducts a randy black mass on a demonic version of the *Blankety Blank* set. He sits, naked, on a plastic stool. The screenplay won a British Writer's Guild award. Heady times, the 1960s.

Various cunning bits of self-referentiality are deployed. Newley, at the projector, heckles his own film before anyone in the auditorium gets a chance – a deft tactic. The Critics, a trio of variously uptight sneering demagogues (including Victor Spinetti) declaim flatulent soundbites rubbishing the entire venture. 'This whole thing is self-glorification on a masturbatory level!'; 'I blame Fellini for this!' Tone's covering his arse metaphorically, if not literally.

Some of the postmodern conceits are clumsy in the extreme. The Mask is introduced – a faceless Newley, clad in a nappy and with an outsize clockwork key sticking out of his back, humping away at various hapless birds. As a clankingly obvious metaphor for the mindless hedonism celebrated throughout the picture, it's second to none.

One thing Newley can never be accused of is dullness. Tone's tone swings wildly about: one minute we see Julian Orchard conducting a funeral procession in the style of Bowie's *Ashes to Ashes* video for the child from Newley's first marriage who died of spina bifida, the next we're treated to *The Princess and the Donkey*, a lewd musical fairytale with gobsmacking lyrics ('They were so surprised that their knees went wonky!') which was apparently so 'dangerous', Gracie and the kids were excused from having to sit through it. 'Now's as good a time as any to go to the potty!' This is well said.

There can be little doubt that Newley's is an amazing story. If he couldn't be bothered to tell it properly here, that's the nature of the beast. Overambitious doesn't cover it: Tone makes Don Quixote look like a Screwfix area manager. Very few people turned out to witness this two-hour therapy session, and while it's hard to look on that as anything approaching a shame, there's reason to lament the fact this sort of monumental folly wouldn't happen now. Celebrities are indulged more than ever before of course, but the products of this cosseting never reach the vertiginous heights or murky depths of *Merkin*. A Newley of today would be frozen out of showbiz before he even got started, and that's a great loss.

As for the Newley of then, he dusted himself off from the post-*Merkin* fallout and went on to compose songs for *Willy Wonka and the Chocolate Factory*, an altogether more down to earth venture.

SPRAWLING SATIRES

The meteoric rise of British satire on TV and in print during the early 1960s is well documented, from Cook to Frost to Cleese to Lance Percival. But the later boom in big, monstrously ambitious satirical films is less heavily charted. Perhaps it's because the films, while involving many of the same personnel, failed to gel in the public mind with an image as plain as Cleese, Barker and Corbett in ordered silhouette, or Cook as Macmillan. Or maybe because, while *That Was the Week That Was* garnered audiences of twelve million, many of these films were lucky to last a fortnight as bemused punters gave them short shrift. All good reasons for them to fall out of the nostalgic spotlight perhaps, but even better reasons for unearthing them again, since what made them so unwieldy then is precisely what makes them so fascinating now.

Now, a three-minute sketch poking fun at the Home Secretary is all very well but, as with rock operas, the inflation of satire to feature length demands that the targets grow accordingly, to take on the whole of society, commerce, religion and all. With such big angry points to make, subtlety and tact are the first things to fly out the window. These films are sledgehammers, it's true, but at their best they're wondrously gaudily over-decorated sledgehammers, and if they disintegrate on contact with their chosen targets leaving barely a dent never mind, as the spectacle remains unlike anything else in film. Bring on the mad prophets of Pinewood!

NOTHING BUT THE BEST (1964)
While *TW3* ruled the airwaves, Frederic Raphael wrote this nifty cross between *Room at the Top* (1959) and *My Fair Lady* (1964). Alan Bates is an ambitious young estate agent thwarted in his social climbing plans by the snobbishness of his bosses, until a grudgeful Denholm Elliot takes him under his wing and coaches him to walk, talk and think like a member of the ruling class. *TW3* stars took part: Millicent Martin is the girl Bates woos with deception after deception and Willie Rushton is a Christmas-camp art dealer fretting over the hipness of Rembrandt.

BEDAZZLED (1967)
Peter Cook's leap up cinema's creative pecking order from the purgatory of *Wrong Box* cameo work takes the same shape as many an entry in this genre – its episodic structure gives the film the appearance more of a themed sketch show than a conventionally progressing plot. In this case it's the simple tale of Cook's suave Devil giving Dudley Moore's burger-flipper seven catch-ridden chances to better himself, leading to seven disparate sketches. Not a satisfying narrative in the old style, but the linear progression from one incarnation of Dud to the next is handled with expert comic nous. The scene where Dud and Eleanor Bron commit tearful adultery in Cook's limo is both funny and oddly moving in a way many conventional romantic comedies would give whole worlds to achieve.

PRIVILEGE (1967)

Peter Watkins makes *The War Game*. The Beeb are told by Powers Unnamed to bin it. The Beeb bin it. Watkins, never a temperate man at the best of times, does his nut. James Heyman turns up with a Johnny Speight script about the oppressive nature of yoof culture for Watkins to direct. Watkins, no teenybopper himself, watches the same Paul Anka biopic for hours on end as homework. Paul Jones is cast as hapless singer Steven Shorter, taking a bizarre prison cell stage act from Birmingham to the international stage in front of hordes of screaming, beehived girls. A fascistic Con–Lab pact butter him up and get him to get the yoof to do their bidding. A conclave of bishops does likewise. As do… er, the apple farmers. Jean Shrimpton turns up to paint a pseudo-Francis Bacon portrait of Jones. Jones shags her. Thus emboldened, they set out to Smash the System. Watkins wraps it all up in his brilliantly observed but slightly too on-the-nose pseudo documentary style. 'I fink the director's a bleedin' nutter!' The Rank Organisation, still under the staunch Methodist hand of J. Arthur, kick the film out of their cinemas for its church-baiting undertones. Watkins gets madder still, and naffs off to Sweden. Jones, meanwhile, goes on to star in *The Committee* (1968), in which he plays an enigmatic drifter who decapitates a businessman with the bonnet of his own car, sews it back on again, and then attends a focus group in a country house to discuss weighty matters such as the optimum roundness of oranges. Well, it's a living.

HOW I WON THE WAR (1967)

Richard Lester, popular purveyor of under-cranked knees-bent running about in *The Beatles'* 'A Hard Day's Night' (1964), took on a more sombre mantle for this 'self-alienating' war epic wherein clueless lieutenant Michael Crawford supervises the construction of an army cricket pitch in war-torn North Africa. The aim was to undercut the then roaring trade in exciting WWII pictures with a dose of anti-jingoistic reality, but such tricks as having John Lennon and Roy Kinnear deliver sober homilies straight to camera, and dead soldiers silently rejoining the platoon coated in coloured paint, preached that little bit too hard, and the gung-ho tide remained stubbornly unturned.

THE BED-SITTING ROOM (1969)

Going to the other extreme, Lester lost a lot of Hollywood kudos after filming Spike Milligan and John Antrobus' ramshackle post-nuclear stage play in the only way anyone could – as an aimless, quarry-bound salmagundi, with character and ideas tumbling over each other, switching from one to the other the moment boredom sets in. This is arguably just the ticket for depicting a chaotic, decaying remnant of Old England, but play well in Poughkeepsie it did not. Still, the roll-call of British acting talent (a feature of many of these films) is exemplary, particularly Michael Hordern as the BBC, wandering from survivor to survivor with burnt-out television front and dinner jacket remnants just ample enough to cover his dignity on the 'screen', solemnly intoning desperate items of non-news before an acapella rendition of the new national anthem, God Save Mrs Ethel Shroake.

SPRAWLING SATIRES

THE MAGIC CHRISTIAN (1969)
Adapted by Terry Southern and Joe McGrath from Southern's own novel, this is possibly the prime exponent of this genre's disjointed vignette approach to storytelling. The high concept is got over in the opening minutes: cynical millionaire Guy Grand (Peter Sellers) and his young cohort (Ringo Starr) set out to mock various areas of society by using Grand's vast wealth to bribe individuals into wilfully belittling their own roles in life. And that's it. Thus the film wavers between sketches on this slender theme which deliver (an on-train board meeting with Dennis Price; the amputation of the nose from a priceless painting as a mortified John Cleese looks on) and those that don't (the phrase 'Laurence Harvey strips while reciting Hamlet' is about as entertaining as the sketch it describes). By the time Yul Brynner and Christopher Lee are wheeled on for arbitrary cameos aboard a luxury liner that symbolises Britain (somehow) the air of self-importance is stifling. Nearly all the films under discussion here punch above their weight to some degree, but *The Magic Christian*'s episodic pomp, coupled with the predictability of its disparate scenes and its tendency to coast along on a wave of borrowed countercultural trappings, make it an easy film to watch, but a hard film to like.

THE RISE AND RISE OF MICHAEL RIMMER (1970)
British political satire was lifted out of the old class war furrow of *I'm All Right, Jack* (1959) by Peter Cook, John Cleese, Graham Chapman and director Kevin Billington, who cocked a snook at the emerging cult of the opinion pollster. Cook is the titular mercurial time and motion man who rises to the top of his polling company, sets the Labour and Conservative parties against each other, introduces hourly compulsory electronic voting for the populace and then sits back and waits for the people to beg him to form a dictatorship to make all the pesky democracy stop. As a Well Made Film it stinks – sketch follows sketch with little regard for shape – but for sheer prescience (not least predicting the 1970 Tory election victory) it's in a class of its own. Once again, an endless succession of acting stalwarts parade before the camera, many of them great fun, such as Arthur Lowe's lazy ad exec, Denholm Elliot's sly rival pollster, Ronald Fraser's bluff Heathesque Tory leader and George A. Cooper's pipe-smoking Wilsonian Labour chief. Any film funded by David Frost which devotes great swathes of its running time to taking the piss out of his 'super!' transatlantic lifestyle deserves applause aplenty.

EVERY HOME SHOULD HAVE ONE (1970)
Marty Feldman's initial venture into the world of feature films was a broad broadside against capitalism, casting him as a hapless advertising executive lumbered with a nightmare account to pitch –McLaughlin's Frozen Porridge – which becomes elided with his number one personal obsession, sex. Shying away from his Mary Whitehouse-like puritanical wife (Judy Cornwell), Feldman daydreams a variety of pastiche vignettes – cartoon ads, *The Wednesday Play* and Swedish films – which meld frozen porridge with his own lewd designs on his Swedish *au pair* Julie Ege. Sadly, a promising premise is fumbled by Feldman and his assorted cowriters (including Barry Took, Denis Norden and Milton Shulman), leaving a few decent gags floating around sets full of the shagpile-and-chrome opulence of adland, and a morass of speeded-up slapstick and easy laughs elsewhere.

THE RULING CLASS (1972)

The film adaptation of Peter Medak's labyrinthine stage comedy set in a rambling country estate takes a sledgehammer to the British aristocracy via Peter O'Toole's disturbed Earl of Gurney, an egotistical, uninhibited creation of his cloistered environment, who believes himself to be the second coming of Christ. After some odd, Biblical electro-shock therapy (involving a life-size crucifix, an Old Testament-spouting Nigel Green and a wrestling match with a gorilla in a top hat) his grasping relatives believe him cured and the family bloodline saved… until he starts styling himself after Jack the Ripper. As ever, celebrity cameos ooze symbolism: William Mervyns's scheming head of the household, Alistair Sim's bumbling bishop and Arthur Lowe's increasingly soused, Stalinist butler. When it has the courage of its singular convictions, the film capers off into weird and wild territory that cleverly masks the occasional clunk of corny symbolism.

IN GOD WE TRU$T (1980)

Now ensconced in America, Marty Feldman turned at least one of his satirical eyes onto that country's burgeoning evangelical movement. Feldman plays a naive Trappist monk threatened with eviction from his monastery by big-time TV evangelist Armageddon T Thunderbird (Andy '*Taxi*' Kaufman), and sets off into the seedier parts of Los Angeles to raise the rent money. A mess of random potshots that makes *Every Home…* seem sober, the film flails randomly at obvious targets (Peter Boyle plays a religious conman with a mobile cathedral) leavened with dollops of cornball sentiment (Feldman finds friendship with a stereotypical 'hooker with a heart of gold').

BRITANNIA HOSPITAL (1982)

Lindsay Anderson, Britain's king of the shrill satirical scream, had put Malcolm McDowell through his paces in the school revolution of *If…* (1968) and the rambling picaresque *O Lucky Man!* (1970) and finally dismembered him in this medical farce in which Britain becomes a crumbling, strike-hit NHS hospital. This much-derided comedy gleefully nicks the mantle of just about every popular British film genre from *Carry On* rudery to Hammer horror, with its cast of symbolic types played by familiar comic actors: Leonard Rossiter's financial director, Graham Crowden's amoral, brain-juicing research scientist and Robin Askwith's bolshy shop steward. Fittingly, it ends with staff and visiting dignitaries witnessing the unveiling of Crowden's latest wheeze – a super-computer poised to take over from the worn-out human race. Delicate it ain't, but as a full-stop to this most wayward of film genres, it's pretty hard to beat.

THE ESSENTIAL PARANOID BLOCKBUSTER

THE STUNT MAN (1980)

The 1970s were the age of the blockbuster with an A-level. Big, sprawling glossily shot films such as *2001* (1969) and *Apocalypse Now* (1978), which combined lavish set pieces with 'Big Things' to say about the world. It was mainstream Hollywood's adolescence, as Tinseltown went off on a gap decade to explore new ideas, experiment with editing, send its laundry home once a month and, naturally, celebrate their individuality by becoming as self-importantly po-faced as every other army greatcoat-wearing campus oaf.

A sense of humour was considered unnecessary by cinema's new sixth form. You won't find much to laugh at in *2001* (a terrible gag about a zero-gravity khazi and the muted appearance of Leonard Rossiter being the nearest thing you get to a grin). Fortunately, one smartarse blockbuster snuck in at the very end of the decade, a fat and frantic paranoid adventure that had its cake of weighty seriousness iced with a fusillade of sly swipes at the very intellectual Hollywood subculture it sprang from.

Steve Railsback is a down-at-heel Vietnam vet who escapes from police custody and goes on the run. The first sanctuary he comes upon is the set of a hysterical World War One film being directed by Eli Cross (Peter O'Toole), a fruitily tyrannical director who expounds on big themes as a huge beach invasion is shot. Cross is under investigation by the FBI after one of his stuntmen drowned in a vintage car; Railsback is not exactly in a hurry to go anywhere, so he's offered the job of replacing – in fact impersonating – the dead stuntman to cover both their arses. Throw in a tentative romance with the film's female lead Barbara Hershey and the stage is set for two hours of wilfully disorientating fun. O'Toole and Hershey are at it behind Railsback's back – or are they? The director is a megalomaniac with the crew united against him – or is he? The cops seem to be rather easily fooled – or are they?

You see what kind of a film this is (or do you?). Director Richard Rush's pet project languished in development hell for a decade. So did Cross's. O'Toole once turned up on set as Cross, wearing exactly the same outfit as Rush. Such practical joking among film crews is the source of many a paranoid moment for Railsback, and the audience. The beach battle scene is enjoyed by watching holidaymakers, politely applauding at every exploding biplane until the smoke clears to reveal what at first looks like real, horrific carnage. The good-natured rough and tumble of Railsback's stunt supervisor often looks scarily like a real attempt to kill him, and looming large is the final stunt: a re-run of the car-off-bridge scene that killed the original stuntman.

The stunt scenes are all immaculate, centring round a lengthy rooftop chase under biplane attack, which leads to Railsback falling through a skylight into a slightly too authentic-looking continental brothel. Shot both as it would be seen in the film and in 'behind the scenes' mode, these are as satisfyingly sumptuous as anything from a contemporary 'war is hell' picture, with added cheek to boot. Even when people are just talking, Rush lays on the unsettling details. Scenery is shifted in and out of shot behind actors. Things are done with reflections in glass. Smoke rings hover into the foreground just as Railsback mimes firing a gun in the background. These aren't lazy borrowings from the Hollywood Boys' book of 'How to Make a Classic Film'. It really doesn't look quite like anything else.

So far it sounds like a mix of action chestnuts and cold, tricksy Chinese box folderol, but the performances give it plenty of wallop in the heart department. Railsback is a refreshingly unsympathetic lead. The audience have to be on his side because they see everything through his eyes, but it's an uneasy alliance. The precise details of his crime are kept secret for ages, and when they do come out, it's in a storm of clumsy wailing violence even Rhett Butler couldn't ameliorate by dusting himself off and smouldering into the lens. Hershey is great too, not taking any crap from anyone and keeping her own motives very secret. O'Toole, naturally, steals the show, spouting self-justifying claptrap like a first language and having a whale of a time both in and out of character, either hovering in a chopper or following Railsback around in his rather nifty crane-mounted camera chair.

The film won critical plaudits and Oscar nominations galore, so how come Richard Rush never made another film until limp Bruce Willis psycho-sauce affair *Color of Night* (1994)? And how come *The Stunt Man* never makes it into the mutually agreed pantheon of clever blockbusters alongside *Deer Hunter*, *Apocalypse Now* and *Mean Streets*? Maybe because it doesn't fit in. Maybe because it's too 'zany', not pompous enough. Or maybe because, if critics included its tightly-coiled demolition of egotistical Hollywood pseuds among their other exhibits, it might lead them to ask what exactly is supposed to be so great and enlightening and true about Marlon Brando chatting fart about a snail in the dark? And that sort of thing would never do.

SPLIT SCREEN

SPLIT SCREEN

Daringly experimental or indulgently distracting? The process of split screen – chopping the celluloid frame up into two or more areas to show simultaneous action – comes and goes in popularity in the cinema as well as on telly. Love it or hate it, it's hard not to get a migraine from it. Here are a few landmarks from the eternal quest to make the silver screen resemble a *Nationwide* regional handover.

NAPOLEON (1927)
Abel Gance's historical behemoth got in on the act early, using multiple projectors to split the life of the inside pocket-fondler three ways, for an arse-numbing five and a half hours.

PILLOW TALK (1959)
Doris Day and Rock Hudson demonstrate what was the technique's main use for decades: the comedy phone call split, so clichéd even by this time it had long been parodied in Tex Avery cartoon *The Bear's Tale* (1940), where the classic gag of someone reaching over from one half of the screen to the other first manifested itself.

THE THOMAS CROWN AFFAIR (1968)
Possibly the most famous member of the splitters' club, this lavish crime caper began chopping the screen up like so much boiled tripe while Noel Harrison was still belting out the title song. This was the high water mark of the split screen era: *Grand Prix* (1966) roped in every available Panavision camera in the land for its six-picture racing scenes, and *The Boston Strangler* (1968) actually had a method to its multi-image madness, effectively recreating the confused nature of the media chatter over the titular killer, and staging a particularly effective police siege showing the action from both sides of a locked door.

THE ANDROMEDA STRAIN (1971)
Split screen looks a bit techy by default, so sci-fi was bound to give it a good home. Doubling up helped post-Watergate rogue nuke thriller *Twilight's Last Gleaming* (1977) get its complicated plot across, but this portentously ponderous plague chiller stood out for a scene where paramedics opened doorways in a plague-hit town, and what they saw through each of them was revealed in a little advent calendar-style window, complete with an unintentionally comical 'ding!' noise.

SISTERS (1973)
The technique fell out of popular use during the 1970s, and might have been lost altogether if it wasn't for the sterling efforts of Brian De Palma. This early feature, starring Margot Kidder as two separated-but-deadly Siamese twins, positively cried out for cinematic partitioning, and the habit stuck through such winningly lurid fare as *Phantom of the Paradise* (1974) and, most famously, *Carrie* (1976).

WICKED, WICKED (1973)
Reducing the whole prismatic shebang to the level of 'come see' gimmickry, this low-rent slasher depicted a detective hunt for a serial killer via the not-at-all-tedious method of having a permanent two-point-of-view split screen (one cop, one culprit) throughout the entire film. Or, if you prefer, 'spectacular Duo-vision!' It didn't do well.

JOHN BLUTHAL

ANARCHIC GENIUS OF THE SUPPORTING ROSTER

Many supporting actors do only that: support. Some work as straight men, providing lines for the stars to prove themselves brilliant at appropriate junctures, whereas others act as comedy relief, falling on their arse when things get too fraught in the foreground. On occasion they are handy as exposition monkeys, chipping in with a timely, 'But I don't understand what's so important about that book of spells/golden talisman/jade monkey, boss!' But every now and again a character actor of real quality comes along who actually helps to drive the plot along with their own unique schtick. John Bluthal is such a man.

Polish-born Bluthal started his career in august company. His first role was as none other than Robert the Bruce in *Father Came Too!* (1963) where he got the chance to exercise his talent for accents early on alongside a front rank cast including James Robertson Justice, Leslie Phillips, Stanley Baxter, Terry Scott, Ronnie Barker and Cardew Robinson. Some fairly straightforward roles followed, including *Carry On Spying* (1964) in which he had a small part (oooh matron!), *The Mouse on the Moon* (1963), the achingly 1960s centrepiece *The Knack and How to Get It* (1965) and a brace of Beatles features – *A Hard Day's Night* (1964) and *Help!* (1965) – before he inevitably became embroiled in that nexus of the supporting actor's craft *Casino Royale* (1967).

By the late 1960s, however, Bluthal was working on television with Spike Milligan and proving himself to be really the only man able to vie with that titan of comedy on screen. So it was no surprise that, as a fully-fledged member of the Milligan repertory company, and the leading one at that, he would soon transfer to the cinema in the company of Milligan and his gang in a leading spot. This eventually came to pass in the genuinely brilliant *The Great McGonagall* (1974). Bluthal played several roles in that extraordinary tribute to the eponymous Scottish poet, as did Peter Sellers, Victor Spinetti and Milligan himself, bringing to life characters such as Dundonian theatre owner Mr Giles and music hall caricature Hercules Faint with an accuracy and skill that most leading actors would be lucky to achieve even after several lifetimes of instruction. His involvement in that superlative piece, accomplished on a miniscule budget, filmed in one location and powered only by the force of the personalities taking part, is Bluthal's finest moment in pictures. Other actors might have been overwhelmed by their surroundings and the sheer scale of the talents they would be working with. However, as on television in the likes of the various series of *Q*, Bluthal demonstrated that he is more than a match for any actor with his extraordinary skill for accent and interpretation, and his amazing versatility. Subsequently, that film is motored not by a famous duo but by the accomplished triumvirate of Milligan, Sellers and Bluthal.

After this there were small roles in such broad mainstream fare as *The Return of the Pink Panther* (1975) as the self-employed blind musician subcontracted to a monkey. Bluthal then started to crop up in bigger-budget features, bringing class and skill to otherwise distinctly average productions. He added depth and interest to *Dark City* (1998) when Keifer Sutherland and Rufus Sewell couldn't manage it and remains one of the few things worth looking at in *The Fifth Element* (1997) that isn't a special effect or costume. However, the tiny part he was given in *Superman III* (1983) – smashing up a load of models of the leaning tower of Pisa, then smashing them again – counts as the biggest waste of material since Cher's tailor gave her a raincoat to wear to the Oscars.

Like many great character actors fallen foul of the dearth of quality film being made in Britain today, Bluthal has found television a medium far more appreciative of his talents especially since it would appear that some sort of *Logan's Run* clause has been places in budgeting contracts for films meaning that no-one over the age of about twenty-five is permitted to be in films. The cinema's loss is the telly's gain as John Bluthal was, and remains, one of the finest actors ever to have appeared in pictures.

VIDEO NASTIES - AN ABSTAINER'S GUIDE

In 1984, the British Government sought to stem the growing panic over the perceived flood of immoral horror films available on chunky Betamax cassettes from the backrooms of provincial newsagents by passing the Video Recordings Act, consigning seventy-four otherwise largely iffy cheapo horror flicks into iconic legal limbo. Among the summarily proscribed titles were a few films that were actually rather good (*The Evil Dead*, *Shogun Assassin*, *Tenebrae* and *Last House on the Left*), some terrible films dilettante chin-strokers have rather daftly insisted are masterpieces (*I Spit On Your Grave*, *The Driller Killer* and *Andy Warhol's Frankenstein*) and, well… the rest. Inevitably, that overlooked grubby majority is where the real, cheap 'n' fearful nature of the nasty video beast lies. For those who eschewed the fiendish delights of the nasties in favour of venturing outdoors, buying Pepsi and Shirlie records and grinning, here's a gristlestop tour of the otherwise unhistorical films briefly conferred mythical status by the ham-fisted manoeuvrings of those zany High Tories.

CANNIBAL FILMS

CANNIBAL HOLOCAUST, CANNIBAL FEROX, ANTROPHAGOUS THE BEAST, PRISONERS OF A CANNIBAL GOD, CANNIBAL APOCALYPSE, CANNIBAL UP THE KHYBER, etc.

Well, it's yer Last Taboo, innit? These grim gizzard-gobbling picaresques tend to be set in either a scrappy-looking bit of South American jungle ('Where life is cheap!') or some dingy basement somewhere in the Deep South. Either way it involves bottom-rung thespians munching awkwardly on a slab of raw pig offal pulled out of a latex head that bears little resemblance to the actor who's just been supposedly slaughtered, while affecting a crazed look as the disease takes hold. *Ferox* is the sleaziest, as they actually cut up real animals for a laugh – the 1980s equivalent of a titchy delinquent's mobile phone footage. Yum.

TEXAS CHAINSAW MASSACRE RIP-OFFS

CALIFORNIAN AXE MASSACRE, TOOLBOX MURDERS

Shamelessly cashing in on the big name *du jour* in gore, and not caring who knows it, these are true no-nonsense, tin-label-fulfilling films – Ronseal Nasties. Literally, in the latter case.

VIDEO NASTIES - AN ABSTAINER'S GUIDE

ELM STREET/FRIDAY THE 13TH **RIP-OFFS**

THE BOOGEYMAN, THE BURNING
If you loved the originals, you'll probably be lukewarm about the rip-offs. If you couldn't be bothered with the originals, well, what are you doing looking at these, anyway? *Electric Blue*'s down the next aisle, chum.

DAS NAUGHTY NAZIS

SS EXPERIMENT CAMP, THE BEAST IN HEAT, GESTAPO'S LAST ORGY
Before endless satellite channels lasciviously dramatised every last machination of the Nazi war machine down to the contents of Rudolf Hess' sock drawer, curtain-dodging Nuremberg nuts had to make do with these badly staged Mengele-style atrocities carried out by duff actors. Whatever amoral action these tapes' prurient purchasers were hoping for, the rather tepid contents thankfully failed to deliver, thus scoring a perverse moral victory, of sorts.

ITALIAN ZOMBIES

ZOMBIE FLESH-EATERS, ZOMBIE CREEPING FLESH, THE BEYOND
Feted in some circles as unsung masterworks of lyrical dismemberment. 'The pierced eyeball scene in …*Flesh Eaters* is pure cinema!' you'll hear someone say if you hang around long enough outside the National Film Theatre. This will be your cue to go immediately home and watch *Brief Encounter*.

FILMS THAT START WITH 'DON'T...'

DON'T GO INTO THE WOODS, DON'T GO NEAR THE PARK, DON'T LOOK IN THE BASEMENT
But you can bet someone does! The rather predictable video nasty equivalent of a Whitehall farce, *sans* Brian Rix.

OBVIOUSLY FAKE PRETEND DOCUMENTARIES

SNUFF, FACES OF DEATH
Really pathetic staged beheadings, executions, gorings by wild boar, etc., interspersed with genuine-but-unremarkable car-crash footage and the like. *Snuff* is especially egregious, with the final segment purporting to be a clip of a real, woman-killing snuff movie. It clearly isn't, though. Put it away, Trevor.

CHEERY OLD 1960s DRIVE-IN FODDER THAT REALLY SHOULDN'T BE ON THE LIST

BLOOD FEAST

Herschell Gordon Lewis was an amiable purveyor of sub-Roger Corman schlock that revolved around southern hicks showering each other in torrents of unfeasibly scarlet fluid on flatly lit sets. Exactly why Leon Brittan felt this presented a major threat to the moral fibre of the UK, while simultaneously letting Kenny Everett's hapless DIY practitioner Reg Prescott spurt equivalent amounts of Kensington Gore on a weekly basis at the Beeb, remains a mystery.

BIBLICAL EPICS

Sin, evil, debauchery, wickedness, devilry, sex, death, power, money... considering the subject matter it should really come as no surprise that Hollywood has always been obsessed with adaptations of the *Bible*. Unlike most of Tinseltown's historical efforts, which typically are about as accurate as Ken Dodd's self-assessment form, when it comes to film versions of the Good Book things are suddenly very different.

On the cinematic release of *The Ten Commandments* (1956) a special feature was shown at the outset of it which demonstrated that not only was the following a faithful adaptation of the Exodus, augmented by the scribblings of mysterious and exotic historians such as Josephus, but the stone tablets used in the film were cut from yer actual Mount Sinai and written in straight up Aramaic (which would now attract a copyright infringement notice from Mel Gibson). One reason for this sudden regard for the source material may be that for sheer wild fantasy and outrageous flights of fancy, no scriptwriter can match sticks turning into snakes or the ten (count 'em!) plagues of Egypt. Producers took excessive pride in ensuring their films were big in scale and equally big on fact... or at least literalism.

The aforementioned *The Ten Commandments* might reasonably be considered the best of the biblical bunch, especially since it prominently features the three things that go together to make any God-bothering spectacular work: big stars, big sights and ludicrous dialogue. For big sights the parting of the Red Sea and the exodus from Egypt are still pretty impressive. For silly dialogue the likes of, 'Dance you straw dogs!' and 'You have the eyes of the wolf!' still take a bit of beating. However, it is the peerless cast that has made this film most famous, including Edward G. Robinson, Vincent Price, Cedric Hardwicke, Yvonne de Carlo, Anne Baxter, Yul Brynner and of course Charlton Heston, proving for not the first or last time in his lengthy career that it is possible to be at the very heart of a massive action piece, yet still do bugger all.

Heston also put his signature 'daringly underplayed' style to use in the equally big and silly *Ben-Hur* (1959), which hardly anyone considers a religious epic anymore. By the time folks bring to mind the sea battle and the chariot race they have as much time for its spiritual aspects as Ben-Hur's mother and sister eventually have for Revlon. Biblical bits are restricted to the beginning and end, signified by the appearance on screen of Balthasar (Finlay Currie), one of the original Three Wise Men who by this time had split up, presumably over creative differences, leaving him ro pursue a solo career. *Ben-Hur* is a straight-up-and-down action film, which is most likely the reason why it gets far more attention than the more overtly religious *The Ten Commandments*, even though it's not nearly as good.

Being an action film, *Ben-Hur* is all get up and go – a radical diversion from most biblical stories, which are extraordinarily slow. Like not tap dancing in church or pointing out that Billy Graham looks a bit like Russ Conway, the quietness in biblical films seems to be one of the protocols of religious observance, most especially those adapted from the New Testament. *The Greatest Story Ever Told* (1965) is so awe-struck by its subject it makes less noise than the traffic in a Harold Lloyd short. 'Twas not ever thus. When Lew Grade was supreme governor of ATV and promised the Pope he'd make a proper adaptation of the life of Jesus, the resultant telly epic was as big and showy a production as Grade ever produced. *Jesus Of Nazareth* (1977), ironically given the medium, is one of the biggest biblical efforts. The sets Franco Zeferelli had made for Grade's mammoth spectacular were put to good use by the Monty Python team for *Life Of Brian* (1979), which has the distinction of being the most controversial Jesus-based feature. However much Mel Gibson's more recent *The Passion Of The Christ* (2004) drummed up newspaper headlines over its graphic depictions of violence, that blood-spattered chunderthon was not banned by provinical town councils, causing a French Underground-style network of bus routes to more liberal boroughs to spring up.

Brian's most solid contender for the title of most controversial adaptation is Martin Scorcese's *The Last Temptation Of Christ* (1988). Starring scary Willem Dafoe as the lad 'imself, it caused outrage amongst people for whom outrage is a particular talent: devout Christians. Leaving the arguments about heresy and blasphemy and all sorts of other words that really ought to be well out of common use by now aside, the real trouble with this is it expands the trend of quietness in Gospel stories to strange and dangerous new levels. By the time the supposedly contentious bit comes along at the end only those looking to be shocked could possibly be shocked as only those looking to be shocked are still awake. Jesus fantasises on the cross about having an ordinary life, which involves an apparently vigorous sex life with his ideal wife, Mary Magdalene. Leaving aside the slight quibble that someone slowly and painfully feeling life being wrenched from them during the course of a brutal and excruciating execution might have something else on their mind other than a tumble with an acquaintance, it is quite clear that no-one is actually suggesting that Jesus did in fact do this, just that he might have done. Still, fact has never been the strong suit of the religious fundamentalist and the film was widely condemned, only to re-emerge into the mainstream years later, just in time to be lumped in alongside other formerly controversial films like *The Exorcist* in the 'what was the fuss all about?' category.

King Of Kings (1961) is not much better as far as the unbearable stillness of being goes. Lines are delivered as if the actors have been recorded in a library. Not the most memorable Good News outing, it does benefit from narration by Ray Bradbury and Orson Welles, but is lumbered with being – as many of these are – exceptionally long. Despite it not being the most ubiquitous version of the story it does feature performances that stick in the mind, and Jeffrey Hunter as Jesus remains many people's enduring image of Him, at least on screen. Rip Torn and Siobhan McKenna are also memorable as Judas and Mary, and it all looks terribly good but eventually the seasoned film watcher starts to wonder what the motivation for these biblical films is. Possibly the producers have a beneficial zeal and, like the Buddhist pizza shop, want to make us one with everything. On the other hand, it's difficult not to conclude that these are all just a cynical exploitation of people's deeply held beliefs. If the latter were the case, they could at least make them a little more interesting, though admittedly there isn't much scope in the Passion story for a sea battle.

BIBLICAL EPICS

Other more interesting films on a religious theme include *The Robe* (1953) which is famous for featuring Richard Burton being acted off the screen by half a yard of red woolly blanket, and for Victor Mature as convert gladiator Demetrius, giving the performance of his life tussling with big cuddly lions. Jay Robinson gives one of his superbly mental turns as Caligula, playing the part for all its worth as a psychotic Kenneth Williams but without the vocal range. Unusually for films of a biblical bent, the source text for which is not noted for being one of an ongoing series, this spawned a sequel, *Demetrius and the Gladiators* (1954), introduced by a short montage of scenes from its predecessor in a definite Saturday night tea-time 'Last week on *The Robe!*' style.

Of the remaining *Old Testament* features, not many make the grade. *Solomon and Sheba* (1959) is a particular crappy effort. Yul Brynner and Gina Lollobrigida are rubbish, and only George Sanders is worth watching, though if the viewer can bear to hang on until the end there's the brilliant battle scene where Solomon defeats the Hammerites (or whoever) by flashing their shields in their faces sending them into a tizz. *Samson and Delilah* (1949) is equally poor, despite the presence of Mature. Probably the most recent entry into the Old Testament canon, *King David* (1985) is the one that killed off the genre as a viable proposition. Starring Richard Gere, deploying his patented 'look down and sigh' style of acting to no great effect, it really is a disaster not even the quite remarkable performance of Edward Woodward can save. The second coming of the whole biblical genre remains a long, long way off.

LEW GRADE

Retirement never suited Lew Grade. He and his two brothers – Jews in exile from Russia in the brick tenements of Bethnal Green – had the work ethic stamped into them as only a childhood of poverty can stamp it. However, odd jobs of tailoring work soon palled, and the brothers were drawn to the stage. The Charleston was the latest craze, and Lew, above even slick brother Bernie, shone in the many hubristically named 'World Charleston Competitions' held in London during the 1920s. Later he toured Europe with his act, the centrepiece of which was a manic Charleston atop a specially made tiny round table. From then it was a logical move for the ambitious brothers to behind-the-scenes management, and Lew and brother Leslie together (and Bernard Delfont elsewhere) rose to become giants of the British variety circuit.

Television was the next medium to conquer, and it wasn't too long out of Baird's attic before Lew declared an interest, snapping up one of the regional commercial station franchises to create what became ATV, that titan of slick transatlantic crime and action series, not to mention *The Muppet Show*. However by the mid-1970s, with forced retirement from fifteen-hour days of scheduling episodes of *The Persuaders* on the cards, the seventy-years-young Louis Winogradsky fancied something a bit more challenging than matchstick models of the Albert Memorial for his dotage.

Bernie was already going great guns chairing the then just about still mighty EMI-Elstree conglomerate, and films seemed to be where it was at for Lew, too. Associated General Films was the result, a US-backed company bankrolling a slate of big films for 1976-77. The first, *The Cassandra Crossing*, allegedly organised in a one-minute conversation between Lew and producer Carlo Ponti at Nice airport, was a rather bloated all-star European 'plague train' disaster flick showcasing Ponti's wife Sophia Loren. It's no classic, but it did the business. Sadly, the other films did not. *The Eagle Has Landed*, with Michael Caine as a go-ahead Nazi on a Churchill kidnapping spree, did good work in Britain but nonplussed everyone else. Another wartimer, worthy doomed refugee boat epic *Voyage of the Damned*, disappointed in all territories. An injured Gene Hackman meant spiralling budgets for Foreign Legion drama *March or Die*, and Hackman also failed to light up lacklustre paranoia thriller *The Domino Principle*. Another conspiracy flick, Mars mission fakeroo *Capricorn One*, was fun, but no box office cigar.

Easily stung, the Yanks pulled out, and Lew relied on an alliance with EMI to keep the ball rolling. Money was back, but quality varied. Idiotic Nazi clone shoot-'em-up *The Boys from Brazil* (1978) was, financially, one of the better bets. *The Big Sleep* (1978), the latest chapter in Michael Winner's mission to royally piss over as many classic films as he could, was one of the worse ones. Slightly better was not-nearly-as-good-as-the-telly adaptation *The Muppet Movie* (1979). Slightly worse were 9/11 predicting (but still rotten) telekinetic tosh *The Medusa Touch* (1978) and Martin Amis-scripted Kirk Douglas-vs-top-heavy-robot bore *Saturn 3* (1980). Not a vintage haul by either critical or accountancy standards. Then Lew was handed the proofs of a sooncome airport novel about the lifting up of a big sunken old boat, and that showbiz instinct started twinkling again.

Taking transatlanticism to its logical conclusion (as only a man with the cheek to name an American-based company Marble Arch Productions could), *Raise the Titanic* (1980) was the film for which, sadly, Lew's cinematic venture will always be remembered. The problem was there from the outset. A mostly talky number, it relied for word of mouth on the spectacular nature of the climactic ship-up, which was never going to come cheap. To ensure maximum realism, the model ship was made as big as possible: fifty-five feet long. Unfortunately, there wasn't a water tank in the world big enough to sink it in, so one was specially built in Malta. It leaked. They fixed the leaks. They sank the ship in it. The ship buckled under the massive water pressure. They fixed the ship… and on, and on; $34 million later, the film opened to tumbleweeds and muted coughs. It wasn't that the model work was anything less than sterling. The water let it down. No matter how big your little boat looks, water remains stubbornly small on screen. The best Grade's men could achieve was a superior episode of (the Grade-produced) *Thunderbirds*. Oops.

After much financial to-ing and fro-ing, Grade regrouped for a final spate of releases, which included popular but queasy Fondafest *On Golden Pond* (1982) and less popular but more fun Hensonia *The Great Muppet Caper* (1981) and *The Dark Crystal* (1982). Sadly, it also included *The Legend of the Lone Ranger* (1981), a high-risk resurrection job that lived or died on the star quality of its then unknown lead actor. Sadly for Lew, the name of Klayton Spillsbury failed to resonate down the decades, and the wooden lassoathon proved the final straw for Lew's film-production empire. Lew resigned, assets were stripped, and the operation flogged to the emergent Tri-Star Company, who would henceforth conform to New Hollywood type and only release films after endless focus groups, meetings and lunches. With Lew died the last glimmer of Old Hollywood, of a single mogul behind a huge desk, making and breaking deals on instinct with a flick of his cigar, in a stubbornly reckless fashion that remains sorely missed.

PULLING RANK

In the annals of British film, no name rings out more sonorously down the ages than the gong-wielding behemoth begat by self-raising flour tycoon and staunch Methodist J Arthur Rank. From 1937, the Rank Organisation went from strength to strength, buying up assorted film production companies, studios and the Odeon cinema chain in short order. By the 1950s, they had five studios, umpteen stars and directors on their books, the charm school in full swing, and the mighty *Look at Life* churning out prim documentaries weekly. By the mid-1970s, however, with the good J. Arthur long deceased, things were looking iffy. Barely 1.5 million quid's worth of films were being made a year, and the only regular banker still in the fold – the *Carry Ons* – were finally starting to wane in takings terms. No-one else, not even Rank's main rivals, Lord Grade's ACC and the mighty Thorn–EMI, were up to much either; things were looking as grim for mainstream British cinema as for much the rest of the islands' industries.

Then, in 1977, the Organisation suddenly, out of the blue, decided to go for it. Rank opened up a sudden slew of productions. All seemed set for a revival. But not everyone else in the company was singing from the same hymn sheet. The distribution company, in charge of all those lovely cinemas, turned a blind eye to many of the new offerings, thus killing them stone dead. If Rank didn't want to show Rank films, what hope had they of selling them to anyone else? What did come out died pathetically in the box office and, while they weren't exactly losing a fortune over multi-million-pound flops, head honcho Ed Chilton got cold enough feet to announce a final, once-and-for-all pulling of Rank's film production interests in 1979, and the board went back to bide their time with the cinemas, back catalogues and shares in the Xerox company to tide them over.

They may have gone out with a whimper, but what a whimper! Yes, the studio got it horribly, hopelessly wrong, but they tried so hard, and so randomly, in the process, it's hard not to warm to these fag-end films. Here are ten of the most intriguing.

THE UNCANNY (1977)

Odd, Anglo-Canadian feline horror portmanteau in which horror novelist Peter Cushing tells three terrible tales of supernatural catty menace to disbelieving publisher Ray Milland. In number one Susan Penhaligon is a maid out to get a slice of her cat-loving ma'am Joan Greenwood's inheritance by suffocating the old cow, only for the feisty felines to scratch her to death in retaliation. In number two a quiet orphan girl has her revenge on her teasing cousin by shrinking her and getting her cat to do her in, with lashings of appallingly-matched back projection shots. Then there is Cushy's special prize: Donald Pleasence and Samantha Eggar are 1930s Hollywood actors having an affair and doing the former's wife in with a non-fake 'fake' *Pit and the Pendulum* film studio prop, only for her ginger tom to have the last miaow. Milland sees Cushing out and burns the script – but did his cat tell him to do so, or did he just think it was rubbish? Lurking in the production credits is good old Milton Subotsky. You can take the lad out of Amicus...

GOLDEN RENDEZVOUS (1977)

A couple of foreign productions helped Rank expand their range, and hedge their bets with various territories at the same time. This South African thriller is pretty close to home though, being a standard Alistair MacLean romp about a gang of terrorists led by John 'stuffy old Dean Worner off of *Animal House*'s Vernon using a nuclear bomb in a coffin to hold Richard Harris' tramp steamer hostage. They were originally led by Christopher Lee, until a barely-coherent Harris fired him in a spate of sauce-fuelled narkiness. The rest of the thing proceeds much as you'd expect, with smuggled enemy agents, some derring-do by an injured Harris, and the inevitable 'blimey, that bomb countdown's taking its time' cliffhanger climax, augmented by such dependable action stalwarts as Burgess Meredith, Gordon Jackson and *Emmerdale Farm*'s Eric Pollard.

HOLOCAUST 2000 (1977)

Hmm... Nuclear power station owner Kirk Douglas suspects his son to be the Antichrist, who's after the controls to the carbon rods for a bit of millennial meltdown mayhem. Cue loads of half-bothered antinuclear sentiment, some stock symbolism about the book of *Revelations* and a crucial equation looking vaguely like 'Jesus' written backwards, a bizarre nightmare sequence wherein the power station rises from the sea and turns into a bunch of grinning dragons in back-projected Supermarionation, some fun proto-*Silence of the Lambs* asylum set design, a rather nifty top-of-head-meets-chopper-blade death for a visiting dignitary, Douglas getting his kit off and being kicked about a padded cell, and some rather nasty stuff about abortion. This Anglo-Italian co-production effortlessly blends all that's ludicrous about both nations' horror traditions into one demented whole. But the laughs are mainly on Kirk Douglas. Especially whenever he's acting 'outraged on humanity's behalf', or pantless.

WOMBLING FREE (1977)

In cahoots with the sainted Dame Wimbledon, Elizabeth Beresford, Lionel Jeffries cooks up an overblown eco-disaster plot, drafts in the agreeable pairing of David Tomlinson and Frances de la Tour as middle-class human foils, then saddles them with Bonnie Langford in regulation St Trinian's gear as daughter, and adds a 'comedy' Japanese couple living next door. The live-action Womble suits are just poor, despite the best efforts of Kenny 'R2D2' Baker inside them, with annoying expressionless faces over which David Jason, Jon P'Twee and Janet Brown are uneasily dubbed. 'My kingdom for a Cribbins!' It's all about as charming as the coniferous terrain of the ubiquitous Black Park, the default, Borehamwood-handy countryside location for many a cheapo fantasy (*Supergirl, Krull, Island of Terror* and, er, *Carry On Cowboy*). And Mike Batt fails to work his usual queasy magic with songs, ranging from the breathtakingly limp (*Madame Cholet*) to the monocle-swallowingly infuriating (*Exercise is Good for You, Laziness is Not*).

PULLING RANK

THE SHOUT (1978)

Alan Bates: a great actor – a minute to learn, a lifetime to master. Here he turns up at a lunatic asylum cricket match, waylaying scorer Tim Curry with a tale of how he terrorised John Hurt and Susannah York with his scary aboriginal mouth noises. Cue the genteel Devonian countryside turning to tribal madness, dead animals, Lazarou-esque wife repossession, York scurrying about in the nip, Hurt doing a Brian Eno with bulky 1970s sound equipment, random close-ups of pebbles, church organs, an exploding scoreboard, soundtrack electronica in excelsis courtesy Tony 'Genesis' Banks and Rupert 'Quantum Jump' Hine, Robert Stephens, Carol Drinkwater and Jim Broadbent dancing about in the nip. As far as weird British horror based around murderous noises and starring a cavalcade of stalwart UK acting talent goes, only the video for Kate Bush's 'Experiment IV' beats it.

THE THIRTY-NINE STEPS (1978)

Hitchcock did it with Robert Donat. Ralph 'Doctor films' Thomas had a go with Kenneth More. The stage was thus set for Don 'Psychomania' Sharp's take on the old Buchan chestnut, which equated to a lot of running about over the heather, and a climactic, Big Ben-set homage to, or if you prefer direct copy of, the Harold Lloyd-alike climax to vintage Will Hay legal comedy My Learned Friend.

THE LADY VANISHES (1979)

This is a fairly faithful (almost shot for shot) but totally unnecessary remake of the much loved Gainsborough train-napping, with Angela Lansbury just fine in the disappearing part, and Arthur Lowe and Ian Carmichael as a dandy Charters and Caldicott… But Elliot Gould as Michael Redgrave? And more to the point, Cybill Shepherd as Margaret Lockwood? Attempts are made to get some screwball banter going between the pair as of old, but Cyb's way off Moonlighting chemistry here, and Gould's more attuned to less well-mannered comedy than this. A better Gainsborough update than Michael Winner's version of The Wicked Lady, but not by much.

TARKA THE OTTER (1979)

'Does snuff exist?' ponders Channel Four, passim. Well, yes it does, it's here, and it's rated A. Screenwriter Gerald Durrell and director David Cobham did the more squeamish kids few favours in their adaptation of Henry Williamson's treasured nature story with multiple, unflinchingly graphic scenes of violent otter mortality, climaxing with the eponymous tyke's grisly fight to the death with the hounds of John 'K9' Leeson's hunt party. Despite the omnipresence of the fur-lined gore, this harrowing film was screened in schools up and down the land. Peter Ustinov's avuncular narration did little to ease the childhood terror brought on by so much shredded otter offal so closely photographed. The subsequent 'Let's have a talk about what we've just seen' topic work turned into a mass trauma therapy session for more than a few fragile souls.

BAD TIMING (1980)

In a nutshell: Theresa Russell takes an overdose. She's been shagging Art Garfunkel behind Denholm Elliot's back. Elliot finds out, and doesn't much care. Art finds out about Elliot and does. Cue shouting and thrown bottles aplenty. Russell takes an overdose, Art turns up and phones an ambulance, but not before shagging her as she lies about, half-dead. Or does he? Or did she? Or will they? Harvey Keitel to the rescue... Nic Roeg's usual temporal trickery slices and dices this ripe bit of noir like so much boiled Haslet for the butcher's window, and the necro undertones so curdled the Rank top brass's Horlicks they denounced the thing as the product of sick minds and ensured this last hurrah for the company came without the customary gong-bashing muscleman up the front end.

SILVER DREAM RACER (1980)

From an original story by 'Colonel Foster' from *UFO!* David Essex is Barry Sheene – well, sort of – urged by his dead brother's widow Diane Keen to take the bike bro' had been building to Silverstone success. The only fly in the ointment is unscrupulous, moneyed Yank rival Beau Bridges. Thus, the scene is set for a rather boring underdog-makes-good story, with a rather shocking 'just when you thought he'd won it' perfunctory ending that was tidied up for overseas sales. Harry H. Corbett, Ed Bishop and Lis Sladen inhabit the authentically 1970s-overcast landscape, and the soundtrack thrums to *The Real Thing*, former *Val Doonican* backing singer *Victy Silva* and Dave's own majestic Silver Dream Machine. Alas, the planet's bums remained obstinately distanced from those all-important Odeon seats, and the Rank Organisation turned back to its photocopier royalties for solace. No more would darkened Oscar Deutsch fleapits reverberate to the dubbed-on strains of Ken Richmond in just his pants stroking a giant plaster crumpet with an outsize cotton bud.

ELSTREE AND SYMPATHY

Great Hollywood film corporations are brought to their knees by the titanic demands of their stars, or multi-million-dollar miscalculations. In Britain, studio woe can emanate from altogether more mundane troubles.

1969: Bryan Forbes assumes his post as head of production at EMI-Elstree, encountering leaking roofs, overgrown backlots and a workforce issuing superhumanly complicated demands. It went something like this. The brothers treated Forbsey, a *wunderkind* in the days when film technicians weren't overly fond of *wunderkinds* and thought them a bit of an Engels-mocking nuisance about the place, with suspicion. His part in making anti-wildcat strike film *The Angry Silence* (1960) probably didn't help matters. So, when Bry started being all 'I'm on the side of the filmmakers, not the moneymen', they didn't buy it.

Let's get down to brass tacks, the lads told Bryan. Just how many free cups of tea per day would each worker be entitled to? 'Unlimited', replied Forbes. Well, that placated two craft unions, but the third wanted more: waitress service. Irene Handl in a pinny pushing a big urn on a trolley, belting out impromptu renditions of *Red Sails in the Sunset* as she plied her wares from sound stage to sound stage, that sort of thing. Forbes, no stranger to the brown stuff, remarked that such an old-fashioned method of tea distribution resulted in a brew 'you could skate mice across', and anyway there's no room in the budget for Irene Handl. You can have unlimited free tea, but get it yourself.

That was it. The brothers retreated for several weeks' industrial action, during which they arrived at the true price of a cup of tea lady tea: about tuppence less than British Rail were then charging. This was too expensive, they told Forbes. Hang on, said Bry, you've just turned down free tea; don't moan to me about your own alternative being too expensive. And so it dragged on, while Robert Fuest waited in the wings, itching to get filming on *And Soon the Darkness*. Eventually everyone got bored and went back, but, never entirely happy with the post, Bryan left within two years to make way for Nat Cohen. Sadly history fails to record Nat's position on the biscuit question.

MARGARET LOCKWOOD

GAINSBOROUGH GIRL

Hollywood had a star system almost as soon as they had film. It took barely a second before the industry went from paying whoever was hanging round the studio gates two bucks to come in and fall off a wall, to Fatty Arbuckle commanding a million a year and getting into all sorts of rum trouble. Britain, however, typically avoided this new royalty, until go-ahead studio Gainsborough, neither blessed with critical success nor mammoth budgets, decided in the 1930s to inject a bit of fun into their melodramas and comedies by rounding up a batch of young actors and promoting them as never before in these Isles. Margaret Lockwood was among that initial intake.

A graduate of the finely named Cone School of Dancing, Lockwood was a canny choice for star status, possessing an appealing calmness alongside a wisely rebellious streak: at RADA, she refused to kowtow to the strangulated 'how verreh verreh love-lay' diction drilled into the other pupils. Appearing as a village dancing girl in *Lorna Doone* (1934), she was plucked from chorus-line obscurity and bunged into the second female lead role – the ideal fairy tale career start, if the film hadn't turned out to be a big honking turd.

Still, it was work, and with the government insisting the country churn out a minimum number of films to compete with the USA – no matter what the quality – there was plenty more where that came from. Lockwood appeared in six 'quota quickies' in 1935, landing her first lead role in *Some Day* as a cleaning girl falling for a lift attendant. She was picked out for lead status in naval swashbuckler *Midshipman Easy* by its star Hughie Green, and began a fruitful association with first-time director Carol Reed.

Her big break came with *The Beloved Vagabond* (1936), in which she played a peasant girl befriended by Maurice Chevalier's architect bumming his way round Provence. Equally high-concept was *Irish for Luck* (1936), with Lockwood as the niece of an itinerant Irish duchess who gets her musical act on BBC radio. This was a popular theme for film comedies at the time. The similarly radio mad *Melody and Romance* (1937) featured Margs alongside Hughie Green again (and his Gang, all trying to get on the Beeb), plus a young Alistair Sim.

Then Gainsborough came a-knocking, and a fine turn as the daughter of the titular Dymchurch smuggler in *Dr Syn* (1937) led to a three-year contract with the studio, who knew a good star when they saw one. However, they didn't necessarily know a good film when they saw one though, as they then stuck her in Cumbrian sheepdog romance *Owd Bob* (1938) – not the best of starts, as Lockwood's supremely dodgy regional accent demonstrated.

But soft! Legend status was just round the corner, as she landed the female lead in a little film Alfred Hitchcock was helming at the Islington studios, *Lost Lady*, soon to become *The Lady Vanishes* (1938), paired with film debutant Michael Redgrave. The shoot, a low-budget affair knocked off in five weeks on a cramped set, did not suggest great things, but the tempting blend of mystery and good old Brit eccentricity (exemplified by Dame May Whitty's scatty title role and the cricket obsessed Charters and Caldicott) is now rightly sealed in the pantheon of cinema greats.

Next stop, Hollywood! This proved to be a step back, if desultory roles in tosh such as *Susannah of the Mounties* (1939), a dire Shirley Temple western vehicle, and *Rulers of the Sea* (1939), a naval epic that owing to Lockwood's sea sickness was shot mainly in dodgy back projection, were anything to go by. Add to that a lot of trouble from the sniping Yank press, and Margs quickly turned tail and fled home, to the sanctity of Carol Reed's quality product.

The Stars Look Down (1940) was what lured her back. Alongside Michael Redgrave's idealistic, reformist miner's son, she was coaxed into the sort of 'hussy' role that caused monocles to fall in martinis the country over. A precedent was set. After a slight return to *Lady Vanishes* territory (and Charters and Caldicott) with *Night Train to Munich* (1940), and a first, uneasy pairing with James Mason in *Alibi* (1942), Lockwood entered her imperial phase with regency romance *The Man in Grey* (1943).

All the Gainsborough trappings are here - corsets, carriages, James Mason, Stewart Granger, Phyllis Calvert, and Margs in – yes – her wickedest role yet. A whale of a time was had by all (except possibly Mason) on set, Margs regularly letting rip with what Granger described as 'the raucous laugh of a truck driver'. *Love Story* (1944) was a more subdued pairing of the two: Lockwood's pianist with a year to live shacking up with Granger's blind RAF pilot.

After a few more diversions – possessed by a murdered girl in *A Place of One's Own* (1945) and hopping into tights but having her singing voice dubbed for dawn of copyright music hall musical *I'll be Your Sweetheart* (1945) – came the role that was to define her, for better or worse, ever after. *The Wicked Lady* (1945) was slagged off something rotten at the time, for its unprecedented sauciness (censors in the USA snipped acres of footage of Lockwood's heaving bosom) and its silly plot (Mason thought it 'utter codswallop'). But the public loved the highwaywoman romp, to the tune of over 18 million British bums on Imperial seats. Margs was now confident enough to turn down piss-poor offers such as Paganini biopic *The Magic Bow*. A star was finally born.

Crinolines and clairvoyance combined in *Jassy* (1947), a florid tale in which future-predicting gypsy girl Lockwood inherits a manor. What Gainsborough gained in budget (better sets and Technicolor) they lost in quality, and a rerun of *Wicked Lady* success didn't quite happen. Lockwood's increasingly star-like temperament finally caused her to fall out with the Gainsborough bigwigs after she flatly refused to take part in the crappy Ralph Thomas comedy *Once Upon a Dream* (1949), instead opting for a role as Nell Gwynne in the Sid Field vehicle *Cardboard Cavalier* (1949), getting a custard pie in the face for her trouble. This was a decision she quite rightly never regretted.

Sadly, with Gainsborough's golden age gone, so was hers. *Highly Dangerous* (1950) was highly silly: Margs as an entomologist with a thing for *Dick Barton* serials, coaxed into Eastern Bloc espionage concerning poisonous insects. *Trouble in the Glen* (1953), a misbegotten Scottish follow-up to the ace *The Quiet Man*, with Margs as daughter to lairy South American laird Orson Welles, was miles worse, not least thanks to the grotty Trucolour process it was shot in, rendering a very brown outdoors indeed.

It was then mainly telly work, including Yorkshire TV's barrister drama *Justice*, as cinema no longer appealed. She turned down what became the Beryl Reid role in *Entertaining Mr Sloane* (1970), though later on, when she guested on *Personal Cinema*, a BBC programme in which stars picked their favourite films, *Sloane* was prominent among her choices. The game Bryan Forbes coaxed one final screen appearance out of her as the stepmother in 'Protocoligorically Correct' fairy tale *The Slipper and the Rose* (1975), but from then on it was a secluded life for one of Britain's first, and best, film stars.

SITCOM SPIN-OFFS

Contrary to popular opinion, most of what constitutes modern cinema originated in Britain. Narrative structure, named stars and all that sort of thing were a creation of the pioneers of the medium on these shores, not America. However, foreign film industries have been responsible for the popularisation of several specific genres. The Yanks, for example, are the progenitors of the Western, for which the remainder of the civilised world may come to forgive them in time. The French have made a speciality of daringly underlit moody melodrama and the Indians have the gaudy and baffling musical. However, one genre that is wholeheartedly British, for good or ill, is the big-screen sitcom spin-off.

Why this should have been is hard to say. Possibly, like the comedy-star vehicle, it made sense in a feckless market to capitalise on an already popular property, but the films themselves mutated over time. Early efforts tended to be films in their own right, merely founded upon characters and their associated situations, but eventually they came to be simply extended episodes of the original series. Tellingly, the quality of the films depended vastly on the quality of the series itself, but that is not always the rule. Great sitcoms such as *Nearest And Dearest* brought forth extraordinarily bad films. However, what matters is not their origins but the films themselves, and some of them are very good indeed. In the risible *Forrest Gump* (1994) Tom Hanks famously says, 'Life is like a box of chocolates, you never know what you're going to get'. In *The Likely Lads* (1976) Bob tells Terry, 'in the chocolate box of life the top layer's already gone. And someone's pinched the orange crème from the bottom'. That's proper philosophy, that is.

LIFE WITH THE LYONS (1954)/THE LYONS IN PARIS (1954)

Starring real life husband and wife team Ben Lyon and Bebe Daniels, and their children Richard and Barbara Lyon, this is probably the first filmed sitcom, although it's technically a film of a hit radio situation comedy, since the television series came after the films. Ben Lyon was an American actor who had been appearing in numerous films including *Hell's Angels* (1930), loony billionaire Howard Hughes' panegyric to pilots. Lyon starred in another radio-based film, *Hi Gang!* (1941) which had little to do with the show other than featuring one of its stalwarts, British comic Vic Oliver, married at the time to Sarah Churchill, daughter of Winston. Lyon joined the RAF and the family moved to Britain, striking their biggest success there, the radio series *Life With The Lyons*, which was as massively popular as only wartime radio series could be. It probably seemed natural to spin the venture off into film, especially since television was still the province of half a dozen families living so close to the studios that they could have heard the announcers by leaning out of their living room windows. The show did make it to television in 1955. It turned out that the radio, television and film versions all had one thing in common: they weren't funny. The films themselves are based on the same premise as their predecessors: family get involved in scrapes, dad gets a bit frustrated, wife tells him to calm down, kids laugh at him, everybody cuddles – a thick seam of boundless hilarity indeed. The one in Paris is the same, but with jokes about frogs.

BOTTOMS UP! (1960)
Unlike the above, this is a full-blown film version of a hit television comedy, and it really is a treat. The programme on which it is based, *Whack-O!* (1956), starred marvelously moustachioed Jimmy Edwards (massively bewhiskered as always to hide the plastic surgery he received after crash-landing his plane during the war) as the appalling headmaster of the equally dismal Chiselbury public school, somewhere in England. Extremely popular and hugely well regarded, the show centered on the efforts of Professor Edwards to chisel his feckless living of drinking and gambling out of the school, while fending off the efforts of the boys to chisel him in turn for whatever they could get. The result was the administering of several *Daily Mail*-pleasing whacks with the cane – hence the title of the show – and the pleasingly naive title of its spin-off. All the shenanigans you might expect in a film centered around a school and its useless staff happen; government inspectors, angry parents, insufferable kids, hopeless teachers, all thrown together in an excellent mix of rather touchingly innocent fun as Edwards extorts, brutalises and nurtures his charges – all entirely against their will of course. The cast is extraordinary too, with Raymond Huntley, Martita Hunt and an incredibly junior Richard Briers. If schools were still run along these lines, well, not much would be any better, but they would at least inspire funnier films.

I ONLY ARSKED (1958)
The long-running smash hit ITV series *The Army Game* (1957) was so ubiquitous its film version only had to be called after the catchphrase of one of its lead characters, namely Popeye Popplewell played by the great Bernard Bresslaw, for the audience to know what it was about. Scripted by eventual *Up Pompeii* and *Carry On...* writer Sid Colin, the premise was the interaction of useless National Service recruits with their dreadful superiors and each other. Since National Service was still mandatory, it's easy to see where the appeal of the show lay. But even without the shared experience of holding back the Russian hordes by peeling potatoes in Aldershot, this is still well worth the effort of circling in marker on the very rare occasions it crops up in afternoon telly scheduling. The cast on their own cannot fail to please, with Alfie Bass as Excused Boots Bisley (who went on with eventual Sergeant-Major Snudge played by the great Bill Fraser to star in his own telly spin-off, *Bootsie and Snudge*), David Lodge as Sergeant Potty Chambers, Norman Rossington as Cupcake Cook and assorted other players including Michael Bentine, Michael Ripper and Charles Hawtrey. Like *Life With The Lyons*, it's a Hammer production. It's often thought that venerable name in British film production, most commonly associated with horror, only got into the way of making sitcom spin-offs when the velvet-lined arse fell out of the bottom of the coffin of the Dracula business. However, as demonstrated here, this is not the case, although *Life with the Lyons* is a bit frightening.

SITCOM SPIN-OFFS

TILL DEATH US DO PART (1969)/*THE ALF GARNETT SAGA* (1972)
Veering into more familiar territory, the former was the first big screen outing for Johnny Speight's legendary bigot Alf Garnett played, as on television, by Warren Mitchell. All of the small-screen cast are here, including Dandy Nichols as Alf's wife Elsie, muttering about her idiotic husband through gobfuls of boiled sweets, and Una Stubbs and Tony Booth as daughter and son-in-law Rita and Mike rowing furiously over almost any subject Alf chooses to mouth off about. Quite different from the above-mentioned straightforward transfers, this takes the characters and premise of the show and creates some back-story for them, depicting the family's survival through the London Blitz. It's therefore one of the more interesting of these films and, thanks to Speight's fantastic script, one of the best, too. Sadly, the follow-up, *The Alf Garnett Saga* (1972), turned out to be something else entirely. Still scripted by Speight but with Stubbs and Booth unaccountably replaced by Michael Angelis and Adrienne Posta, this second stab was a bit of a shambles, especially since the situation – a crucial constituent of any situation comedy – was changed dramatically to relocate the family to a block of high-rise flats. By doing so Speight falls into the worst sitcom spin-off trap, that being the relocation of action to another place for no real reason; the most diabolical example of this is *Are You Being Served?* (1977) when the entire cast goes on holiday together at the same time to the same resort – no need to explain why! Similarly, the characters themselves were altered needlessly. Angelis plays son-in-law Mike as a sort of feckless drug-addled womaniser, probably only to expedite the diabolical sequence where Alf takes an acid trip. Even the briefest of viewings, however, suggests if anyone had some sort of run in with narcotics during the film's production process, it was probably Speight.

STEPTOE AND SON (1972)/*STEPTOE AND SON RIDE AGAIN* (1973)
A far more successful spin-off duo is this superlative pair produced under the aegis of the great Nat Cohen. The two rag and bone men from Oil Drum Lane in Shepherd's Bush are given two shots at big screen fame with a pair of excellent set-ups. In the first, Harold (Harry H Corbett) marries a girl recognised by dad Albert (Wilfred Brambell) as being dead common. Albert knows this, of course, because he's as common as own brand muck. Nevertheless, the marriage goes ahead between Harold and Zita (Carolyn Seymour) leading scriptwriters Ray Galton and Alan Simpson (also responsible for the telly series) to dance into the jaws of the relocation trap by sending the cast to Spain for the honeymoon. This time the production merely tickles the tonsils of disaster, and escapes unharmed by the halitosis of mediocrity. The result is both funny and touching – not an easy combination to achieve in any genre, let alone a sitcom transfer. The second outing for the lads is more of a straight out farce. Harold cripples their horse Hercules by driving his cart into the back of a Pickfords van bound for York, from which exotic destination he then has to return to London. There follows a series of vignettes involving alcoholic doctor Milo O'Shea, washed-out nympho housewife Diana Dors (that'd be a cameo part then) and disgusted insurance agent Frank Thornton, at one point unaccountably refusing from Harold some champagne delightfully chilled in a toilet pan. Both the *Steptoe* films are not only as funny and moving as the series, but also fantastically contemporaneous, stuffed to the gills with

achingly 1970s set-ups, from mosaiced Burton the Tailor shopfronts to desperately tatty parks. Furthermore, the latter production remains the best example ever of a follow-up as an improvement on the original. Whenever anyone tells you that the most successful instance of a sequel being better than its predecessor is *The Godfather: Part II* (1974), tell them it's actually *Steptoe And Son Ride Again*.

ON THE BUSES (1971)/*MUTINY ON THE BUSES* (1972)/ *HOLIDAY ON THE BUSES* (1973)

The *Buses* trilogy encompasses almost every aspect of the sitcom spin-off genre, good and bad. *On The Buses* is a straight telly transfer of what was a mammoth hit series, with Reg Varney's Stan the bus driver working alongside Bob Grant's toothy conductor Jack. Stan's supposedly riotous bachelor existence is severely cramped by his dreadful family. Mum, Doris Hare, brother-in-law Arthur, played by the great and sorely missed Michael Robbins, and of course Stan's sister Olive, played by Anna Karen whose character is still, after nearly forty years, a byword for plug-ugly women, all live at home, creating Stan's Sisyphean struggle to keep their supremely crappy establishment afloat. At work, Stan and Bob try to get their end away with a plethora of tight-topped (and seemingly visually impaired) female workmates while doing their best to avoid legendary Inspector Blakey (Stephen Lewis), a character as ingrained upon the national consciousness as any Dickensian grotesque. In the first film, Stan's miffed that Mum and Olive keep buying things on HP which he has to pay for with endless overtime. Disaster looms as the bus company threaten to let women do the driving too, meaning less overtime and financial ruin, which he and Jack try to thwart. And that's it! In *Mutiny...* Stan gets engaged, much to the consternation of Mum and Olive as they wonder what they're going to do if he moves out. As a solution, Stan gets feckless Arthur a job as a driver, and moves himself onto a better gig. Hilarity, naturally, ensues. Lastly, the action is transferred to a holiday camp where Stan, Jack and even Blakey end up after losing their jobs at the bus depot. Stan's family, of course, follow. Wagnerian this cycle of works isn't, but worthy it most certainly is. Quite apart from being funny – the darts match in *Holiday...* is near genius, and awed whispers can still be heard regarding the scene where the toilets blow up – what these films celebrate is unabashed working class life. Not polished up or sanitised for the more comfortably off, and certainly not reinterpreted for the foreign markets, the depictions of working class 1970s Britain in these Hammer gems is as complete and true as in any hefty documentary series. In a time when the acceptable face of British filmmaking seems to consist entirely of a pair of jeans and blazer combo under a mop of floppy hair fannying about in fashionable London-centric locations, the tradition of working class entertainment for working class people deserves a bit of recognition.

MAN ABOUT THE HOUSE (1974)

The mid-1970s was the high water mark for sitcom films, when even second-stringers such as *Father, Dear Father, That's Your Funeral* and *Never Mind the Quality, Feel the Width* (all 1972) were blown up to silver screen dimensions with a King Cone stuck in the middle. Many sank like stones, but this stretched edition of the O'Sullivan/Thomsett/Wilcox versus Murphy/ Joyce flatsharing brouhaha lasted the distance, with a tempting mix of a ' bickering cast unite against mutual enemy' plot, a poisoned Steak Diane, and a finale that bids a cheery farewell to narrative, opting instead for a mad dash through the Thames Television studios to meet Spike Milligan, Bill Grundy and the stars of *Love Thy Neighbour*, all playing themselves (though confusingly Michael Robbins plays a studio guard, and not Arthur from *On the Buses*). It was clearly getting crowded in celluloid sitcom land. Something had to give.

RISING DAMP (1980)

Here's where everything that could go wrong went wrong. This lamentable effort proves even the very best source material does not ensure a quality film. While the likes of *Porridge* (1979) and *The Likely Lads* (1976) had first-rate material to translate into a brace of excellent films, director Joe McGrath managed to take Eric Chappell's titanic sitcom and turn it into one of the most tragic and empty pieces of work ever put on screen. There is a disturbed air hanging over proceedings from the very first due to the absence of Richard Beckinsale, brilliant in the series as medical student Alan and an integral part of the show, but tragically dead by the time this was made. The decision to effectively replace him with Christopher Strauli hobbles the production from the first. Beckinsale's absence casts a pall over the whole thing. Of course it doesn't help that the viewer also knows Leonard Rossiter himself wasn't long for this world either, or that Chappell's magic touch seems to have deserted him somewhat. He falls into the trap of the big screen adaptation of *Dad's Army* (1971), cobbling together a story from several old plots, which is a massively foolish ploy, since it has to be presumed that the vast majority of the audience will already have more than a passing knowledge of the original series, and therefore recognise the set-ups. *Rising Damp* is the nadir of the genre, and understandably the fashion for small-screen transfers petered out shortly afterwards. To an extent, that was unfortunate, as the cinema was robbed of full-length features of the likes of *Yes, Minister* and *Never The Twain*, and the absence from the cinematic landscape of Messrs Peel and Smallbridge is a lasting tragedy.

BILL FRASER

THE GRUMPIEST NICE MAN THAT EVER DID LIVE

The contribution by actor, comedian, director and genius Bill Fraser to the world of British entertainment, and therefore to the welfare of all mankind, might never be fully measured. He gave Peter Cushing his first acting gig, he took part in Thora Hird's interview for Ealing Studios, he saved Eric Sykes' life, he was funny, menacing and inventive and remained so until his dying day. Not as hugely prolific as some of his contemporaries, or even his former young apprentices, he did, however, run up a fine tally of quality material in between being one of television's biggest stars in, among other things, *Bootsie and Snudge*.

Fraser's first film appearance was in bizarre comedy vehicle *Helter Skelter* (1949) which, by its cast list, seems to have been a showcase for almost every comedy star either working at the time or otherwise hanging around the Express Dairy in Charing Cross Road waiting for work. They all seem to have found it here though with the likes of Mr Pastry, Jimmy Edwards, David Tomlinson, Jon Pertwee, Terry-Thomas, Wilfred Hyde-Whyte, Esma Cannon, Valentine Dyall, Kenneth Griffith, Dennis Price and Harry Secombe all taking part. Fraser's part is given, bafflingly, as Oliver Cromwell. Quite how that fits in with Mr Pastry is anyone's guess, though, sadly, it does not seem to have entailed Pastry's parliamentary trial and summary execution, which would certainly have raised more than a few laughs. Terry-Thomas appears as himself, and gets to perform his famous cabaret sketch, 'technical hitch,' whereby he is a disc jockey forced to recreate the voices on the records lost in an accident, from Paul Robeson to Yma Sumac, with increasing desperation. Whether or not Fraser was required to recreate the Battle of Naseby or the closing of the Long Parliament is open to conjecture.

Just to demonstrate that he kept only the best of company in his early roles, Fraser also took part in telly-hating curio *Meet Mr Lucifer* (1953) in which Joseph Tomelty retires from his job only to be given a television set, wonder of the modern world that such an object was then, which turns out to be a curse as neighbours, friends and family crowd in on him to experience the marvels of a half-hour programme, three inches across, that no one can hear. The set is then sent onwards like an electronic Flying Dutchman (on hire) with increasingly bizarre consequences. The film also featured Barbara Kelly, Gordon Jackson, Raymond Huntley, Frank Pettingell, Joan Sims, Ian Carmichael, Irene Handle, Dandy Nichols, Fred Griffiths, Stanley Holloway as the Devil and Gilber Harding as himself, which comes to much the same thing.

Military shenanigans followed in *Orders Are Orders* (1954), the film upon which sitcom *The Army Game* was eventually based, Fraser's involvement providing a nice ironic twist since it was *Army Game* spin-off *Bootsie and Snudge* that created for him a position at the very centre of national cultural life for decades to come. Further star-spangled banter in *The Fast Lady* (1962) came after a clutch of less memorable fare, then fondly remembered silent (mostly) madness in *A Home Of Your Own* (1964) and the extraordinary musical vehicle *I've Gotta Horse* (1965) in the company of the never again repeated combo of Billy Fury and Fred Emney. All are films that languish on the shelves of telly companies or their pernicious allies in the film world who conspire to keep them in the dark while every week on television endless Westerns and war films are trundled out. If a horse has to be seen on afternoon TV, it shouldn't be trotting up Monument Valley, it should be cantering along the Thames Valley… with Amanda Barrie on it.

Slightly more Hollywood fare comes next on the Fraser CV with *Masquerade* (1965), the only spy caper ever to have the sense to put together Cliff Robertson and Felix Aylmer, providing a wider audience for Bill's brilliantly gruff schtick, then the frankly odd *Captain Nemo and the Underwater City* (1969) with Robert Ryan as the titular mythical matelot and Fraser as a gold-hungry schnook in the company of a similarly odious sidekick, played by the great Kenneth Connor, and Allan Cuthbertson, fresh from being made sap of by every other major comedian in Britain on television, from Tommy Cooper to Morecambe and Wise.

However, Fraser's finest hours come in two rather different British film comedies, *Up Pompeii* (1971) and *That's Your Funeral* (1972). Both film versions of sitcoms, Fraser gets to utilise his trademark angry but still funny technique to full effect in both, though the first has the edge if only because it has rather flightier ambitions than the latter. Bill plays Prosperus Maximus, consul of Pompeii, prospective assassin of Nero, scourge of Michael Hordern and perpetual tormentor of our hero, Lurcio as played by Frankie Howerd. Hokum as a description doesn't even begin to cover it. Neither does corny, daft or downright silly. Funny does though and Fraser is excellent as the husband of volcanic vamp Voluptua, aptly described as the 'last of the red hot pokers'. *That's Your Funeral* on the other hand is just crackers, with Bill and Raymond Huntley appearing alongside David Battley, Dennis Price, Richard Wattis, Roy Kinnear, Michael Ripper, Bob Todd, Frank Thornton and Hugh Paddick in a tale of drugs and coffins that has to be seen to be believed.

Fraser eventually made for the sunny uplands of television after a while, much as his long-term compatriots had done, and he fully deserved the wider recogntion that being back on the small screen again brought him. He still made the odd film appearance, such as in Roman Polanski's massively stupid – not to mention bad – *Pirates* (1986) but he was still good to watch and got, creditably, funnier the wrinklier and crumblier he became. When he died in 1987 most people knew they had lost Sergeant Snudge but little did they realise they had also lost a true giant of the entertainment world and one of the few men who had positively influenced the industry on his own. The man was a giant and is still sorely missed.

HANDMADE FILMS

The British Film Industry (the UK's leading oxymoron) is a strange and mutating creature. Once upon a time there were home-grown film companies turning out 'product' from premises ranging from palatial studios that could vie with the best the Yanks could offer down to sheds somewhere in Manchester. These have gone now to be replaced by the odd cafe-dwelling, achingly middle-class producer with a fetish for floppy hair or Restoration bosoms, whose films can only be considered 'British' in the sense that they probably took the call from America to confirm the budget somewhere in London.

Once money for British pictures came from bread tycoons or the War Office, and the lads who landed the cash made great films everyone wanted to watch. Now there's Lottery cash to be put at the disposal of producers who make bad films that no one wants to watch. In the fuzzy middle ground between pleasingly ramshackle cottage industry and US colonial outpost there was at one point the odd rabble of misfits determined to make proper British films in Britain with British money. Well, not including the producers of the kickers and boobs comedies there was really only one: HandMade Films. After the collapse of Ealing, Gainsborough, London Films, Hammer and British Lion (which consisted of pretty much everything that was still struggling on at the time cobbled together to create a sort of cinematic British Leyland) it fell to the likes of EMI and ITC to come up with the goods on the film front. Controlled respectively by the legendary showbiz brothers Bernard Delfont and Lew Grade, make films they did and, would you believe it, sometimes they were quite good. However, by the 1980s Lew and Bernie had started to get the jitters. After all, as producer Saul Zaentz once said, the way to make a small fortune in pictures is to start with a large fortune. Still the 'industry' limped along after its own weary fashion in the late 1970s until fate leant a pointy hand – a hand with a camera sticking out of it.

In 1979 the Monty Python team were about to embark on the second of their features up to that point, *Life Of Brian* (1979) which they were producing under the unlikely aegis of Bernard Delfont's EMI. Having already hijacked the subconscious of every catchphrase-repeating nerd on the planet with the pretty threadbare but superbly maniacal *The Holy Grail* (1975) the lads resolved to further disturb the peace with their gentle religious meanderings. However, at some point well into the production (actually, three days before shooting was to start) Bernie decided he had better actually have a look at the script, and was much perplexed by what he found therein. He cast the work aside and withheld his shekels, whereupon there was much wailing and gnashing of teeth in Python Towers, for Lo! however clever and witty they may have been verily they had not as much money as Bernie and they were right in it and knew not what to do. It was celebrity pal to the rescue as, to cut a long story short, Eric Idle had a word with George Harrison and he had a word with his lawyer Denis O'Brien and HandMade Films was born, completing *Brian* in fine style. Malcolm Muggeridge hated it so much everyone realised it must be great and it went on to make a fortune. Hurrah!

Originally it was to be British Hand Made Films (since Harrison had liked the sound of the British Hand Made Paper mill in Somerset) but it was carefully pointed out to him that this made the company sound like a nationalised business, and at that point in history nationalised businesses were in perpetual financial crisis. After *Brian* scooped a truckload of cash, HandMade consolidated their position as the most exciting company in a field of one with their next and arguably best feature, *Time Bandits* (1981). Festooned with the sort of cast producers and directors can only land by being on first name terms with the talent, director Terry Gilliam was able to rope in John Cleese, Michael Palin, Ian Holm, Peter Vaughan, Katherine Helmond, Sean Connery, David Warner and a brilliant turn by Ralph Richardson, whose sole character at the time – dotty old fool – happily coincided with what was required for a change. Normally a pantomime walk-down list of British characters like that is enough to elicit a tired sigh from the most fervent of supporting roster fans, but the difference here is that the participants are given something worthwhile to do, especially Cleese and Connery (sans toupee) who are both brilliant as an upper class Robin Hood and brilliantly gruff King Agamemnon. Taken altogether, and not to leave aside the excellent cast of Bandits themselves, it makes for a genuine contender for Best British Film Ever and is also one of the most identifiably HandMade films. Considering over the next few years the company also brought forth *The Long Good Friday* (1980), in which minicab drivers' totem Bob Hoskins took on the US-dominated gangster genre and won hands down, and *A Private Function* (1984), which proved that Michael Palin was one of the great leading men of British films, it's difficult to see how they could possibly have gone wrong; but they did.

During the making of *A Private Function* in Yorkshire, another production was underway in the slightly more glamorous surroundings of Puerto Rico. *Water* (1985) starred Michael Caine and appeared to be HandMade's tiresomely inevitable attempt to 'crack the American market'. O'Brien was determined that it play in Des Moines and chucked trunks of cash at it, in the process starving the production of *A Private Function,* rather miffing writer Alan Bennett, who might have expected a little more respect. *Water* was awful and bombed and *A Private Function* proved itself one of the gems of 1980s cinema and turned a nice profit, while gaining masses of critical praise and a real audience in America. The problem with *Water* (apart from a duff story and Michael Caine) was it enlisted the help of a plethora of character actors in support – William Hootkins, Leonard Rossiter, Brenda Vaccharo and Fulton Mackay – but unlike *Time Bandits* gave them nothing to do. A foetal Billy Connolly was there too, and was actually quite good, but this was before he impaired his acting ability by climbing up his own arse and disappearing. Everything about *A Private Function* worked and it is still a joy to watch. Expect to see *Water* again only if eternal damnation turns out to be a reality.

These two examples from the HandMade CV neatly illustrate what went wrong with the company. The notion of an eccentric bunch of film-making renegades seems to have been cast aside at about the time O'Brien sought to do more than just succeed by making a bit of money producing good films. He wanted to make tonnes of money making any sort of film, even if they turned out to be shit. At least it can be surmised this was his objective, since most of the films he brought forth in the following years were indeed shit. The problems began when the tonnes of cash that were supposed to follow them failed to materialise. This unfortunate tendency to turn out crap is neatly surmised by rubbish adaptation of rubbish stage show *Bullshot* (1983) and Madonna vehicle *Shanghai Surprise* (1986). Hoskins' directorial effort *The Raggedy Rawney* (1988) is worth a brief peek if you can look away at well-judged intervals in order to avoid Dexter Fletcher. *Bellman and True* (1987) is bearable in a late-Saturday-night-in-1989-ITV-Autumn-Season-of-Films kind of way. Hardly tunes of glory. The quality of HandMade's output became a shadow of what had been.

Still in the plus column are: the fantastic *The Missionary* (1982), in which Palin gets the chance to outshine the likes of Maggie Smith and Denholm Elliott; *Privates On Parade* (1982), an adaptation of the Peter Nichols play with a slightly too convincingly brilliant performance by Michael Elphick; and the not as good as it ought to be *Mona Lisa* (1986) which features brilliant turns by Robbie Coltrane, Bob Hoskins and Cathy Tyson but suffers from having no real point and featuring Michael Caine.

Then of course, there's *Withnail & I* (1987), the most overrated film of the 1980s. Lionised to all get-out nowadays it has attracted to itself a fully fledged cult for reasons that escape the most rational of minds. It has some nice moments but they rather tellingly involve seasoned professionals Richard Griffiths and Michael Elphick whereas the rest of it suffers from just having no point. This was director and writer Bruce Robinson's first film and by Jove, it shows. Since its production and (extremely) latter success Robinson has described how he conceived of the film from a series of moments that he had a clear picture of, such as the traffic policeman shouting 'Get in the back of the van!' The problem was that what came in between, i.e. most of it, had far less attention lavished on it. The resultant story of two blokes going to the country for a weekend seems less like a devastating indictment of the failure of the 1960s and more like a particularly turgid episode of *About Britain*. The singular benefit of the film's newfound status is that that it's too expensive to be put on the telly that often.

Some projects never made it to the screen. *Travelling Men* was slated to have starred Michael Caine and Sean Connery with a script by Peter McDougall. Considering that the class average had dipped disastrously by this point, anyone would think that O'Brien would have been desperately keen to have two world class stars appearing in a film scripted by the country's best screen dramatist, thereby providing the global appeal he was desperately after. But the useless O'Brien tinkered too much with the project and the stars, who had hitherto been itching to take part, buggered off, leaving McDougall to find meagre recourse by pouring a tin of Evo-Stick over O'Brien's car.

The last throw from HandMade, just as the whole enterprise came tumbling down, was ironically one of the more successful. *Nuns On The Run* (1990) is a work for which the adjective 'slight' might well have been created. Although ostensibly a proper feature, it manages to convey an atmosphere more akin to a particularly dry episode of *After Henry*. An acceptable way to pass an evening hunched over a plate of mince, it is a TV movie and nothing more, a fact confirmed by its limited success on general release but its position among the ten biggest audiences in Channel Four's history. And then… that was it. Denis

O'Brien, the man rock stars trusted to make tax on their money disappear, was in fact making one particular rock star's money – George Harrison's – disappear entirely and production ceased. This was a crying shame because at its peak Handmade was turning out stuff, especially with Palin in the lead, that was as good as anything that Balcon, Rank or anyone else who had ever signed a cheque for a film budget on these shores had ever managed. The only possible silver lining to this immense cloud is that Terry Gilliam's long-mooted sequel to *Time Bandits*, whereby the diminutive stars will be the daughters of the original Bandits, will never be made as that is a really, really terrible idea. Though it would still be better than *Bright Young Things* (2003).

RED TRIANGLE FILMS

RED TRIANGLE FILMS

In autumn 1986, Channel Four unveiled what would become a lastingly notorious 'experiment to discover the advantages and disadvantages of using a visual warning for some films...' Late on Friday nights, some of their regular arthouse films would have a red warning triangle graphic superimposed over the picture, to indicate 'special discretion required'. The nation's moral guardians were, possibly as planned, not amused. Mary Whitehouse remarked: 'It's not good enough to slap on a warning symbol and then indulge in sadistic madness of this kind.' Poor audience feedback meant the scheme foundered after five months, but not before the following had escaped:

THEMROC (1972)
Sacked French worker drops out of society for life of barking, incest and cannibalism.
Controversy: incest, killing and eating of gendarme (who suspiciously resembles a barbecued pig).

PASTORAL HIDE-AND-SEEK (1974), THROW AWAY YOUR BOOKS; LET'S GO INTO THE STREETS (1971)
Surreal coming-of-age shenanigans in rural and urban Japan.
Controversy: drowned babies, sexual attraction to rabbits, inflatable women, penis-shaped punch bags.

IDENTIFICATION OF A WOMAN (1982)
Self-indulgent Antonioni misfire about a bored film director who shags around.
Controversy: shagging around, and the copious amounts thereof.

PIXOTE (1981)
Tough life of ten-year-old Sao Paolo street urchin.
Controversy: juvenile violence, sexual abuse.

THE CLINIC (1982)
Riotous goings-on in a Melbourne STD clinic.
Controversy: 'ripe' language, presence of Mark 'Joe Mangel' Little.

MONTENEGRO (1981)
Bored American housewife poisons dog and falls in with a bunch of deranged Yugoslavians with knives embedded in their heads.
Controversy: extended scene of scantily clad woman being chased by a toy tank with a dildo mounted on the gun barrel.

NO MERCY, NO FUTURE (1981)
Schizophrenic woman has various squalid sexual encounters in the seedier parts of Berlin.
Controversy: sex, suicide, strobe lighting.

OUT OF THE BLUE (1980)
Punk teenage girl runs from incestuous dad and junkie mum in US small town.
Controversy: school bus carnage, paedophilia, smack, Dennis Hopper... what more could you ask for?

THE WALL (1983)
Director's reminiscences of Turkish prison life.
Controversy: near-continuous rapes and beatings. Sleep well...

DAVID WARNER

If there's one thing that needs to be made clear about David Warner, it's that *he doesn't always play baddies*. Got that? It's just that, as the man says, 'when I play good guys nobody recognises me'. Even the most cursory glance at the early years of his bulging CV puts the stereotype into perspective.

After graduating from RADA to a few filmic bit parts (including *The King's Breakfast* ((1963)), a short film adaptation of AA Milne's *'I do like a little bit of butter on me bread!'* poem), Warner was plucked from the stage by Tony Richardson and cast as Blifil, the Walter the Softie-esque rival of Albert Finney's virile *Tom Jones* (1963). However, it was his title role in *Morgan: a Suitable Case for Treatment* (1966) which cemented his reputation as a rising star with one big toe dipped in the counterculture, an image that thankfully his portrayal of Adam in John Huston's ponderous epic *The Bible… in the Beginning* did little to dent.

In 1968 Warner appeared in two of the thirteen films that Universal studios, keen to grab a piece of swinging London, bankrolled in the UK to, as it turned out, financially disastrous effect. Fortunately, he appeared in two of the better films, which, since *Heironymus Merkin* was among them, admittedly isn't saying much. *The Bofors Gun* was a solid adaptation of John McGrath's polemical play, with Warner, along with everyone else, upstaged by Nicol Williamson's manic Irish gunner.

Work is a Four-Letter Word, however, is something else. An adaptation of *Eh?*, a play by Henry Livings about a rebel in a *Brazil*-esque future society of subservient industry, it upped the 1960s ante by having the narky Warner obsessed with the cultivation of outsize magic mushrooms, and Cilla Black as his long-suffering fiancée. Warner, nagged endlessly by 'La Black' about his employment status, figures a job in the boiler room of a power station would kill two birds with one stone, and goes about annoying everyone in the place with his contrary behaviour before installing his hallucinogenic crop and marrying Cilla so he can have someone to help with the tidying up. As with countless other films of this period, no-one could be bothered thinking of a proper ending, instead opting for a mass mushroom-fuelled love-in, complete with speeded-up chase scenes and a giant computer exploding, all to a *Delia Derbyshire* soundtrack. *Very* Peter Hall.

Equally Peter Hall was *Perfect Friday* (1970), a caper comedy in which heist supremo Stanley Baker ropes louche, decadent but cash-strapped upper-crust couple Warner (in pinstripe suit and footballer's blow-wave) and Ursula Andress (in big floppy hat) to help him make off with 200 grand from deposit boxes. Nothing if not varied in his choices, Warner then did *Straw Dogs* (1971), playing the backward child molester whose presence in Dustin Hoffman and Susan George's holiday cottage is the catalyst for one of the most celebrated controversies in film history. Buying a haunted mirror in *From Beyond the Grave* (1973) was light relief by comparison.

The counterculture called Warner back for one last fling, in the Beatles-funded film version of satirical stage success *Little Malcolm and His Struggle Against the Eunuchs* (1974), as Dennis Charles Nipple, argumentative foil to John Hurt's titular campus rebel turned dictatorial leader of the Dynamic Erection Party. *The Omen* (1976), however, is what really cemented his career, which inevitably took a turn for the horrific after that, from the good – playing Jack the Ripper against Malcolm McDowell's H.G. Wells in *Time After Time* (1979) – to the rotten – killer bat silliness *Nightwing* of the same year. In between, there was a jumbo ham role with added relish as a timewarped pirate king in *The Island* (1980), a film of one of Peter Benchley's 'other' books.

It was Terry Gilliam to the rescue, plucking him out of pish fantasy purgatory and dragging him up as the Evil Genius in the wonderful *Time Bandits* (1981), a ripe piece of casting. Warner, in his element turning dwarves into pigs and growing an impromptu merry-go-round out the top of his head, more than holds his own in a film packed with perfectly judged star turns. A similar all-over costume with a hole in the top for him to scowl out of was employed in glorious faulty-photocopiervision for Disney's computerised knockabout *Tron* (1982).

By the time he was clapping his hands dementedly like a seal in *The Man With Two Brains* (1983), an agreeable pantomime dotage of rogues and villains was on the horizon, and indeed he's busier now than he's ever been… But he does good guys too, you know.

THE ESSENTIAL
MAINSTREAM HORROR

THE OMEN (1976)

Of all horror films made in the 1970s the most successful, certainly the most famous, are *The Exorcist* (1973) and *The Omen* (1976). While the former basks in the reflected glory of being the scariest picture ever made, with no proper explanation ever given or deemed necessary, the latter is largely dismissed as bubblegum pap – Hollywood schlock horror bearing no comparison to its respected predecessor. But look more closely at *The Exorcist* and it soon becomes apparent that the silver sheen is the cheap flash of EPNS, while that comforting glow emanating from *The Omen* is glorious twenty-four carat gold.

The fact is, *The Omen* is miles better than *The Exorcist*. The legend that's grown up around William Friedkin's child-possession fable is more myth than anything else. Richard Donner's fantastic fable of apocalyptic prophecy deserves all the praise that can be shovelled upon it. While *The Exorcist* has had the benefit of being banned from release for a long period, building up people's expectations of it and and therefore a totally understandable deduction that it therefore must be really, really scary, *The Omen* has plodded on entirely under its own steam.

Nostalgia plays its part too. Memories of teenage nights huddled around a hired telly with a tenth generation copy of *The Exorcist* playing through a top-loading Videostar and appearing on screen through more snow than is usually visible on a documentary about weather patterns in the Arctic adds massively to the appeal. Anyone who wanted to see *The Omen* only had to wait long enough for it to crop up on telly. When *The Exorcist* went back on general release and the snow lifted, it transpired it was never that good to begin with. Only lovers of American period furniture could ever be scared by the goings on in the bedroom of little Regan. And while there are some people who find the sight and sound of a teenage girl with bad skin and lank hair and a speaking voice tempered by forty Capstan Full Strength, most have seen worse hanging around city centre bus stops on a Saturday night.

The Omen is quite, quite different. Permeated from start to finish with a marvellous air of dread, it draws the audience in by setting the most pertinent action in comfortably normal situations – hospitals, churches, parks, offices – but then distorts them just enough to keep them recognisably real, but horribly so. All of the most diabolical incidents in *The Omen* take place in the most ordinary of settings. Lee Remick is finally offed in her hospital room, her last sight (prior to the roof of the ambulance below) being, unfortunately, her dreadful nylon bed jacket. Billie Whitelaw is dispatched to hell from her kitchen. When Gregory Peck finally cashes in his chips, it's at the hands of a policeman acting in the name of the law rather than a slavering apostate of hell. Though the difference between the two rather depends on your opinion of the police.

THE ESSENTIAL MAINSTREAM HORROR

The most famous exit for any of the leading characters is that of David Warner, Peck's photographic sidekick during the investigation into little Damian's real identity. What makes Warner's eventual demise doubly shocking is that it doesn't take place in the hugely creepy catacombs he and Peck visit immediately beforehand, in order to receive instruction from the similarly hugely creepy Leo McKern into how to teach Damian a lesson he'll never forget. Donner is too clever for that. He allows Peck, Warner and the audience to leave the claustrophobic atmosphere of the underground caverns and breathe a sigh of relief in the sunny afternoon, only for Warner to be decapitated by a sheet of glass sliding off the back of a runaway truck escaping from a building site presumably not in possession of the necessary Health and Safety certificates. The effect of what would already have been a shocking death is therefore massively increased and comes as far more of a jolt than Freidkin's surly teenager could ever manage by ralphing up some pea and ham.

The demonic execution of the priest played by Patrick Troughton is a little different. Being skewered by his own church's lightning rod may count as the most ironic end to a character in cinema history, but hardly the most shockingly realistic. Troughton's character, necessary for some brilliantly histrionic exposition, is probably the most hysterical and extreme in the whole film – his eye-rolling delivery of the famous, 'When the Jews return to Zion...' passage from the imaginary book of Hebron is one of the film's highlights – and makes Billie Whitelaw's Satanic nanny seem like a model demonstration of The Method. A suitably demonstrative destruction was required and doesn't jar.

The Exorcist is quite different. The level of mania surrounding the possession is no more than cartoonish in its realisation. Tellingly, the most successful moments of the film involve the all too real medical procedures carried out on Regan, possessed by a demon with the voice of Wolfman Jack and the skin tone of Derek Jameson, and the fantastically terrifying ethnic music listened to by Father Karras' mother on a tiny radio. The rest is just pantomime.

Most of the performances in *The Omen* might also be described as one-note. Lee Remick isn't really required to do much, an expectation she lives up to spectacularly well. Even supporting actor stalwarts Bruce Boa and Julian Glover do not add much, though they scarcely get the opportunity. Critiscisms are forever being levelled at the portrayal of Robert Thorn, the US Ambassador and adoptive father of juvenile antichrist Damian, on the part of Gregory Peck. Too wooden, it's said, too conservative. Ambassadors are not known, however, for their sense of gregarious élan, with probably only Shirley Temple Black standing as the only one in the history of the State Department who could have carried off a decent anecdote. Peck's decidedly wooden performance is as accurate as any would ever get, at least in a tale of demonic possession.

The Exorcist trades on the rather silly precept that it is in some way based on an actual series of events, as described in the book by William Peter Blatty on which the film is based. But as the Coen Brothers showed by falsely claiming that their *Fargo* (1996) was based on a real-life incident and watching the alarm that built up on the part of the audience, such a claim is incredibly easy to make and the attendant fuss is hardly ever justified. The only thing that *The Omen* ever claimed to be was silly, fun and scary. A mission it accomplished with frightening ease.

TV CREAM'S ANATOMY OF CINEMA

POST-APOCALYPTIC FILMS

Celluloid musings on the great cataclysm have been with us since the war. First off the blocks was *Five* (1951), in which just that number of lone survivors battled to stay alive, paving the way for the more famous Astaire/Peck submarinations of *On the Beach* (1959). In the same year, trapped miner Harry Belafonte emerged into a desolate New York City in *The World, the Flesh and the Devil*. All worthy (and occasionally preachy) efforts to be sure, but the majority of conflagratory chronicles have less noble fish to fry.

For the filmmaker with their heart in the world of sci-fi schlock but their head desperate to tackle weighty topics, this genre is a godsend. Topics, after all, don't come much weightier than the end of civilisation, but since nobody knows what that might look like, there's little need to pay tedious lip-service to realism, research or other boring chores that get in the way of the fun stuff. The RKO oddity *Captive Women* (1952), where a ruined New York in the year 3000 becomes a battleground for gangs of assorted ugly stick targets, is a fine early example of this hybrid confusion. After lashings of mushroom cloud stock footage and a ponderously solemn 'When will people learn?' introduction, what transpires is a great big punch-up little different from any other.

The second big draw is the price. When a film's set design budget runs to rubble, a knackered barn and several acres of sod all, studio bosses suddenly find a renewed enthusiasm for sci-fi cinema. The depopulated nature of the film instantly takes care of the need for troublesome extras... and think of the saving on costumes, laundry and hairdressing! George Miller's original *Mad Max* (1979) is the paradigm here, costing less than half a million and taking over 200 times that amount. It's surely no coincidence that *Mad Max: Beyond Thunderdome* (1985), with its gallumphing, committee-written title, mythological tweeness of Franklin Mint proportions and Tina Turner as the overly-barbered Aunty Entity, saw the pain-in-the-arse factor inflate in line with the tariff.

So, more is less, less is more – the laws of Hollywood appear to be breaking down along with civilisation. But the bottom line still holds true: a load of old toot is a load of old toot. While some of these pictures are weird and wonderful, and some just plain weird, many are as fun and thought-provoking as the wildernesses they depict. However, a battered flying jacket and a rusty old Triumph do not a deep insight into the human condition make. Still, for its unique combination of pretension and tattiness, the solemn and the screwy, there's nothing to beat the genre that picks up where society leaves off. And after the last remnant of mankind has succumbed to the inevitable and collapsed groaning into the polluted stream, please don't forget to switch off your set.

THE OMEGA MAN (1971)

Clearly having learned nothing from his recent sojourn to that terrible *Planet of the Apes*, Charlton Heston once more finds himself representing The Last of America, as the lone compos mentis survivor of a Sino–Soviet biological war, on the run from a gang of drooling zombies known as The Family out to get him for his evil wheel-using ways. The Heston solution? Hole up in a penthouse flat, drinking scotch and making wisecracks at a bust of Julius Caesar. Well, it's a living. Textbook post-hecatomb thriftiness is evinced in the abandoned cityscapes; instead of building a massive and costly set, they merely filmed

THE ESSENTIAL MAINSTREAM HORROR

Charlton moping around a shopping centre in the early hours of a Sunday for that all-important desolate feel.

IDAHO TRANSFER (1973)
Peter Fonda and Keith Carradine hang out in Idaho's imposingly barren National Park. They think it's rather super. They gather a bunch of kids together to immortalise the place on film. They cook up a vague story about a team of young scientists travelling into an eco-buggered future via a threadbare time machine that bizarrely requires young women to remove their trousers before use. Once there, the kids talk their way through a load of slackerish angst before doing each other in with rocks. One week after the film is released, the distributor goes bankrupt. These events may or may not be connected.

THE FINAL PROGRAMME (1973)
Avengers/Phibes director Robert Fuest is let loose on Michael Moorcock's time-tripping novel of swinging psychosexual splother, producing a muddled tale of a race to stop the blueprints for a genetically modified Superman falling into the wrong hands as the missiles drop. Jon Finch cuts a dashing cross between Martin Shaw and Tony Bastable as unstable, black nail varnish-wearing, chocolate digestive-munching fop Jerry Cornelius, and Jenny '*Jubilee*' Runacre is fun as the catsuit-clad, predatory Miss Brunner, but really, as with *The Avengers*, this is all about the set-pieces. And what set-pieces. Heaps of wrecked cars along the Thames? Check. Multicoloured poison gas clouds? Check. Underground supercomputer powered by rows of scientists' disembodied brains? Check. Hypodermic-firing drug pistols? Check. Chic restaurant with in-house mud wrestling? Check. Giant pinball arcade featuring women rolling about in those inflatable spheres James Burke used to try out on Tomorrow's World? Check. Hermaphrodite ubermensch revealed as a manicured monkey doing a crap Humphrey Bogart impression? Er, check. The soundtrack? Why, jazz-Moog, of course! Never has the holocaust been so groovy.

WHERE HAVE ALL THE PEOPLE GONE? (1974)
A reasonable enough question for Peter '*Airplane!*' Graves to ask, you might think, after a family picnic is somewhat spoilt owing to the annihilation of mankind (save for a handful of handily immune individuals, natch) by solar flares that reduce humanity to piles of white powder, leaving only their clothes behind. Cue a gruelling slog from deserted town to deserted town, scavenging anything left lying about, with a particularly memorable Jaws-style shocker as Graves siphons petrol from what he believes to be the car of another hapless dustee.

A BOY AND HIS DOG (1974)
The inspiration for *Mad Max*, no less. A pubescent Don Johnson ambles across a barren wasteland with a haughty telepathic sheepdog, which speaks to him with a voice strangely reminiscent of *Knight Rider's* KITT, constantly correcting his grammar and berating him for his overactive libido. Looking for a bit of the other, Johnson stumbles into a fallout shelter containing a semi-functioning micro-society based around some kind of *Stepford*

Wives distillation of homely, all-American, village fete-holding wholesomeness. Despite the odd homicidal clown-faced hick, Johnson decides this is better than scratching a living on the surface, where crumpet is somewhat thin on the ground. He soon changes his mind, however, when they tie him down and attach his nob to a milking machine. Adapted in part from a Harlan Ellison story, this downbeat and daft tale is certainly not your average apocalyptic actionfest, though that didn't stop the producers trying briefly to market it as such by altering the title to the meatier-sounding *Psycho Boy and His Killer Dog*.

DAMNATION ALLEY (1977)
Button-down sergeant George Peppard and wayward comrade Jan-Michael Vincent drive specially-constructed armoured cars across a post-nuclear wilderness of giant cockroaches to a ruined Las Vegas. In a rare turn of events for this genre, the film ends with the desolate Earth getting better, and everyone going off to live on a cosy farmstead. Which is nice.

THE LAST CHASE (1981)
One of Hollywood's countless *Mad Max* road rip-offs. In a Clarksonian nightmare future where eco-fascists force America's populace into dinky electric cars, free-thinking rebel Lee Majors dusts off his trusty old racing machine and bombs across the desert to California. Burgess Meredith in a jet fighter is sent to shoot the mother down, in a temptingly daft blend of *Revelations* and *The AA Book of the Road*.

MEMOIRS OF A SURVIVOR (1981)
This is a decidedly wayward adaptation of obtuse sci-fi scribbler Doris Lessing's tale of a marble-shedding Julie Christie holed up with a teenage girl in a feral future London. An odd mixture of *Survivors* (Christopher Guard runs a back-to-nature commune) and any number of 'spooky' children's TV serials from the 1970s, when Julie finds – or probably hallucinates – a portal to a Victorian household headed by Nigel Hawthorne behind a rubbery wall in her flat. It all leads up to Guard's kiddie commune rampaging the dirty streets, before a big egg turns up in Julie's flat and everybody climbs into it. The combination of iffy effects, egg-and-chips direction and an omnipresent plonking Radiophonic-esque soundtrack lock this future firmly in a very specific past... and all the better for it, of course.

NIGHT OF THE COMET (1984)
Once again, everyone save a few well-sheltered Californian teens and sinister boffins have been wiped out by the titular celestial encounter (they turn into red dust this time, for the sake of variety). Rather sensibly, with the risible *Beyond Thunderdome* on the horizon, the makers saw the writing on the wall for the post-apocalypse genre, and play it for none-more-eighties headband-toting teen laffs while Cyndi Lauper provides a rather less haunting musical backing.

CITY LIMITS (1985)
In the year British television served up mighty nuclear fallout frightener *Threads*, Hollywood rounded up some of its regulation twenty-something 'teenagers' to form skull-helmeted

motorbike gangs and do each other in, until a standard-issue sinister corporation tries to bring them to heel using that failsafe signifier of bottom-feeding cinema, Kim Cattrall, as saucy intermediary. In the event of a holocaust, only cockroaches and films like this will survive.

FELIX AYLMER

PRIESTS, PRIME MINISTERS… AND TIMELORDS?

There existed for several hundred years in the 1950s and 1960s a certain cadre of British film actors for whom the parts they played fitted like gloves and those gloves were oft-worn and comfortable. Cecil Parker played stuffy upper-class idiots, Raymond Huntley played officious upper-class idiots, Miles Malleson played rather agreeable upper-class idiots, Sam Kydd played 'all' the idiots who were not upper class (apart from taxi drivers, which was Fred Griffiths' job) and Felix Aylmer played Archbishops.

Well, actually Aylmer only played such clerical luminaries a couple of times, the earliest being for Michael Powell in his *Life and Death of Colonel Blimp* (1934) then for Olivier in his comedy of manners *Henry V* (1944) and latterly in *Becket* (1964). Other than on film Aylmer's holy orders led him to dodder across our telly screens as Father Anselm in *Oh, Brother!*, which was also a splendid vehicle for Derek Nimmo.

But back to the pictures. Leaving the warm waters of recognition for the cold currents of anonymity aside Aylmer put together a film CV that makes Sam Kydd's read like a bus tickets. Aylmer's fruity vowels were first heard in the fleapits of the West in 1930. He set out his stall as the man of choice in matters official as a prison Governor in properly forgotten feature *Escape* (1930) alongside the great Nigel Bruce and the formerly legendary Gerald Du Maurier, a man once so famous that he was made the star of a limerick so filthy people had to look away when they wrote it on bog walls. During the next eight years of peacetime Aylmer managed to rack up a further forty-eight films in which he performed roles as wide and varied as Prime Minister Lord Palmerston in *Sixty Glorious Years* (1938) and Prime Minister Lord Palmerston in *Victoria the Great* (1937), though Aylmer was most likely the sort of chap who considered all of this a diversion (and that's the sort of word he would probably have used, too) from his proper work on the legitimate stage where no doubt his tights hardly had a chance to air.

On a more serious note, during war Felix remained as busy as a bee with not even Hitler and his entire Wermacht able to prevent his career in pictures, no matter how hard they tried. Busier than Vera Lynne's hairdresser Felix turned out a further forty films during the war years but of slightly better quality than of old with the aforementioned Blimp probably the best, but with *The Young Mister Pitt* (1942), *Major Barbara* (1941) and, in a brilliant display of versatility, *South American George* (1941) with George Formby among the best.

There's also a very tenuous case for Felix being the first – or, if you're being pedantic, as fans often are, 0th – *Dr Who*. Consider the evidence. In wartime Gainsborough silliness *Time Flies* (1944), Tommy Handley, spade-jawed comedy spiv of radio's *ITMA* fame, happens upon a wily old man who's just invented a time machine – an iron sphere that's bigger on the inside than it is on the outside – with which to travel back to the Elizabethan era for historically semi-accurate fun, giving Shakespeare ideas for plays and suchlike. If that isn't an early episode of *Dr Who* with added gags about nylons, what is? Aylmer's appearance in this – all pince nez, neckerchief and tweeds – is strongly reminiscent of Peter Cushing's much reviled turn as The Doctor in the Amicus *Who* films, to boot; curiouser and curiouser.

Victory in Europe may have meant a bit of slacking off for soldiers, sailors, airmen and others who had a less busy time during the conflict but for Aylmer it was time to make some films fit for heroes and it was during the fallow period of his last fifty or so features that he really came into his own and got the roles he had been heading towards for so long: *Trio* (1950), *The Lady With The Lamp* (1951) taking a real step into the unknown as Prime Minister Lord Palmerston, *Ivanhoe* (1952), *The Master Of Ballantrae* (1953), *Separate Tables* (1958), *The Mummy* (1959), *The Road To Hong Kong* (1962), *Quo Vadis?* (1951) and *Masquerade* (1965) are just a few of the really very good films that fell to his banner before he finally turned up his comfortably slippered toes at the age of ninety.

Born of another century (1889 actually), he started acting before cinema was even invented. However, he managed to make the genre his own in that brilliantly understated way that the best character actors in Britain always did: not by making great, big films with their names over the titles but by turning in great big performances in what might otherwise have been small roles and making sure they were the characters audiences remembered for a very long time. Sometimes confused with Frank Royde (who never really made any films) simply because Kenneth Williams' impressions of them both sounded exactly the same, it is worth singling out the great Felix Aylmer for special mention even though, of course, 'as to his character God alone can tell'.

COMEDY STAR VEHICLES

There are few less edifying spectacles in cinema than actors more used to positioning Howitzers or tossing submarines from hand to hand trying to raise a laugh. Almost any proper actor will say the hardest thing in the world to do is extract a chuckle from an audience. No less a barmpot than Sir Anthony Hopkins once insisted to get a tear from a story of a dog being run over is easy, but to get a laugh from same flattened canine, now that's acting.

This is a lesson most straight actors never learn. The odd one can do it (Donald Sutherland and Paul Newman), some can do it sometimes but not others – Gene Hackman in *Superman II* (1980) versus Gene Hackman in *Loose Cannons* (1990) for example – but most just can't do it at all (Arnold Schwarzenegger, Sylvester Stallone, Nicolas Cage and everyone else). Sadly, the grating denizens of the latter category never learn and, like a dog returning to its own vomit, they sin again. To this very day big ticket stars will try their hand at comedy only to be sent yelping back to their Malibu beach houses by audiences who don't wish to spend money to discover what they already know: most film stars are not funny.

Directors and producers, largely intelligent people, know this and have done for several thousand years which is why the comedy star vehicle is as old as any other genre in film. Not the comedy film, which is a quite different thing and is safe in the hands of the merry but limited band of proper comic actors, but instead the films which are made on the back of the popularity of a comedian. During its golden age, before the telly came along and spoilt everyone's fun, a comedian who has spent years playing every part of the country with their act was seen as a shoo-in for success in films. The audience already knows them, loves them, laughs at them and more importantly pays good money to see them. How could such a project fail? That's the terrible logic anyway and almost every major comedian of their generation fell for it, with results for which the adjective 'mixed' may be the understatement of the century.

THE CRAZY GANG

This titanic bunch of maniacal comedians were an amalgam of three of the most popular double acts of their day: Bud Flanagan and Ches Allen, Jimmy Nervo and Teddy Knox and Charlie Naughton and Jimmy Gold. The legacy of the Gang is pretty much lost now or known only to the last few survivors who saw them perform on stage – Dennis Norden, basically – so it's a relief that something of their magic, however pale a reflection it is, remains on film. Individually, the lads were extraordinary people in their own right. Teddy Knox was the brother-in-law of Fu Manchu creator Sax Rohmer and was at one point employed by the family of his successful pseudo-Sino semi-sibling to ensure he sat down to write every day, mostly by locking him in his room and refusing to let him out. Jimmy Nervo hailed from a successful and established circus family and was adept at all the multifarious arts therein, even the high wire which he detested but mastered. He took his stage surname from a comic character of the day and formed a massively popular double act with Knox providing the impetus for the Gang. Jimmy Gold and Charlie Naughton were Glaswegian labourers who took to the stage comparatively late in life but proved a hit almost immediately. Their double act went on to last longer than any other in history: fifty-three years. Their entire time together was marked by a deep and unselfish friendship that saw Gold handle all of the financial and business affairs of his partner, who never learned to read or write, which Naughton paid back by continuing to split his earnings with his partner years after Gold was no longer fit to perform. Bud Flanagan was probably the most famous individual of the troupe thanks to his distinctive singing voice and bumptious personality. Born Reuben Weintrop, when hard up he once walked from London to Glasgow in search of work having already, at the age of fourteen, walked out of his house one day and hitched to New York to find a gig. Ches Allen was the most 'legitimate' of the bunch. Having been a straight actor he retired from the Gang early to work as their agent and was replaced on an informal basis by eccentric juggler Monsewer Eddie Gray, a bizarre man with a splash of real genius about him referred to more than once as 'The funniest man in the world'. The films the lads made together are a similarly mixed bunch. The best is *Alf's Button Afloat* (1938) the third version of what is incongruously billed as 'WA Darlington's famous farce'. It tells the tale of Aladdin's genie (Alistair Sim) imprisoned in the tunic button of Alf Higgins (Flanagan) after the lads have mistakenly enlisted in the Royal Marines. The best sort of mayhem results involving Flanagan being striped pink, first class stooge Wally Patch being hypnotised, the Gang masquerading as eastern potentates and the remainder of the cast being eaten at the end by a bear. A forgotten cinematic treasure indeed. Before this had been the film industry in-joke-stuffed *Okay for Sound* (1937) then the extraordinary *The Frozen Limits* (1939) featuring a compelling mixture of prospecting, drag, singing Mounties and Bernard Lee. On a more serious note, the war, and *Gasbags* (1941) saw the Gang enlisted to impersonate Hitler & Co. and in the process retrieve a secret weapon of pleasingly daft conception in the company of Wally Patch and lunatic's lunatic Moore Marriott. Finally came *Life is a Circus* (1958), which was more or less a retread of the glories of *Alf's Button* but with added rheumatism, the Gang by this time having a combined age of about 12000. The inclusion of Lionel Jeffries and Shirley Eaton nudged things along a little but it was most certainly time for the boys to bow out from films, which they also did on stage a few short years later.

GEORGE FORMBY

If the Crazy Gang made some of the best films in this genre, then George Formby probably made the most. The gormless banjolele-strumming simpleton made over twenty films, the first being *By The Shortest Of Heads* (1915) for which no banjo was required, as he was hired to play what he was in real life – a jockey. He didn't make another until *Boots! Boots!* (1934) after he had ditched his horse in favour of a slightly less attractive wife, Beryl. She also appeared with him in this slight tale of a comedy bootblack in a posh hotel, the only time they appeared together in their careers before she withdrew to the background to run every aspect of his life, famously insisting that no leading lady be permitted to kiss him (a contractual stipulation that presented no real deal-breaking problems at any point of negotiations for any of his female co-stars). She was not the most popular person on set and when it was announced one day that Beryl couldn't make it the crew gave an ovation. *Boots! Boots!* (also featuring eternal Rovers Return barmaid Betty Driver) was a resounding success and George, banjo in hand, turned out plenty more. The most often seen are *Come On George!* (1939), where he returned to the saddle in order to ride past anonymous extra Dirk Bogarde, and *Turned Out Nice Again* (1941), a sort of proto-*The Man In The White Suit* in which George invents a new kind of thread while dodging the attentions of an incredibly juvenile looking Wilfred Hyde-Whyte. Formby's last outing, *George In Civvy Street* (1946), is notable for an extraordinary climactic *Alice in Wonderland* dream sequence where George plays the March Hare, a prospect more horrifying and curious than anything Lewis Carroll ever dreamt.

Now the centre of a full blown sinister cult whereby grown men sit in the dark and strum together in Blackpool, Formby must be counted as the most successful of the comedians that made films. Whether that means the films are any good is another question.

SID FIELD

The almost-forgotten Sid Field is a perfect example of the worth of the films in this genre, at least as a record of performers long gone. Having toured the variety circuit for twenty-seven years before he found fame as an 'overnight success' in a London revue staged by impresario George Black, Field was more than ready to get into picture halls. The best of the three films he made was *London Town* (1946), which provided him with the chance to perform some of his acclaimed stage act alongside the unbelievably arch Jerry Desmonde and 'Two Ton' Tessie O'Shea. Later came probably his most influential film *Cardboard Cavalier* (1949) in which, as Sidcup Buttermeadow, he manages to both overthrow Cromwell and display the shtick countless comedians ever since, from Frankie Howerd to Catherine Tate, have purloined. 'Titter ye not!' and 'How very dare you!' are both Sid's. The film itself is quite cute, but no more. Field died tragically early at the age of forty-five, so he never got the chance to do any better, but at least *London Town* remains to remind us of what excellent business he could get up to.

THE GOONS

Individually the Goons covered the entire waterfront of cinema success, from Harry Secombe pottering along with minor star vehicles *Davy* (1957) and *Sunstruck* (1972) to the titanic and unparalleled career of actual proper genius Peter Sellers. Spike Milligan racked up perhaps the most eccentric mix of features, getting involved in the likes of *Postman's Knock* (1962) and *Invasion Quartet* (1961) before trotting out his own maniacal product with such seminal works as *The Bed Sitting Room* (1969) and *The Great McGonagall*

COMEDY STAR VEHICLES

(1974). However, the team as a whole made only two films that could justifiably be called Goons films: *Down Among The Z-Men* (1952) then *The Case Of The Mukkinese Battle Horn* (1956). The former is a classic example of How Not To Do It. Sellers, Milligan and Secombe – then still augmented by Michael Bentine – are thrown together with BBC announcer Andrew Timothy and dance troupe the Television Toppers in a pointless and cheap sort-of spy story that goes nowhere and accomplishes nothing, especially not laughs. Clearly an exercise in 'for God's sake get them on film before the popularity wears off', it's actually quite painful to watch. ...*Battlehorn*, however, is vastly different. Only a half hour or so long, it's the closest thing there has ever been to a Goon show made visual. Bentine was well away by this time so the numbers are made up by an embryonic Dick Emery, who adds brilliantly to the mayhem. The Goons never matched this, and only when they went their (almost) separate ways did their top-flight work really start to happen.

TONY HANCOCK

Hancock was probably the most respected of the comedians who got the opportunity to make comedy vehicles. Massively successful on television as well as radio, Hancock's film career was short-lived and disappointing by comparison, but still notable. The first of his two efforts, *The Rebel* (1961), is often criticised as being merely a protracted version of *Hancock's Half Hour*. It has the same main character who has the same traits, the same landlady, and finds himself in the same sort of scrapes, as penned by the same scriptwriters, Ray Galton and Alan Simpson. But for fans of Hancock (well, anyone with any sense) this is far from a negative, since more of a good thing is just, well, good; and *The Rebel* is very, very good. Hancock himself detested it, however, thinking its humour too broad, and though it made a shedload of cash it received no critical praise, which mattered to him hugely. His second and last starring role was in *The Punch And Judy Man* (1963). Cowritten by himself and made this time in black and white – as opposed to the full colour of *The Rebel* – it's a more winsome and slightly darker tale of frustrated ambition and domestic stagnation. It plays much more slowly than its predecessor and suffers as a result, and Hancock's lugubrious figure is a little overwhelmed by the situation. Quite apart from that though, it's also a bit boring. There is a scene, however, where Hancock is watched by a small boy who copies his every move as they both eat a giant knickerbocker glory in a café – the dead spit of a scene in *Jaws* (1975) where Roy Scheider's character is copied by his young son. Perhaps it's a coincidence, but Tony Hancock influencing Spielberg is too good a theory to dismiss.

MAX MILLER

Thomas Henry Sergeant - that's Max Miller to you, lady - was the legendary plus-four wearing comic who ruled the music halls for thirty years demanding of his audience whether they wanted jokes from his 'white book' or 'blue book'. The audiences, on one occasion including a voluble Queen Mother, always demanded the blue stuff. For his surprisingly large catalogue of film appearances, it was, sadly, always the white. Miller's first film appearance was in an adaptation of music hall fetishist JB Priestley's play, the extraordinary *The Good Companions* (1933) alongside a celluloid virgin at the time, John Gielgud, playing a character with the irresistible name of Inigo Jollifant. Miller is well down the cast list among the likes of dependable Wally Patch and a nascent Jack Hawkins, in a story of three friends forced into taking to the open road along with a performing troupe called the Dinky Doos. Sadly, none of the Doos are played by Gielgud. Miller played himself in his next film *Channel Crossing* (1933) but really, he always played himself, right up until his last film, *Asking For Trouble* (1942). Unfortunately, Max never got the chance to commit his proper act to film in any of these, mostly because no one had the nerve to let him rip on such a big stage. As a result, his films are worth a look only to remind the interested viewer of what he looked and sounded like, and not much else.

MORECAMBE AND WISE

Eric and Ern's short and pretty unspectacular film career is one of the great tragedies of both comedy and cinema. Their three well-known efforts (well known for all the wrong reasons), *The Intelligence Men* (1965), *That Riviera Touch* (1966) and *The Magnificent Two* (1967), are not nearly as bad as most would have, but neither are they particularly good. Eric, regardless of the material, always bears watching. Remarkably, these three features all came before the lads really hit the cosmic heights of the 1970s. The trouble is, the characters played by Eric and Ernie are those that were used in the ATV *Two of a Kind* series written primarily by Sid Green and Dick Hills (and who were also involved in the screenplays for these) where Eric was a simpleton and Ern was a bit of a bully. Successful on TV, this didn't work on film. Imperial phase Morecambe and Wise, after they'd been reconstructed by writer Eddie Braben with Ernie as the world's worst playwright and Eric as the world's funniest Dad, never made the big screen. *Night Train To Murder* (1983), sadly, did. This was the first of an optimistically planned series of films made under Thames TV's Euston Films banner, and was the bait that famously took the boys from the BBC. The result – an Agatha Christie spoof. Eric's niece (Lysette Anthony) inherits a vast fortune, and attempts on her life take place on the titular nocturnal locomotive. It's as if Ernie the playwright had finally got the upper hand over Eric, and we get to see the fruits of his artistic labour almost uninterrupted. What humour there is is so tragically muted you could play *The Last Post* on it. Director Joe McGrath did no further films after this. In a face-saving plea, Eric insisted Thames only ever showed the film in mid-afternoon slots. To be honest, even that's too good for it.

THAT'S NOT *CARRY ON*!

A handy guide to the many non-canonical films which have laboured under those magical two words at one time or other.

CARRY ON SERGEANT (1928)
Silent, Canadian-backed tale of two Canucks who go in for a bit of Boche-bashing action and capture a German spy. Made waves of controversy at the time, and cost a coffer-busting half a million dollars to boot. No Monkhouse, though.

CARRY ON LONDON (1937)
Short programme filler starring a young Eric Barker, later to be an early, bluff mainstay of the *Carry On* series proper, alongside a younger Kenneth More. Takes its title from the catchphrase that used to end popular radio chatathon *In Town Tonight*.

WHAT A CARRY ON! (1949)
Jimmy Jewel and Ben Warris join the army in another putative *Sergeant* scenario. Originally intended to be *Somewhere on Parade*, another in the long-running series of Frank Randle escapades, though Randle at the time was thought to be getting a bit peas-above-sticks, and was replaced with the more compliant Jewel.

CARRY ON ADMIRAL (1957)
Based on *Off the Record*, a creaky old stage farce. Rogers and Thomas allegedly decided to lift the 'Carry On' part of the title for the following year's inaugural *Sergeant*. Naval officer Brian Reece and politician David Tomlinson get giggly-pissed on ginned-up water and decide to switch uniforms for a lark, landing in deep trub. Joan Sims provides the sole link with the *Carry On* gang as a chambermaid chatting about broken door numbers.

DENTIST ON THE JOB (1961)
A.k.a. *Carry On TV*. The second and best of the orthodontic Monkhouse vehicles, with Sir Bob and Kenneth Connor flogging toothpaste in a variety of ways. Eric Barker and Charles Hawtrey add to the cross-franchise confusion.

TWICE ROUND THE DAFFODILS (1962)
It gets more convoluted still. This sanatorium-based whimsy started life as a (fairly) serious Patrick Cargill play, before being Carried-up by Gerald Thomas as *Carry On Nurse*. Then came this (slightly) more subdued reworking, wherein On-sters Kenneth Williams and Joan Sims cross swords with *Doctor* stars Donalds Sinden and Houston.

NURSE ON WHEELS (1963)
A.k.a. *Carry On, Nurse On Wheels*. This Rogers/Thomas extra-curricular romp (it even has Norman Hudis on script and Eric Rogers on scoring duties) features Esma Cannon as mum of rookie district nurse Juliet Mills, plus Jim Dale in a caravan.

FRANK RANDLE

HE'S SUPPED SOME STUFF TONIGHT!

Try mooting in polite company that one of the greatest British comics was a trampoline artiste whose chief catchphrase was 'Geroff me foot!' and you'll solicit exactly the sort of raised eyebrow you're probably sporting right now. However, the former Arthur Hughes, son of Wigan, childhood friend turned professional rival of George Formby, accomplished tumbler and monologist, was precisely that.

Frank Randle specialised on stage in a variety of 'rambling old drunk' personas, indulging in lengthy monologues with plenty of 'blue' content that delighted northern audiences but, along with unashamedly thick Lancastrian accents, ensured that he never came close to the sub-Watford success of the more sanitised Formby's cheeky chappy routine.

Stories of Randle's ale-fuelled 'esoteric' behaviour range from the delightful (Randle responding to an obscenity charge from the mayor of Blackpool by dropping tons of bog roll onto the town from a light aircraft; offering a tin of dog-ends around the table during a dinner with snooty entertainment bigwigs, then ostentatiously bunging the waiter a hand-rolled luxury continental smoke) to the disturbing (Randle demolishing a dressing room with an axe after an iffy performance; a pissed Randle firing a Luger randomly at an extra). Ah, showbiz.

The stories would be all that remained of the man if John E Blakeley, founder of the Mancunian Film Corporation, one of the few British production companies to have studios outside the Home Counties (a converted Manchester church later to house early *Top of the Pops*) had not set Frank up with a franchise – the *Somewhere…* films. The first three of these, *…in England* (1940), *…in Camp* (1942) and *…on Leave* (1943) were all the same film, with minor variations, involving Randle and posh-talking 'dude' comedian Dan Young rubbing big, docile sergeant Harry Korris up the wrong way.

The comics shared screen space with 'Proper Actors', whose job it was to provide some half-arsed attempt at a plot with which to tie the gags together. This being the 1940s, these 'Proper Actors' all stiffly forced their dull expository lines out in 'simply wonderful!' strangulated RADA tones through clenched teeth, while Lancashire audiences no doubt talked amongst themselves until the next Randle scene, which was always guaranteed to be something of, in Randle parlance, a hot 'un.

The comics not being big on literary matters – Dan Young either couldn't, or wouldn't, learn a script – Blakeley reduced these scenes to a basic situation, a few props and a smattering of gags, then cranked the cameras into action and shouted 'OK boys, be funny'. And funny they were, in a chaotic, woozy sort of way. Modern-day purveyors of 'naturalistic' comedy – every 'umm' and 'ah' painstakingly placed into the script – could learn a thing from the stream of semi-consciousness that threatened to burst its banks whenever Randle, Young and Korris got into full cross-purpose flight. Add the obligatory showcase for Randle's tumbling skills – cleaning a billiard table, or the ever-popular comedy boxing match – and the winning formula was set in stone that never received so much as a light sanding of the corners thereafter.

Somewhere in Civvies (1943) was made – shock horror – 'Down South', and ditched Randle's army pals in favour of an inheritance plot, a special effects-heavy scene in a fake haunted house, and a suitably coarse female foil for Frank in the shape of the brazen Mrs Spam. After that it was back to Mancunian for *Holidays with Pay* (1948), featuring Randle's opera-signing pal Josef Locke, with whom he'd spend many a lost weekend drinking and dodging the taxman, and the fabulously self-explanatory *School for Randle* (1949).

His popularity beginning to wane, Frank fell back on a few remaining crumbs of comfort: sell-out Blackpool tours, his Aston Martin and yacht. His final film, *It's a Grand Life* (1953), had the fortunate distinction of being his best. The barracks milieu is back (minus Korris), and what ensues is a (slightly) more refined version of the *Somewheres*, with stock RADA girl replaced with Diana Dors, who's given plenty of unsubtle close-up inserts during which to smoulder at length. Randle runs amok from soup to nuts, losing a defecting soldier in a pub, turning an interrogation by his colonel into a polite discourse on how to draw a chicken, conducting a lecture on the bazooka, competing in a wrestling match, of course, and finally saving La Dors from drowning (in reality a stunt double, one Pat Phoenix).

Sadly, bankruptcy and booze caught up with him, and after gamely touting enticing-sounding film proposal *Wigan Peer* about the place, he succumbed to gastroenteritis in 1957. *It's a Grand Life* was likewise the swansong of Mancunian Films, and as the film comedy flavour of the month shifted first to radio, then telly stars, a whole entertainment era slid quietly in remission, preserved only by the odd strip of grainy, sludgy film showing an improbably aged hiker threatening gamely to 'take on anyone of my age or weight, dead or alive... I'll run 'em, jump 'em, fight 'em... aye, and I'll play 'em dominoes!'

DOWN UNDER

Britons bemoaning the knackered state of UK cinema, spare a thought for Australia and New Zealand, who until very recently toiled in less-than-splendid isolation on miniscule box office takings and peppercorn government grants, working with whatever semi-amateur talent they could lay their hands on. But in the manner of the countries themselves, this stifling lack of resources led Aussie and Kiwi directors to work that bit harder, which subsequently grew in strange new, yet somehow oddly familiar, shapes.

The tour of both countries' output will be whistlestop to say the least, taking as read the more celebrated and successful films (regretfully glossing over *Mad Max* but thankfully avoiding the cinematic oeuvre of Paul Hogan). However, there is just as much interest to be had surveying the earlier careers of those 'down-under' directors who went on to conquer Hollywood, that odd post-war period where indigenous Australian film still hid behind the country's infamous 'cultural cringe', and the first flowerings of both countries' government-funded independent explosion. As befits those former colonies that began their lives embracing the misfits, these films can be oddball indeed.

AUSTRALIA

THE OVERLANDERS (1946)
Early films in both countries were, by necessity, largely the product of writers, directors and companies from the colonial 'motherland'. But indigenous acting talent was springing forth to put a national stamp on these celluloid invasions. The most famous of these early stars was John William Goffage, better known to the continent and the world as the Australian Cary Grant, Chips Rafferty. If you see an Australian film made between the outbreak of WWII and the mid-1960s, chances are there'll be a fair dinkum, rugged-but-loveable Aussie in there, not necessarily in shorts and bush hat, played by Chips. In this Ealing Studios production, Rafferty oversees the historic movement of thousands of cattle across the Northern Territories to Queensland to shore up the country's supplies in the face of Japanese invasion. It's great fun, albeit steeped in 'hard yakka and hard tucker' cliché from top to toe. The no-probs persona is here in excelsis, with Rafferty rounding up his crew in none-more-laid-back style (*Rafferty*: 'Hey Jacky, fancy a thousand mile trek to Queensland?' *Aborigine Jacky*: 'How long yer gonna be?' *Rafferty*: 'About three years.' *Jacky*: 'Right, I'll tell the wife. Back in ten minutes.') although the film is dated by Rafferty's dreams of leaving Australia for the brave new world of... the Soviet Union ('Moscow here I come!'). There's more of a roguish tinge to the bloke in proto-Children's Film Foundation favourite *Bush Christmas* (1947) with two fish-out-of-water children using bush survival skills to track down Rafferty's gang of horse rustlers.

TV CREAM'S ANATOMY OF CINEMA

THE SUNDOWNERS (1960)

The isolation felt by new arrivals in the wide open spaces of the New World was a major theme for the subsequent wave of immigration-based dramas. In this American-funded film, Robert Mitchum and Deborah Kerr take up the itinerant sheep-shearing life with Peter Ustinov, under the aegis of no-nonsense shearing chief (Rafferty again). The contrast between a clean slate land of opportunity and an empty, rootless existence was the order of the day here, the bucolic excitement of sheep-shearing contests and games of two-up being small compensation for the lack of a real home. The style of this film – as close to documentary as mainstream Hollywood got in those days, with plenty of natural history footage of Oz's bizarro widlife thrown in – was a fittingly downbeat one, and one that would almost become the default pastoral style for many a 'pom in purgatory' film to come.

THEY'RE A WEIRD MOB (1966)

Post-*Peeping Tom* brush-off, Michael Powell fled to Sydney to create, what else – an Italian neo-realist romantic comedy. The result is properly odd. An Italian journalist emigrates to the 'You Beaut' country to become a journalist at the behest of his cousin, only to find the promised job waiting for him has vanished, as has the cousin, and he's left with debts that have to be met by taking gruelling work on a baking hot construction site – cue a strange and wonderful silent sequence of frenzied earth digging in full suit, tie and hat, and a slow-mo, exhausted collapse. Romance ensues with one of his cousin's creditors, who gradually falls in love with him, though her cantankerous, dagophobe dad – played by, natch, the man Chips – proves a tougher hurdle. It sets the 'fair go' idealism of the country against its latent xenophobic streak to brilliant effect and broke box office records for a native film. Powell later made *Age of Consent* (1969), in which globetrotting aussie artist James Mason finally returns home, and hooks up with dodgy old pal Jack MacGowran and very young muse Helen Mirren on remote Dunk Island. Meanwhile Walter Chiari, the journo from ...*Weird Mob*, became a down under-bound Italian monk relocating his vineyard for wine comedy *Squeeze a Flower* (1970), featuring a host of latterly big Aussie names, as well as Dave Allen.

WALKABOUT (1971)

Nicolas Roeg's fragmented outback meander ripped into the then still repressively buttoned-down nature of middle-class Australian life by confronting a suicidal businessman's plummy children (and, latterly, some equally plummy geologists) with both aboriginal and small town mores, although the landscape photography (and, for some, the Jenny Agutter photography) probably made more of an impact than the culture clash invective could hope to. In similar moody vein, short children's film *Storm Boy* (1976) followed the mute adventures of a young boy in remote south Oz, an aborigine called Fingerbone Bill and orphaned pelican Mr Percival.

OUTBACK (1971)

By the 1970s, of course, Australia was the number one destination for British ex-pats. *Outback* saw Brit teacher Donald Pleasence stranded in The Yabba, a remote scrub wilderness where sun, chronic boredom and dumb drunken insolence are the inescapable order of the day, the week, and the year. The Australian tourist board didn't take kindly to this warts-and-more-warts portrayal (which incidentally was Chips' last film), and several counter-message films were pushed through, mainly in a lighter, more continent-promoting mood, such as *Sunstruck* (1972), a whimsically romantic tale of rather more ebullient and eager teacher Harry Secombe upping sticks to Oz for sun, surf and Sheilas, but finding himself in an outback girls' school instead. Still, it all turns out all right in the end (what would you expect from a film made by Immigrant Productions?).

THE ADVENTURES OF BARRY MCKENZIE (1972)

Barry Humphries can be an amazingly subtle comedian when he feels like it. Not so with this creation, an endless fusillade of 'Pommie poofter' jokes and innovative but ultimately wearying Ocker euphemisms for lager, piss and vomit, prized from the pages of *Private Eye* and ham-fistedly shackled to the sort of crumpet-seeking subplot that would not be out of place in a minor *Carry On*. Barry Crocker, later to warble the *Neighbours* theme, is the Akubra hat-toting bludger, seeking fame and fortune in London with his Auntie Edna (Humphries) in tow. Cameos from Peter Cook, Spike Milligan and Joan Bakewell come and go in perfunctory manner, though Dennis Price's pervy Home Counties schoolboy fetishist is memorable. Humphries-isms still shine through the wall-to-wall coarseness: Barry advertising 'High Camp Cigalettes (sic)', the band Raspberry Ripple and the Y-Fronts, the headline 'Leprosy panic sweeps Birmingham', etc. Director Bruce Beresford ladles on that slightly off-kilter, slightly threadbare style present, to varying degrees, in all manner of Antipodean films from this through *Mad Max* to Peter Jackson's pre-*Rings* efforts. It's hard to define, but the basic elements are: lots of wide-angle close-ups of faces, often made all the more jarring when they're not being employed for any dramatic effect at all; one- and two-person shots frequently filmed 'straight on', with the characters seemingly pressed against the wall; the AFC money often appearing to stretch to a lighting rig that must number two in total, giving a kind of pasty flat look, with loads of too-dense shadows; and loads of showy low angles and long zooms, as if trying to make up for the previous points. Add to that the general shapelessness of the film as a whole (what's that Aboriginal dream sequence doing there, exactly?) and you have a kind of cheerily ramshackle quality that is unapologetically gung ho in its sheer lairy, uneven, government-funded oddness. The sequel, *Barry McKenzie Holds His Own* (1974), moved to Paris, where evil Transylvanians, under the aegis of a marvellously bloodless Donald Pleasence, kidnap Edna, assuming her to be the Queen. The cameo roll call features John Le Mesurier, Roy Kinnear, Clive James and Edna-ennobling Prime Minister Gough Whitlam.

THE CARS THAT ATE PARIS (1974)

Joining Beresford in an emergent wave of home-grown directing talent was Peter Weir, who made this immensely enjoyable low-budget sci-fi romp, in which the inhabitants of a surreally quaint outback town (as with Melbourne suburbs, still stuck in the Victorian era, though in this case they even wear bonnets, stovepipe hats and entertain themselves with mind-numbingly dull tea dances) who engineer accidents for passing cars to keep their community ticking over, until youngsters in souped-up custom cars (including a bondage VW beetle) literally start tearing the town apart. It's witty, knockabout stuff – basically an extended student film, in the best sense of the phrase. More Victorian types get it in the neck in Weir's follow-up, the far more conventional and respected *Picnic at Hanging Rock* (1975), based on a not-really-all-that-true story of a bunch of schoolgirls disappearing in mysterious circumstances during the titular outing. Again, it's all about repressed Old World values getting the boot from the untameable wilderness of the new country. A theme would appear to be developing.

DON'S PARTY (1976)

Beresford, after calling the shots for Humphries-starring glam rock showcase *Side by Side*, turned his camera on the emergent, liberalised middle classes in an adaptation of a play set at a raucous suburban party on the night of the milestone 1969 election. The coming change in political and social climate is offset with the unreconstructed behaviour of the party guests, predating (and going much further than) Mike Leigh's *Abigail's Party* in its ruthless mockery of wayward suburbia. It couldn't be more of a contrast with Beresford's later *'Breaker' Morant* (1980), a sober Boer War period piece with Australian Lieutenants including Edward Woodward and Bryan Brown being court martialled as scapegoats for maltreatment of PoWs. Ray 'Alf off *Home and Away*' Meagher and the almost-as-ubiquitous-as-Chips Charles 'Bud' Tingwell are among a superb cast. For historical veracity it knocks Weir's Mel Gibson-tainted Anzac tribute *Gallipoli* (1981) into a cocked hat. Wildly changing tack yet again, Beresford then served up *Puberty Blues* (1981), a teen movie which, all big hair, surfing, 'fancy a root?' chat-up lines and beach alcoholism, was simultaneously trashily camp and incredibly grim.

HARLEQUIN (1980)

Simon Wincer was a director attuned to the sinister possibilities of Oz, with *Snapshot* (1979), in which a model is stalked by her boyfriend in an ice cream van, and this beautifully-shot mystical chiller. Aussie politician David Hemmings falls under the spell of eerie Rasputin-like magician Robert Powell, who holds the senator and his ailing family in a firm grip with healing powers, telekinesis, and a wardrobe of increasingly outlandish costumes – clown, monk, Jesus robes, natty leather jacket-plus-trousers, and the climactic harlequin suit – set against unforgiving Perth landscapes. It has an eye for colour and composition that gives it the look of an Australian counterpart to *The Shining*, which its release predated by two months.

MALCOLM (1986)

In a predictably blokeish cinematic milieu, female directors did start to gain a foothold. Gillian Armstrong was propelled by Judy Davis and Sam Neill to world stardom with the pleasant if slightly static feminist period drama *My Brilliant Career* (1979), while Jane Campion put the fun into dysfunctional with weirdo sister curio *Sweetie* (1989) before moving on to the Oscar-trousering melodrama *The Piano* (1993). More interesting is unsung heroine Nadia Tass, director of this excellent caper comedy. An exercise in doing 'quirky' without becoming a pain in the arse, *Malcolm* takes a plot that could easily nosedive into sentiment – reclusive, borderline-autistic bloke with a talent for making gadgets falls in with a lowlife criminal and his girlfriend, and helps them with a robbery – but treats it in exactly the right head-on manner, like an Australian Ealing comedy, for want of a better comparison. The dialogue is brazen, the gags are sound and the gadgets, from Malcolm's personal tram to the split-in-two getaway car to the robot ashtrays, are great. The only thing that dates it is the Penguin Cafe Orchestra soundtrack, which was really lovely once, before it appeared on every mobile phone advert ever.

NEW ZEALAND

RUNAWAY (1965)
As with Australia, the early years of New Zealand cinema were marked by colonial concerns. Lana Turner and Van Heflin fled to the land of the long white cloud in US melodrama *Green Dolphin Street* (1946), and Jack Hawkins colonised it in the rugged nineteenth century colonial epic *The Seekers* (1954), with help from a rather unrugged Kenneth Williams, no less. John O'Shea's interracial Maori romance *Broken Barrier* (1952) made local impact, leading to this new-wave story of an angsty teenage boy escaping the repression of small-town NZ by, well… running away, meeting various characters and passing the obligatory majestic New Zealand scenery on the way. Then came *Don't Let it Get You* (1966), New Zealand's answer to *A Hard Day's Night*, in which a displaced Aussie drummer seeks fame, fortune and Kiri te Kanawa in Rotorua.

SLEEPING DOGS (1977)
Another Aussie émigré, Roger Donaldson, really put the wind up Kiwi cinema with this near-future actioner. It's a familiar enough conceit: the islands are overtaken by a totalitarian regime, various renegade armies are formed to fight back using any means necessary and an innocent bystander (Sam Neill, in this case) gets mixed up in their insurgence while trying to avoid contributing to the bloodshed. It is shot in a heady style and the novelty of the locale got it an international release, and it became the first NZ film to screen in the USA. Following on from that, Donaldson helped found the New Zealand Film Commission the following year, a funding and distribution organisation along similar lines to Australia's.

SMASH PALACE (1981)
Donaldson really hit his stride with this harrowing melodrama, in which a middle-aged car-obsessed father (played by cult NZ star, ex-Brightonian jazz drummer Bruno Lawrence) responds to his collapsing marriage by kidnapping his daughter and making for those photogenically remote landscapes. *Smash Palace* helped put NZ cinema firmly on the map and launched Donaldson into international league. After helming *The Bounty* (1984), a lavish telling of the naval chestnut with Mel Gibson as Mr Christian and Anthony Hopkins as Captain Bligh, came the likes of *Cocktail*, *Species* and, er… *Cadillac Man*.

TV CREAM'S ANATOMY OF CINEMA

SKIN DEEP (1978)

Then there was documentary maker Geoff Steven, who hit paydirt with this fictional study of an isolated NZ township which, under the auspices of its dictatorial burgermeister, decides to 'put itself on the map' by raising funds for a massive publicity campaign, at the centre of which is the hiring of a big-city masseuse to work in the local health spa. This last appointment really puts the cat among the pigeons, as several previously tightly repressed male townsfolk start to unwind at speed over the streetwise new arrival. This is all set against a keenly-observed background of 1970s mundane small-town life, instantly recognisable to anyone from the UK (the giant thermometer showing money raised, the various parochial community events, etc.) but with many typically Kiwi quirks (a log-chopping contest) thrown in.

UTU (1983)

Geoff Murphy started out self-funding his own spare-time productions on 16mm. Early efforts included action comedy *Tankbusters* and *Uenuku*, the first Maori-language film, followed by *Wild Man* (1977) starring Bruno Lawrence as one of a pair of conmen finding rich pickings in late nineteenth century gold-mining communities, and *Dagg Day Afternoon* (1977), a zany vehicle for Wellington boot-wearing Kiwi comic Fred 'That'll be the door!' Dagg. Then came a real popular success: *Goodbye Pork Pie* (1981) sees a jilted husband hook up with a local nutball to drive from top to bottom of the country in a yellow mini to try and win her back, getting into many high-speed run-ins with the law and other New Zealanders along the way. Murphy's follow up, *UTU*, was even more off-the-wall, a western with Maori rebels led by Te Weke (an acting debut for former trade union leader Anzac Wallace), an ex-army corporal who swaps sides to exact revenge on the colonial government who have reneged on their land agreements and attacked villages. It's chock full of action and gun battle scenes, shot in a fast-paced, wide-angle style for which the term 'bravura' could have been invented. But there's more to it than straightforward white/black hat fare, as distrust and ambiguous motives are felt and held by nearly all the characters. It's a serious tale, but black humour seeps through, as does a hefty dose of violent slapstick: one memorable running gag sees settler Bruno Lawrence, descending into paranoid obsession after Te Weke kills his wife, trying to invent a Maori-stopping supergun by strapping first two, then four, then eight rifles together, with disastrous recoil results.

THE QUIET EARTH (1985)

Murphy's next film couldn't have been more of a change of pace. Bruno Lawrence is a worker on a nebulously-defined 'government scientific project', which goes wrong and wipes out every living thing on Earth, except for (it seems) Lawrence. For the first half of the film, Lawrence wanders the deserted country, looting shops, pissing about with trains, berating cardboard cut-outs of historical figures and slowly descending from anarchic delight into lonely depression. Then he discovers another, female, survivor, and the inevitable romance starts to develop, only to be stymied when a third survivor, a massively-built Maori, turns up. The film then becomes a three-way emotional stand-off, before further scientific 'events' lead to an ambiguous, if not downright weird, ending.

DOWN UNDER

DEATH WARMED UP (1985)

Peter Jackson's blue-shirted zombie comedy *Bad Taste* (1987) was, surprisingly, not the first sicko splatter flick on the islands. That honour goes to this David Blyth no-budget gorefest, wherein a mad scientist hypnotises a young man to shoot his parents, and on his release, the kid goes after the old man in his zombie-ridden island laboratory. With plenty of flying gore played for shock/comic effect (including our old friend Bruno Lawrence as a hunchbacked zombie whose head explodes), it plays like a slightly more warped version of a Peter Jackson film, if such a thing is possible.

THE ESSENTIAL
TOP SECRET LAIR

THE ABOMINABLE DR PHIBES (1971)

It's 1929. You're a well-respected doctor, theologian and musical genius about town. You're horrifically scarred in a car accident, which also claims the life of your beautiful wife. You harbour a major grudge against the nine eminent surgeons who failed to save her life. What to do?

In the warped world of *Avengers* director Robert Fuest and art director Brian Eatwell, where there's blame, there's an elaborate series of baroque assassinations themed round the nine biblical plagues of Egypt, launched from an imposing marble-lined secret hideaway-cum-ballroom. Truly, the lair of Dr Anton Phibes (Vincent Price) is a thing of camp and sinister glory. Surgeons are drained of blood, strangled by frog masks, impaled on a brass unicorn head, coated in pureed Brussels sprouts and devoured by locusts. All the while, Phibes gleefully prances about his malevolent Alhambra dungeon with silent companion Vulnavia, in a horror film so free of realism, logic and sensibility it's of another genre altogether. Here are the main ingredients if you fancy trying this sort of thing yourself on a spare Sunday afternoon.

A. A great big Wurlitzer organ of Odeon fleapit vintage, on which to dramatically rise from the pit at the start of proceedings.

B. Dr Phibes's Clockwork Wizards – a mechanical dance band to accompany your diabolical doings. (In the proposed third sequel Brides of Phibes, the Wizards were to gain the power of locomotion, in a running battle with massed coppers.)

C. Symbolic busts of the cursed doctors, to theatrically destroy in commemoration of each successful execution, as your mute accomplice plays a mournful violin solo.

D. That all-important dance floor, complete with secret device to ensure that the bumbling coppers never bring you to rights.

E. (Out of view to left) A shrine to your beautiful wife, as also seen in another life variously accompanying James Bond, Dusty Bin and a bottle of Lamb's Navy Rum, to whom you longingly converse via an artificial voice-box which plugs into the back of your head. They made their own entertainment back then.

God Save Mrs Ethel Shroake – Spike awaits the inevitable in *The Bed-Sitting Room*.
(Stefano Archetti/Rex Features.)

Eye of the Keyholder – Anthony Newley polishes up his memoirs on the set of *Heironymus Merkin*.
(George Konig/Rex Features.)

In the grim aftermath of *Sergeant Pepper's Lonely Hearts Club Band*, George Burns leads the *Bee Gees* and Peter Frampton to the benefit office of Mr Kite. (Globe Photos Inc / Rex Features.)

'It's not a question of losing my nerve...' Peter Ustinov prepares for the *Topkapi* heist.
(Everett Collection/Rex Features.)

'This'll be Jeffrey Archer's flat one day, you know!' Vincent Price horrifies the critics' circle in *Theatre of Blood.* (Snap/Rex Features.)

Roll out the barrel – Richard Harris at your disposal in *Juggernaut.* (Everett Collection/Rex Features.)

'We're the beautiful people, aren't we?' Gregory Peck and David Warner await the rising of the Holy Roman Empire in *The Omen*. (Snap/Rex Features.)

'If that's a girl, then I don't know what my sister is!' Jayne Mansfield and Tom Ewell phone in a performance for *The Girl Can't Help It*. (Snap/Rex Features)

Up and under – **Lynda Bellingham and Robin Askwith wrap up warm for** *Confessions of a Driving Instructor.* (Chris Capstick/Rex Features.)

'It's lovely out, y'know! – Godber and Fletch find themselves playing away in *Porridge*.
(Chris Capstick/Rex Features.)

Very Peter Hall – the director (in beard) dusts off David Warner for *Work is a Four-Letter Word*.
(Reg Wilson/Rex Features.)

'I'm not a bleedin' fish finger!' *Slade* take to the stage of the Rainbow Theatre as *Flame*. (Andre Csillag/Rex Features.)

Francis De La Tour and Leonard Rossiter search for the permissive society in *Rising Damp*.
(Chris Capstick/Rex Features.)

Joan Collins at ease, shortly before welcoming her new insect overlords in *Empire of the Ants*. (Globe Photos/Rex Features.)

Now hear the word of the Lord – Michael Bryant and Arthur Lowe square up to Peter O'Toole in *The Ruling Class*. (Everett Collection/Rex Features.)

'Tch! These modern girls!' Margaret Lockwood is *The Wicked Lady*.
(Everett Collection/Rex Features.)

Special Op-art Operations Executive Monica Vitti, aka *Modesty Blaise*.
(Everett Collection/Rex Features.)

A boiler-suited Hazel O'Connor proves to be a problem man had not forseen as yet in *Breaking Glass*.
(Rex Features.)

Beastly bric-a-brac – Peter Cushing leads cinemagoers into Temptations in *From Beyond the Grave*.
(Everett Collection/Rex Features.)

Smashing Time – Rita Tushingham and Lynn Redgrave, hot off the train and gobsmacked at London's 'scene with the built in trip'. (Sharok Hatami/Rex Features.)

'Live and let live, that's my motto.' *Flash Gordon*, still – just about – alive.
(Everett Collection/Rex Features.)

A rare shot of Peter Sellers and Orson Welles on the set of *Casino Royale* together, shortly before **Princess Margaret turns up.** (Everett Collection/Rex Features.)

'Ship's concert, I shouldn't wonder.' Raquel Welch keeps *The Magic Christian* on an uneven keel. (Snap/Rex Features.)

'A perfect coagulation of the plasma.' – Sheree Hewson inspects the Monkhouse molars on the set of *Dentist in the Chair.* (George Konig/Rex Features.)

ROBERT MORLEY

FRUITY WINDBAGS A SPECIALITY

Robert Morley was a giant among giants in the theatre. No less than Cecil Beaton eulogised: 'Whether hanging a necklace around his latest lady-love, drinking pink champagne, being jeered at by the populace or rouged in preparation for Victoria's christening, Mr Morley gives a performance of rare quality and style from the tip of his chestnut curls to the last button of his gourd-like waistcoat'. To the cinema audience, however, he was better known as 'that fat old loon with the eyebrows who ponces about in front of the sideboard and publishes a book of humorous anecdotes every Christmas'. Such is the power of the typecasting machine.

It was not always so. Back in the days when film and theatre were still on nodding terms, MGM poached Morley from the Old Vic to star as Louis XVI in *Marie Antoinette* (1938), and it was off to Hollywood for Morley and old acting mucker Peter Bull, cast as his barber. Thereafter, he turned down *The Hunchback of Notre Dame* on the grounds it was more a grunting than a speaking part, before the war (and lack of cash) necessitated a trip back to Blighty to churn out propaganda quickies from the misshapen (Will Hay acting straight in 1940s *The Big Blockade*) to the wonderful (*The Foreman Went to France* ((1942)), as a duplicitous mayor with a rather wayward French accent).

Morley's fruity theatricals were finally given full reign in *The Ghosts of Berkeley Square* (1947). Morley and Felix Aylmer are a pair of Queen Anne-era military bumblers appearing on a weird sort of heavenly *This is Your Life*, telling the tale of how they tried to trap a general in a house in the titular square in a naive attempt to stop the war, but killed themselves in the process and remain doomed to haunt the house until they can persuade a monarch to visit. Such pantomimic capers allowed Morley full rein to pull faces of all kinds, and at that point the wind changed. This was Morley on film from now on.

Decadent kings, bumbling ministers, pompous double-barrelled aristocrats – any hope of a varied film acting career had given way to the chance to exhibit varying degrees of Morleyness. There was the occasional serious success such as *Oscar Wilde* (1960), but the public image of untrammelled windbaggery remained rock solid. There were great things to be wrung from this formula, though: the idiot heir to an Edinburgh tweed firm in *The Battle of the Sexes* (1959), rubbing shoulders with Bogie in *The African Queen* (1951) and *Beat the Devil* (1953), a pettifogging W.S. Gilbert in *The Story of Gilbert and Sullivan* (1953), a fruity inventor in *Topkapi* (1964) and a butterfly-obsessed computer programmer in *Hot Millions* (1968).

Honourable misses include his turn as a thinly veiled Cedric Hardwicke in Evelyn Waugh's Los Angeles funeral satire *The Loved One* (1965), which fast became an all-star campathon, Morley struggling to outgun John Gielgud, Jonathan Winters, Rod Steiger and Liberace. This delirious feast of 'black, protruding tongues' even has a shocked toff's monocle falling into his brandy glass, which of course is the apotheosis of western humour. Morley did manage to outact Jerry Lewis of all people, in the multicoloured, Bakelite-festooned moonbase sexual frustration farce *Way... Way Out* (1966) – no small feat.

After cinema's swinging-era sea change, Morley's old school puffer fish act found fewer ports of call. As a judge in boringly controversial Charles Bronson/Susan George underage romance *Twinky* (1969) all he could do was take the money and think of the Inland Revenue. On the other hand, there were gift parts in knowingly camp serial killer romps *Theatre of Blood* (1973) and *Who is Killing the Great Chefs of Europe?* (1978), both haughtily superior but still childish critics (one of theatre, one food).

The odd mix of dignity and mortification that is Morley's screen persona can be summed up by two less-than-stellar roles from his anecdotage. *The Blue Bird* (1976) looked prestigious – an all-star fantasy marking the first joint US–USSR co-production. The result was a breathtakingly shoddy pantomime fraught with technical difficulties, not to mention Jane Fonda rampaging round the studio trying to out-Commie the Soviet crew. Morley at least has some dignity in his role as the avuncular Old Father Time – a better deal than Harry Andrews (playing a tree) and George Cole (a dog). In *Second Time Lucky* (1984), New Zealand's incorrect comic answer to *Bedazzled*, he went one better, cast as God having a wager with Robert Helpmann's drag queen Devil over endless historical permutations on the Garden of Eden. Even when turning histrionic tricks for a fistful of used fivers in tenth-rate garbage, he still commands a slightly battered respect.

THE ESSENTIAL CAPER COMEDY

TOPKAPI (1964)

In 1955, top noir director Jules Dassin made top serious heist drama *Rififi* on a budget of sod all, and stormed Cannes with it, mainly thanks to the lengthy, elaborate and near-silent sequence at the centre of the film where the jewel robbery is taking place. Americans, as is their wont, started copying it. The copies became gradually more outlandish and overblown until, with the dawning of the 1960s, that unique film genre with almost no connection to criminal reality, the caper comedy, was born.

The rules of this genre faithfully followed Dassin's original dress pattern. Start with the assembling of the gang (a rag-tag band of misfits each, preferably, with a special skill), move on through outlining of the plot and training, and build up to the (hopefully) ingenious, suspenseful and showstopping heist itself, before rounding things off with a 'best laid plans' coda where it all goes horribly wrong. When it works, it works like nothing else in cinema. There's nothing like watching an immensely satisfying harebrained scheme being carried out like clockwork, allowing the audience to root for a bunch of unreconstructed career criminals (violence, tellingly, is rarely used), before hypocritically switching to a 'yes of course, well they had it coming' position when the fall inevitably arrives. The spectator gets to feel part of this hyper-smart gang, while enjoying the diplomatic immunity conferred by their ticket stub, and a deeply satisfying cake is had and eaten in the stalls.

Dassin, understandably, felt he was not getting his due for starting the whole ball rolling more or less single-handedly. What to do? Write a sniffy article in *Cahiers Du Cinema* rubbishing his imitators? Withdraw pompously from making films altogether and take up macramé instead? No, he decided to beat the caper copyists at their own game, and *Topkapi* is probably the most eloquent 'Look mate, if you're going to rip me off, *this* is how you should do it' riposte in the history of film.

Saucepot Greek jewel forger (and future Mrs Dassin) Melina Mercouri hooks up with her ex-squeeze, scheming criminal genius Maximilian Schell, to nick a Sultan's priceless emerald-inlaid dagger from a museum in the titular Turkish locale. Along the way they recruit foppish gadget maverick Robert Morley, a circus strongman and a 'my body is my tool' acrobat-cum-mime. A sound gang, but when they look for an arms courier the best they can find is small-time conman Peter Ustinov. The Turkish police get wind of something fishy when they catch Oosti-Boosti at the border with a load of grenades, so enlist him to spy on Schell's gang from the inside. This, of course, is a rubbish thing to do as he's a bumbling fool who knows damn all about what's going on, and has to fight off the amorous intentions of a deranged chef who keeps popping up for no concrete reason at all, before an accident forces him reluctantly into the strongman role, and the heist is on.

THE ESSENTIAL CAPER COMEDY

From the broad comedy of the early scenes, through the occasional longueur (the romantic banter twixt Schell and Mercouri falls mighty flat), we're treated to a slow, steady build-up to the inevitable climax, with the odd pitfall followed by ingenious change of tactics along the way, as per genre regulations. This being the 1960s, there's also lashings of travelogue-style footage of Turkish locales (bazaars, docks, mosques, and a decidedly odd mass oiled-up wrestling tournament) – all exquisitely photographed.

The forty-minute, near-wordless heist is not only gag-packed, but truly nail-biting. While Mercouri, Morley and a mechanical parrot distract the guards, the intrepid trio scamper across museum rooftops in a vertiginously filmed sequence that makes the viewer almost as queasy as height-fearing Ustinov. Then, Schell and Usters brace themselves at the top of the rope while the acrobat is lowered through a window and down onto the display case via an elaborate pulley system, to avoid setting off the pressure-sensitive floor alarm. It is a brilliantly ingenious excuse for high-wire acrobatics and heart-stopping slip-ups, and naturally it has been cheerfully ripped off countless times by productions including, in descending order of merit: an episode of *Thunderbirds, Herbie Goes to Monte Carlo* and *Mission: Impossible*. Needless to say these were tarted it up with noise and orchestral scores, whereas Dassin chose this point to cut the film back to bare bones: silent chambers, anguished grimaces, the creak of the rope and, most importantly, no incidental music whatsoever.

The performances are, admittedly, not all so breathtaking. Schell is phoning his act in from the suave exchange and Mercouri is on hands-free from the Blackwall Tunnel – she's supposed to be a criminal legend-cum-impetuous nymphomaniac, but sub-Eartha Kitt come hither purring is as well-developed as that gets. Fortunately, the Brits come through with the goods: Morley's eccentrically childlike gadget lover could have been written for, even by, him.

Ustinov's hapless Arthur Simpson, however, is another matter. It is common practice to make the bumbling liability in any criminal gang the broadest of broad comic turns – think Benny Hill's 'big lady'-mad professor in *The Italian Job*. Ustinov could have done that in his sleep, but instead goes in entirely the other direction, and hits on a mumbling, realistic way of speaking (in a soft midlands accent) which seems on a different planet from Mercouri and Schell's stilted continental slickness, which as they're meant to be worlds apart anyway is entirely appropriate. Thus, the bumbling comic relief is elevated to key figure and focus of audience sympathy – Dassin gleefully tramples all over one of the sacred rules of the genre he unwittingly helped create.

Ustinov was originally offered the Clouseau role in *The Pink Panther* about the same time Peter Sellers landed Simpson in *Topkapi*, but they both turned them down and ended up swapping jobs. Peter U then won the 1965 supporting role Oscar while Pete S lucked out of the starring role award for *Dr Strangelove* the same year. Ustinov promptly installed his gong in the lav. Nice one, Arthur.

SWINGING SPIES

Bond cast a shadow over 1960s cinema that is hard to fully appreciate these days. Once the series got going, it pulled the rug out from under the industry's feet, then wrapped it up in it, put it over its knee and spanked it until it revealed the whereabouts of the secret undersea base. Before film franchises were cheapo, support feature affairs (witness detective potboilers like *Ellery Queen*), but this one was big news. It just begged to be copied. But how? With Bond's unique combination of po-faced Cold War espionage, knowingly daft OTT villains and saucy asides, there was no way of producing a direct facsimile without being found out big time. Some avoided this via *The Ipcress File* route, playing down the glamour and amping up the grit. Others, however, forsook respectability and plunged headlong into camped-up overdrive.

What this genre's really all about is pop film eating itself. Hitching their wagon to the 'in' crowd, the makers of the 'second wave' of espionage confections brought pretty much everything else 'in' with it – in-jokes, in-references, and quite frankly incest, as ever more desperate producers cannibalised previous cannibalisations for bits of undercover business. Not a healthy way for a film genre to carry on, and as a result it burnt itself out in a few years, while the dinner-jacketed original agent toddled on undefeated into comfortable middle-age. None of the below fulfil any of the criteria of the 'well-made film', and frankly they're all the better for it. Which would you rather have? A straightforward, tightly-plotted Len Deighton snoozefest, or a DayGlo, knickers-down, glorious mess of gadgets, girls, guns and great big gaudy sets? Misguided attempts to pastiche the unpasticheable they may have been, but the road to cinematic hell is paved with delightfully silly set-pieces. And who cares about the contents of that microfilm anyway?

THE SECOND-BEST SECRET AGENT IN THE WORLD (1965)

If there had to be an acknowledged king of the cut-price Bond knock-off, self-financing string-and-sealing-wax auteur Lindsay Shonteff would be your man. Here he casts Tom Adams, latterly famous as the grey-haired stiff in a long-running DFS ad campaign, as shop-soiled Endsleigh League Bond Charles Vine, drafted in to guard an antigravity device from the Russkies. Comparisons with Bond proper are played for cheap laughs, Adams exhibits an un-Bond-like amoral streak by shooting folk in the back, and Sammy Davis Jr warbles the Bondesque theme. Adams/Vine returned for two sequels, *Where The Bullets Fly* (1966, featuring Sid James and Wilfrid Brambell) and the ultra-threadbare, Spanish-produced *OK Yevtushenko* (1968, featuring nobody), but by then the wayward Shonteff had moved onto other things...

SWINGING SPIES

MODESTY BLAISE (1966)
Peter O'Donnell's much-loved comic strip assassin-thief was modded up by Joseph Losey, a director hitherto best known for claustrophobic English class study *The Servant*. Modesty was played by Monica Vitti, smouldering with breathy continental semi-intelligibility, with a wisecracking bleach blond Terence Stamp in tow. The pair are hired by secret service head honcho Harry Andrews to safeguard a Middle Eastern diamond bribe from the hands of camply villainous, fan-toting, lobster-boiling Dirk Bogarde (in grey quiff and slit-vision sunglasses). O'Donnell's original script was discarded in favour of a swinging montage of op-art wallpaper, explosive doorbells, multi-coloured smoke bombs and very high hair. Everything about this film's modus operandi is completely, almost wilfully, wrong. The result is a swinging spadeful of downbeat camp fun, if such a thing is possible.

DEADLIER THAN THE MALE (1966)/SOME GIRLS DO (1968)
Ralph Thomas, mastermind of the *Doctor...* comedy franchise, had dipped a toe into Cold War comedy with *Hot Enough for June* (1964), casting Dirk Bogarde as reluctant agent 008¾, but really scored with these two camp-outs, dragging HC McNiele's hardboiled 1920s creation Bulldog Drummond into the swinging era. One-time potential Bond Richard Johnson incarnated as the suave Hugh D. is pitched against deadly but naturally ravishing female baddies such as Elke Sommer and Daliah Lavi. The first film was packed with gadgets and set-pieces such as the climactic giant chessboard shoot-out, but the sequel reached new heights of preposterousness, with a tale of a supersonic airliner hijacked by a squadron of scantily-clad robot lovelies as an ultra-camp Robert Morley demonstrates how to cook an egg.

THE PRESIDENT'S ANALYST (1967)
Fresh from playing Derek Flint, perhaps the most famous 'name' spoof Bond of all, James Coburn is cast as the titular White House shrink in this dayglo swinging conspiracy comedy, summoned to relieve his boss of the trauma of office (and a few state secrets besides) via an omnipresent flashing red alarm. Soon both American and Russian agents are after him, and many violent counterculture-related incidents lead Coburn to the real enemy – the all-powerful phone company, headed by the sinisterly smooth Pat Harrington Jr, who imprisons him in a phone box and screen their world domination plans in the form of quaint UPA-style cartoons, before a violently festive 'happy' twist ending. What with the obligatory censorship controversies (the names 'CIA' and 'FBI' altered with bad dubbing, apparently at the authorities' behest), a murderous William 'KITT' Daniels, inevitable psychedelic trip scenes, excellent *Casino Royale*-type sets and a whole Lalo Schifrin goin' on scorewise, this film gets dangerously close at points to becoming 'Quality Cinema', but thankfully veers off on yet another wild tangent before anything so boring can happen.

CASINO ROYALE (1967)
One of the most notorious botch-ups in film history, of course. Seven 007s! Five directors all filming at once! Peter Sellers and Orson Welles at loggerheads on set! All well documented, but what's the film like? It's a genuine, copper-bottomed, non-ironic hoot. You can be all

humourlessly nitpicky and play Spot the Joins, as the 'plot' veers from Niven's creaky knee routine to Woody Allen in front of a firing squad to Sellers and Andress on that circular double bed to op-art torture chamber after op-art torture chamber. Or you can just sit back and be swept along by the gloriously mad incongruity of it all, from the absurd (a bagpipe-playing Peter O'Toole as himself) to the genuinely great (The *Look of Love* beats all 'proper' Bond songs hands down). Throw in more than twenty celebrity cameos, ranging from Ronnie Corbett to Stirling Moss, and you've two solid hours of brightly-coloured mindless joy, a Fisher Price Activity Centre for the Nehru-collared set. Cause and effect be damned!

OK CONNERY (1967)

For sheer cheek, this takes the biscuit. Cheapo Italian filmmakers cast Sean Connery's younger, non-thespian brother Neil as Dr Neil Connery, bearded, badly dubbed, karate-chopping, lip-reading plastic surgeon brother of Bond proper, hired by Bernard 'M' Lee and Lois 'Moneypenny' Maxwell in lieu of 'The Other Feller' to fight criminal mastermind Adolfo '*Thunderball*' Celi. Ennio Morricone provides a parping pastiche of a Bassey-esque theme song. Skating as close as possible to the Bond franchise at all points while skillfully avoiding actual trademarked names and designs, this is the cinematic equivalent of nabbing a big pie left cooling on next-door's window sill and running away chortling loudly. For that, if nothing else, respect is due.

CAPRICE (1967)

Stanley Donen kickstarted the mid-1960s trend of lavish, one-word-title, Hitchcock-alike international espionage romps with the marvellous *Charade* (1963), and continued it with the only slightly lesser *Arabesque* (1966). Former Warner Brothers cartoonist Frank Tashlin, however, took the format to dizzying heights of daffiness with this hairspray-based spying mish-mash. Doris Day (in a variety of 'swinging' outfits and outsize round sunglasses) becomes involved in cosmetics-based intrigue and drug-smuggling, with a blue eyeshadow-wearing Richard Harris and debonair cosmetics chief Edward '*Knight Rider*' Mulhare, all whipped up into a knowingly deranged Mod frenzy of OTT set design and jet-set glamour (ski-slope shootouts, private jet interiors, a chain-suspended double bed, the Eiffel Tower – check). Both Day and Harris loathed Tashlin's messaround antics, but it's a wonderfully unrestrained piece of fluff, as exemplified by the scene in which Doris takes a break from the intrigue to visit the cinema – which is showing, er, *Caprice*.

SALT AND PEPPER (1968)/ONE MORE TIME (1970)

This genre's all about cinematic in-japery and self-indulgence, so how could it be complete without a visit from the Rat Pack? Dean Martin spent the sixties stumbling through a series of low-rent, girl-crazy *Man From UNCLE*-style adventures as Matt Helm, but that was *The Godfather* compared with this. An ageing Sammy Davis Jr (Charles Salt) and Peter Lawford (Chris Pepper) are a pair of Soho nightclub owners inducted by John Le Mesurier into the British secret service to gallivant around the Home Counties in a gadget-heavy car. The sequel, directed by Jerry Lewis, was even more foolish, featuring Lawford in a dual role as his upper class British cousin and a bit of business where Davis opens a secret passage behind a bookcase to discover Peter Cushing and Christopher Lee in costume as Frankenstein and Dracula, seemingly put there for no other reason than the lairy old Packers rather liked Hammer films. Two more Martinis over here, pronto!

TIFFANY JONES (1973)

It was inevitable that the sexploitation industry would eventually turn their attention to Bond spoofery. Pete Walker adapted raunchy *Daily Mail* cartoon strip Tiffany Jones for the big screen, with Anouska Hempel as the eponymous wide-eyed fashion model finding herself wooed by the dictator of a made-up Eastern Bloc country as well as its displaced Crown Prince who's out to overthrow the former, with the standard arms deal MacGuffin floating about somewhere. It's nominally a comedy romp, but Walker, no comic director at the best of times, is on autopilot, and the plot is an imagination-starved bore. Comedy foreign accents and cross-dressing are the order of the day. The 'highlight' in this fiercely unmemorable mess is a scantily-clad Hempel being captured by a gang of Marxist chefs and whipped with strands of spaghetti. It feels like a sad hangover from the old 'dolly bird in jeopardy' days rather than a working pastiche.

BIG ZAPPER (1973)

Another secret service knock-off from serial budget-dodger Lindsay Shonteff. Buxom Diana Rigg-alike Linda Marlowe is secret agent Harriet Zapper, driving round London, straddling a gatling gun and marking time in between martial arts bouts with horny boyfriend Rock Hard. A gobsmacking scene where Marlowe stuns a hapless assailant with a bolt of badly superimposed lightning from her nether regions, apropos absolutely nothing whatsoever, ensured this film's place in the annals of cult. Enough cash was raked in to justify a sequel, *Zapper's Blade of Vengeance* (1974), which upped the body count and beheadings, and lowered the camp comedy angle – slightly. Shonteff carried on in this ramshackle vein, returning in the late 1970s with two films based around uber-randy secret service agent Charles Bind (sic), played variously by Nicky Henson and Gareth Hunt. And so the wheel of the customised Lotus Esprit turned full circle.

CHIC MURRAY

CHIC MURRAY

COMEDY GENIUS ADRIFT IN A SEA OF TAT... MOSTLY

Billy Connolly, who may not be much cop as an actor but certainly knows his comedy, once remarked of his hero and friend Chic Murray that with better management he could have made some great films, but all he seemed to get were Big Fat Policeman types in the sorts of comedies Connolly wrongly described as 'mildly sexy', but which might be properly described as rubbish. There's a lot of truth in this.

Greenock-born actual proper comedy genius Murray was involved in more than his fair share of crap. Why remains something of a mystery, but Chic was an enigma anyway. At a time when most comedians either told jokes or fell over to music, Chic's act consisted of whimsical stories laced with subtle one-liners, so perhaps, unsurprisingly, producers found it difficult to make the best use of his talents.

His film parts, such as they were, included the likes of Big Fat Policeman in *Secrets of a Door-to-Door Salesman* (1973), Big Fat Policeman in *The Ups and Dows of a Handyman* (1975) and then a series of pointless nobodies in various hopeless entries in the sex comedy canon *I'm Not Feeling Myself Tonight* (1976) and *Can I Come Too?* (1979). Involvement in further dubious product followed with *What's Up Nurse!* (1977) and *What's Up Superdoc!* (1978), making Murray one of the mainstays of the whole lamentable genre. What the hell someone of the calibre of Murray, a trade comedian well respected by the industry quite apart from his dedicated audience, was doing getting embroiled in all this tat is anyone's guess, but then sexcoms traded heavily on the appeal of popular stars, usually to little effect. Most likely the collapse of his traditional professional stomping grounds due to the closure of theatres and clubs all over the country drove him into their mucky paws. Perhaps he needed the money. Perhaps he was just flattered to be asked. The real reason probably died with him, but none of the above give any proper insight to the sort of glorious business he was capable of.

Not all Chic's big screen work deserves to be swept under the shiny nylon carpet of yesterday. His first film appearance, in Charles K Feldman's brilliantly demented *Casino Royale* (1967), typically had little to do with his day job, though the same might be said of anyone's involvement in that grand folly. But while the sexcoms sought to exploit his comedic faculties, *Royale* cast him as a hit man, the logic of which is as baffling as some of Murray's own jokes. He made the most of the part though, and came across as genuinely sinister as he reached out of a television screen to assassinate Orson Welles before loping through the rest of the film as an oasis of mildly amused calm in the shambolic but entertaining whirlwind that constitutes the rest of the film.

By the 1980s Chic had settled into his place as Grand Old Man of comedy. The sex comedies were over and Murray found himself in a small-scale no-budget feature that was to provide him with almost his most famous legacy. The part of the Headmaster in *Gregory's Girl* (1981) finally gave Chic the chance to exploit his extraordinary character to full effect. Despite having extremely limited screen time he manages to dominate the whole film. When he's not in shot, the audience waits patiently for the next time he is, and the success of the film has as much to do with him as any of the leading players. Indeed his exhortation to a clutch of pupils, 'Off you go, you small boys!' while contentedly tinkling the ivories is easily the most famous line in the film. His total belief in the role is what makes him so compelling, as he stares intently while trying to decide how many doughnuts to buy. Sadly, Chic never lived to capitalise on this late flowering, but there's just enough of him on film for his genius to be recognised.

THE GENIUS OF
SEXPLOITATION

Although just about every previously *verboten* film genre has by now come in from the cold to warm its hairy backside at the fire of 'Proper Critical Acclaim', the sexploitation films of the 1960s and 1970s still find themselves standing in the snow, pressing their noses (at least, it looks like their noses) up against the leaded windows in envious dismay. Which, for a genre that almost single-handedly (in all senses) carried the British film industry through its darkest hour – the post-1960s slump after the major US studios panicked and pulled out of the country – is extremely unfair. After all, there was more to this varied genre than the threadbare *Confessions* romps and their rip-offs. Much more. In fact, in its own braless way, the sexploitation industry was a miniature replica of the whole gamut of filmmaking. Here are a few sub-sub-genres of particular scholarly note.

DOCUMENTARY

PRIMITIVE LONDON (1965)
Sexploitation kingpin Stanley A Long teamed up with writers Donald and Derek Ford to launch this salacious tabloid exposé on unsuspecting cinemagoers, promising to lift the lid on the seedy underbelly of modern London living. What you actually get is an hour and a half of... well, anything the producers fancied putting in, basically. It's roughly equivalent to two dozen editions of *Man Alive* chopped into bits and then reassembled at random, all showing various aspects of the decade's creeping moral decline. Interspersed with a liberal amount of bare norks, of course. Choice items include:
Wayward yoof – represented by Mods (a goofy Roger Daltrey type in a too-small pork pie hat buying a scarlet jacket), Rockers (seen at legendary bikers' Mecca the Ace Cafe in Alperton) and, best of all, some Beatniks at the One Tun pub on Goodge Street. While the Rockers are monosyllabically sardonic ('What would you do if you were Prime Minister?' ((Pause)) 'Get out of it, quick!') the generally rather posh Beatniks ('Where were you educated?' 'Oh, prep school, grammar school, university... and my bedroom mostly!') are not afraid to chat fart, postulate and recite some of their poetry ('That's all I can remember, I'm afraid') while sporting unabashed beards-without-moustaches and pulling thoughtfully on briar pipes.
Violence – helpfully introduced by a suit of armour coming to life, shambling over to a trestle table where bludgeons and swords are helpfully laid out, and swinging them stiffly about a bit, as the portentous voice-over drones on about mankind's neverending conflict. It all builds up to footage of Mick McManus in wrestling practise, accompanied

by one of those comedy piano pieces with a twittering bird effect over the top.

Advertising – Barry Cryer tries to coach a haughty actor through endless takes of the line 'Senor Coffee is real good!' A trad gag, drawn out for slightly too long; and if they're only recording a voice over, why do they start every take with a clapperboard?

Comedy – whereas up until 1959, comics apparently all sported 'a red nose and the baggy checked pants of the bookmaker', now they're blue-tongued, antigovernment and vicious to a man. Evidence consists of Ray Martine, playing a set at The Establishment Club, which here looks drab as anything. Martine cracks wise about Mrs Wilson as a nervy young couple shovel boiled cabbage down their faces. The man's sharp, but the place is a dump. There was a £5 waiting list for this?

General gruesomeness – consisting of: gratuitous battery chicken slaughter footage; a goldfish treated for fin rot in an intensive three-man operation, revived with 'a squirt of whisky'; and close-up footage of a corn being removed. The narrator manfully tries to tie these gruesome bits of footage into the big 'life in the raw' theme, but he isn't fooling anyone.

On top of all this there's wife swapping, Jack the Ripper, car accidents, Billy J Kramer, stripping and, er… millinery. A heady brew indeed.

HARD-HITTING, KEN LOACH-ESQUE DOCUDRAMA

COOL IT CAROL (1970)

Socialist auteur Ken Loach's *Cathy Come Home* broke seven shades of new ground for reality-based crusading social drama. Decidedly un-socialist auteur Pete Walker's grimy magnum opus may only be able to boast two at most, but was still revolutionary for the sex film genre in its own way. 'Based on a true story', the film sees the titular petrol pump attendant run off with butcher's boy Robin Askwith from their dreary Shropshire town for the bright lights of London. There they fall under the insalubrious wing of Jess Conrad, who introduces them to gambling, starring in porn films, and for Carol, 'entertaining' a series of wealthy businessmen. Walker lays on the grime and seediness with cynical aplomb; Askwith in particular is great, and far from his cheeky stereotype – even his arse exhibits a certain grittiness. As with *Cathy*, *Carol* attracted a fair old dollop of critical opprobrium, not least when Walker revealed he'd changed the ending of the real story – where Askwith's prototype was caught and slung in Borstal – for a more upbeat return to the country. Astonishingly enough, this slice of parochial British sleaze was a hit in the States to the tune of $2 million.

TV CREAM'S ANATOMY OF CINEMA

PERIOD DRAMA

THE BAWDY ADVENTURES OF TOM JONES (1976)

Tony Richardson and John Osborne may have gathered the glory with their 1960s version of Henry Fielding's monstrous six-volume picaresque epic, but Cliff 'That Riviera Touch' Owen and Jeremy 'Allo Allo' Lloyd made a suprisingly good fist of things thirteen years on, with Nicky Henson in the lead, Trevor Howard as a fantastic drunken, spank-happy narrator, Arthur Lowe and Terry-Thomas in Tom Baker wigs as Henson's teachers Thwackum and Square, and a cameoing Joan Collins as pantomime highwaygirl Black Bess. What's more, it's a musical, with the requisite gloriously tortuous lyrical contrivance present and correct in the songs. The hapless squire who discovers the infant Tom dumped in his bed opines 'How can I possibly explain it/That I've found a baby in my bed?/If nobody will claim it, on who shall I blame it?/Eloise, Mary-Anne, Hector, Jeremy or Fred?' The sub-Gilbert and Sullivan fun continues when Lowe and T-T perform Modus Operandi, a duet that initially resembles Flanders and Swann's 'I'm a Gnu' ('To survive (diddle-dee-dee)/To stay alive (diddle-dee-dee)/You must/Have a modus/Operandi'), brought to a close in the only manner possible – Lowe accidentally treads in some cow shit and Terry-Thomas grimaces in disgust. It all looks wonderful too; no gloopy browns, faded greens, underlit interiors and telly aerials looming into shot as you'd get with Carry On Dick. Veteran lensman Douglas Slocombe ensures that exteriors beam with ruddy colour, and interiors exhibit chiaroscuro candlepower to match anything Kubrick got in the over-fussy Barry Lyndon. And all this for a throwaway slap-and-tickle comedy!

SPACE OPERA

ZETA ONE (1969)

Semi-clad female aliens cavort in and out of increasingly outlandish Pop Art sets. It's a capsule description of well-loved Jane Fonda camp-out Barbarella – and this rather less cared-for Tigon production, give or take a few odd things. Those few odd things are: veteran actress Dawn Addams and ubiquitous screen siren Valerie Leon as the heads of alien operations and, as the hapless Earth duo out to foil the topless invaders, none other than James Robertson Justice and Charles Hawtrey. The spectacle of these two rent-paying Britcom stalwarts trying to cut it as the heads of an anti-bare-breasted Amazon insurgency in various Bacofoil-bedecked locations is, well, otherworldly.

PORTMANTEAU HORROR

SECRETS OF SEX (1969)

Yes, the sexploitation gang muscled in on this genre too, with this delirious bitty saga in which a mummy with the voice of Valentine Dyall links half-a-dozen short stories ranging from sub-Mayfair cartoon 'clothes fall off' titillation to full-on grotesque body horror, by way of a man splitting himself in two astride a razor-augmented vaulting horse. You can't accuse the 'twists' in these tales of not being up to scratch, as it's hard to believe they're meant to be twists in the first place. Wilful *non sequiturs* is nearer the mark. This was masterminded by William Burroughs acolyte Anthony '*Horror Hospital*' Balch.

PUBLIC INFORMATION FILM

TAKE AN EASY RIDE (1975)
A forty-minute wonder that distills the scaremongering essence of the many 'don't talk to strangers' films that were shown in school across the realm (with local bobby in attendance), this salacious slice of cautionary sauce is rendered in the same overcast, washed-out colours as any conventional example of the Central Office of Information's fear-stoking output. Various tales of hitch-hiking woe at the hands of sleazy truckers, rich 'swinging' couples and an unseen black-gloved monster in a sports car are stiltedly acted out, linked by the obligatory stentorian voice-over. A thoroughly grim little flick from the director who brought you 'me too' comedy *The Ups and Downs of a Handyman*, this was originally intended as a genuine cautionary programme for Southern Television, until the usual Soho suspects offered the makers more money to tailor it for the raincoat brigade.

SURREALIST MASTERPIECE

THIS, THAT AND THE OTHER! (1969)
Granted, this delirious product of the long-running Stanley Long–Derek Ford partnership is unlikely to owe its disjointed, spaced-out nature to close semiotic study of the works of Luis Bunuel, but nevertheless, the strange, disorienting atmosphere of this chips-cheap, three-handed sauce portmanteau would have had the giraffe-burning artisans of 1930s Paris doffing their berets at its uncompromising oddness. Dennis Waterman conducts a fetishistic glamour photo shoot. Morose loner Victor Spinetti finds his lonely nights at home listening to tapes of road accidents interrupted by the arrival of a random sex-suicide theme party. Finally, randy cabbie John Bird crashes his carriage and hallucinates a psychedelic orgy in the swimming pool of a remote cubist mansion. What this all means goodness knows, but the beyond-ramshackle filming and editing, as well as the fact that, for a sex comedy, there's precious little that is sexy or funny about it, earns the film every right to take its place amongst the most heroically obtuse works of the pre-war fish botherers. *Ceci n'est pas un saucy romp!*

TV CREAM'S ANATOMY OF CINEMA

ESKIMO NELL (1975)

A semi-autobiographical tale of the making of a typical x-rated film from exploitation veteran Michael Armstrong (made at the behest of Stanley Long), *Eskimo Nell* stands head and shoulders over its tit-'n'-bum cousins. Film-school graduate Dennis Morrison (Armstrong) seeks directorial work in Soho, but the only person who'll have him is shabby tit-film producer Benny U. Murdoch (Roy Kinnear) of B.U.M. Productions. Finding his lofty ambitions to arthouse profundity undercut by Murdoch's insistence on lashings of norks, Morrison hooks up with producer Clive Potter and virginal, penguin-obsessed scriptwriter Harris Tweedle (Christopher Timothy) to produce a cinematic version of the eponymous dirty poem, using money derived from three different backers (who inevitably all have their own designs on the finished film).

Cigar-chewing Yank impresario Big Dick pushes for a hardcore film starring the singular talents of his ditzy bit on the side, Billie Harris (a self-styled cross between Brigitte Bardot, Marilyn Monroe and Peggy Ashcroft). Wealthy banker Ambrose Cream ('Through my investment company Cream Holdings, I've been able to give many young people a helping hand') wants a *Sound of Music* knock-off tailored to the strengths of his opera-singing, karate-chopping protégé Millicent Bindle. Vernon Peabody, meanwhile, offers cash for the first all-British gay western, with young companion Johnny in drag as Nell. While Tweedle busily types out three different scripts, Murdoch legs it out of the country with the cash, with the hapless trio left legally obliged to satisfy the backers. Morrison's girlfriend (a husky-voiced Katy 'Dr Who' Manning) suggests tapping her mother Lady Longhorn, a Whitehouse-alike moral crusader, for the cash. She, however, is under the impression this is to be a family film, and thus a fourth version is born, starring Manning and Longhorn's drippy son (Christopher Biggins). Somehow, all four films get made, on the same set, with actors from each version bustled in and out in shifts. Morrison spouts flowery nonsense to the actors ('You symbolise the dialectical collection of opposites coming to a listless, distanced unreality') while the various Nells behave with diva-ish arrogance, and genitalia are inevitably caught in clapperboards. To cap it all off, there's the time-honoured comedy chase to stop the dirty version being accidentally screened to Her Majesty at Leicester Square.

Despite an ending shamelessly swiped from *The Producers*, Armstrong's script is uniquely sharp among sexcoms. He nails various figures in the business (Murdoch is a very thinly-veiled version of Tigon supremo Tony Tenser). The squalid absurdities of Wardour Street's operations are captured with a gimlet eye. Best of all, the dialogue pushes the usual sexcom string of 'big one' single entendres into a non-stop flow of off-colour puns and filthy Spoonerisms ('I see fur clad figures, set against vast panoramas of whining shite...'), coming thick and fast ('almost Joycean' as Morrison would no doubt muse). It's the smartest sex script on the block, but one which still appreciates the comedy value of a well-timed 'Oh, bollocks!'

UNTIED NATIONS

UNTIED NATIONS

With one war down and another on the boil, Europe exerted a fearful fascination for Golden Age Hollywood. Taboos being what they were back then, a strange genre of 'almost satire' sprang up, involving the invention of a European state just fictional enough to avoid accusations of finger pointing. These imaginary backwaters included:

SYLVANIA/MARSHOVIA

German émigré Ernst Lubitsch payed homage to the old monarchies of Europe with this pair of winsome Maurice Chevalier/Jeanette Macdonald musical comedies. In *The Love Parade* (1929) she's the Queen of Sylvania and he's her prince consort. In *The Merry Widow* (1934) she's Marshovia's richest taxpayer and he's out to stop her legging it out of the country with a Frenchman. Double entendres and Chevalier's ironic ignorance of French alternate with lavish ballrooms and chandeliers. It got a lot less sedate from here on in…

FREEDONIA

The most famous of all the bent Balkans, presided over by Groucho Marx as the ebulliently corrupt Rufus T. Firefly in *Duck Soup* (1933). War is stirred up partly by Trentino, a supposedly devious (i.e. entirely innocent) ambassador from neighbouring – yes – Sylvania, but mainly because Groucho's already paid a month's rent on the battlefield. Is it satire, or just an excuse to fart about with a broken mirror and belittle Margaret Dumont? And while we're about it, what has four pairs of pants, lives in Philadelphia, and never rains but pours?

KLOPSTOKIA

Soup producer Herman J Mankiewicz previously oversaw *Million Dollar Legs* (1932), a similarly deranged European free-for-all with WC Fields as president of this cash-strapped but superhumanly athletic nation (whose inhabitants are all called either Angela or George), seeking to pay off its debts by winning every event at the 1932 Los Angeles Olympics; after a hearty meal of roast goat stuffed with eel, of course. Demented fun is had with an old Klopstokian love song ('Woof bloogle jig/Mo jig bloogle woof!') and Fields' impressive row of presidential call buttons ('Call the guard.' 'Show the ambassador in.' 'Show the ambassador out.' 'Ham on rye.'; 'With mustard.', etc.)

MORONIKA

Anything Fields and the Marxes could do, the Three Stooges would do several years later, and sure enough they turned up as glove puppet dictators of this extremely thinly veiled Germanic country in the timely *You Nazty Spy!* (1940). The boys had a thing for daft place names: *Malice in the Palace* (1949) featured a map of hilarious made-up other countries (Great Mitten, Jerkola, Atisket, Atasket, that sort of thing) which involved a long, slow pan of the camera around the map, so the audience has time to read the side-splitting names, thus killing the slapstick pacing stone dead, and looking very weird indeed.

GRAND FENWICK

Tiny, English speaking and boozy Duchy located somewhere between Switzerland and France, ruled by Grand Duchess Gloriana and forever riling the Americans. In *The Mouse that Roared* (1959) it declares war on the U.S. for ripping off their trademarked wine, hoping to instantly surrender and reap the reparations, but finding themselves in possession of a 'Q-bomb' instead. The *Mouse on the Moon* (1963) sees them beat the superpowers in lunar exploration via David Kossoff's wine-fuelled rocket, and all because Ron Moody wanted a nice hot bath.

TONY BOOTH

TONY BOOTH

LADDER-TOTING LOTHARIO

Coming to the theatre via a stint in the merchant navy, organising blue-as-you-like on-ship concert parties, bolshy Liverpudlian Tony Booth's career was always going to favour the gritty. Though the stage gave him the latitude to appear both as the White Rabbit in *Alice in Wonderland*, and among the original cast of trouser-dodging *cause celebre Oh! Calcutta!* in between lugging spaghetti in dingy Fleet Street nosh houses, the belt-and-braces world of British cinema had rather more down-to-earth plans for him.

After an unhappy stint in *Ice Cold in Alex* (1958), wherein director J Lee Thompson repeatedly berated him for making the heavy breathing sound which turned out to emanate from John Mills' pet spaniel (Booth's scene was cut anyway), came a period of classic 'wilderness years' sustenance. A small role in Boulting Brothers germ warfare drama *Suspect* (1960) here, a stock heavy in amnesiac safecracking intrigue *Pit of Darkness* (1961) there. Thereafter, small roles in standard hard-boiled thrillers followed, until he secured the lead in Butcher's drama *The Hi-Jackers* (1963), as a long distance lorry driver who has his cargo of whisky snatched, and goes after the wrongdoers with a lady hitchhiker in tow.

In 1965 everything changed, as his role as Alf Garnett's 'Scouse git' son-in-law in *Till Death Us Do Part* made him a household name in a way no amount of Butcher's second features would ever do. He still kept his oar in, however, taking bit parts where time allowed. A prudent decision, though some of the roles that abounded in British film at the time were to set a dodgy precedent. *Corruption* (1967) was a swinging horror nasty from the leaky Pentel of Robert Hartford-Davis, in which Peter Cushing played a deranged, prostitute-decapitating surgeon. Booth's role as a stereotypically lascivious Bailey-esque fashion photographer was perhaps mercifully small.

Neither the Sea nor the Sand (1972) was one of those 'ah, but are they already dead? Woooo…' horror chestnuts set on a Jersey lighthouse, taking its lead from a novel by newsreader Gordon Honeycombe, and its plot's accessibility from a novel by James Joyce. A role in this was followed by an obligatory billeting in Equity-placating John-Wayne-in-London creakathon *Brannigan* (1975), along with just about every other available thespian in town. During an interrogation scene, Booth was in hysterics at The Duke's prudish inability to whisper a motivation-giving line about biting a man's bollocks off. 'He bit this guy in the place where a guy shouldn't bite a guy!' was the best the upstanding Marion could come up with, as Tone collapsed to the floor in tears.

It wasn't that great a leap, then, to his cinematic gold seam the same year. Dandy Nicholls, in between popping endless uppers and downers on set (cheekily bunging a few the way of an unwitting Warren Mitchell to boot), asked Tone his opinion on a role she'd been sent as the cranky old mum of the main character. Booth, perhaps reminded of the knockabout of his seagoing days, thought it was a great script, and got on the blower to Columbia to see if the role of the main character's brother was up for grabs. It was, he got it, and in short order *Confessions of a Window Cleaner* (1974) began shooting.

The four *Confessions* films may be full-blown wildernesses in terms of wit, style, set design, cinematography, narrative, etc., but when it came to the box office, they stuck more bums to seats than all the discarded chewing gum in Soho. But while Robin Askwith's own rear end is the abiding (to the point of unshakeable) image left by the films, Booth's Sid Noggett leaves the outline of mad eyes and gnashed teeth on the cinemagoer's retina. Take the opening scene in *Confessions from a Holiday Camp* (1977). Sid and Timmy (Askwith) are running a holiday camp (rather foolishly in March, as the narration belatedly sees fit to mention – presumably after the goose-pimply rushes were viewed). Sid asks Tim to distribute beauty contest leaflets. That's it. But Booth's performance, starting with a roll of the eyes, progressing through a fixed gurn and ending with shape-throwing wails of frustration, prehensile choppers in search of a juicy bit of carpet to gnash on, is so incongruous among the rent-paying performances as to be otherworldly. His effervescing fizzog wouldn't have been out of place among the melting Nazis of *Raiders of the Lost Ark* (1981). He's a trouper, our Tone.

It was telly work in the main after that film wrapped. The non-canonical *Confessions from the David Galaxy Affair* (1979) was an unsavoury parting shot, and although the occasional celluloid role has popped up since – Jimmy McGovern's *Priest* (1994) being a prime example – it's been an easy dotage of *Albion Market*, Equity stewardship, Labour activism and professional thorn-in-the-PM's-side ever since. Not quite pipe and slippers time, then.

THE BIT-PARTERS

They're not stars. They glide effortlessly under the media radar. They are never going to be mouthing gushy platitudes on an MDF podium while clutching an outsize paperweight. But that doesn't mean that British bit part actors, reliable workhorses of the industry, are unrecognized by the public. 'Oooh, look at him, wasn't he in that…?' 'It's her off of, ooh…' 'You know, I could swear I've…' Indeed, the busiest bit-parters are every bit as much old friends to the cinemagoer as big name stars such as Julian Sands and Dabney Coleman. Here, ranked by number of clocked-up appearances (all figures approximate – it's hard to keep track of these folk, they get around), are ten of the most oft-spotted and well-loved twentieth-down-the-credit-list players.

MARIANNE STONE (188 FILMS)

Specialities: the queen of the bit part, Marianne specialised in glamour-free dogsbody roles – charladies, secretaries, reporters, nurses and barmaids – over a period of forty years. *Carry Ons*, sexcoms, horrors, Ealing comedies – she's done the lot.

Most prestigious role: Vivian Darkbloom in *Lolita* (1962), a literary character, no less! Not too meaty on the dialogue front, though.

Finest hour: bizarro cigar-smoking upper class dilettante The Duchess in aristocratic Satanist low-budgeter *Devils of Darkness* (1964).

SAM KYDD (181 FILMS)

Specialities: a career of two halves: policemen and soldiers in the 1940s and 1950s, later tending to move on to 'gormless lanky lummox' territory.

Most prestigious role: an officious warrant officer hampering Douglas Bader's Spitfire acquisition in *Reach for the Sky* (1956).

Finest hour: shocked copper discovering the first victim of the bone-sucking Sillicates in sci-fi horror *Island of Terror* (1966).

MICHAEL RIPPER (133 FILMS)

Specialities: Innkeepers in horror films, gravediggers in horror films, people about to suffer a violent death in horror films.

Most prestigious role: to prove it wasn't all horror, spouting party rhetoric in the first film version of *1984* (1956).

Finest hour: a rather sizeable role as turncoat innkeeper Tom Bailey, saving a young couple from snake-cum-vampire Jacqueline 'Servalan' Pearce in Hammer's immaculate *The Reptile* (1965).

THE BIT-PARTERS

MILES MALLESON (119 FILMS)

Specialities: doctors, clergymen, and chinless bourgeois twits in general.
Most prestigious role: the seedy chap buying 'views' off Carl Boehm in *Peeping Tom* (1960).
Finest hour: the unforgettable hearse driver in *Dead of Night* (1945). 'Just room for one more inside, sir!'

DAVID LODGE (97 FILMS)

Specialities: military types mainly, with a side-order of dodgy criminals.
Most prestigious role: military policeman in *Ice Cold in Alex* (1958).
Finest hour: as he kept exasperatedly reminding the audience in Spike Milligan's TV shows, 'I was in *Cockleshell Heroes* (1955), you know!'

GRAHAM STARK (80 FILMS)

Specialities: policemen, and standing just behind Peter Sellers.
Most prestigious role: combining the two as Clouseau's befuddled second-in-command Hercule in *A Shot in the Dark* (1964).
Finest hour: auteuring his own silent Britcom short *Simon, Simon* (1970), featuring Eric Morecambe, Peter Sellers, Michael Caine and a great big crane.

ARTHUR MULLARD (79 FILMS)

Specialities: pig-ugly cockney oiks from start to finish, called things such as Basher, Hasher, Bruiser or Big Jim.
Most prestigious role: right at home in Babs Windsor's East End conjugal melodrama *Sparrows Can't Sing* (1962).
Finest hour: annoying fisherman Spike Milligan in a variety of guises in oddball comedy short *Fish and Milligan* (1966).

GEORGE WOODBRIDGE (76 FILMS)

Specialities: more innkeepers and rustic types, with an extra helping of 'ripe gentlemen'.
Most prestigious role: opening doors for Moira Shearer in *The Red Shoes* (1948).
Finest hour: manning the pumps in the original Hammer *Dracula* (1958), as a Transylvanian landlord with a strangely bucolic, English turn of phrase.

FRED GRIFFITHS (72 FILMS)

Specialities: morose cockneys in charge of working vehicles (taxis in particular, Fred being a fully licensed London cabbie who plied his trade between roles).

Most prestigious role: in model Eiffel Tower-smuggling Ealing classic *The Lavender Hill Mob* (1951) – at the wheel of a taxi.

Finest hour: in *Carry On Regardless* (1960), rejecting Kenneth Williams and his chimp from behind the wheel of – yes – a taxi; 'I'll take you mate, but not yer bruvver!'

ESMA CANNON (63 FILMS)

Specialities: Independent-minded eccentric ladies of a certain age, performing outrageous facial contortions wherever possible.

Most prestigious role: Agnes in Powell and Pressburger's *A Canterbury Tale* (1944).

Finest hour: the 'merry spinster' in *Carry On Cruising* (1962), running rings round Kenneth Williams during a table tennis match.

COOKING WITH FINSBURY

Sunday morning, eleven o'clock. You've nipped out for a paper and some Oxo, so the task of preparing the Sunday roast is nigh. It's a tightly timed process, so you'll need some organizational help, so what better than a film, the sort of film so familiar you can pick it up and put it down, as it were, in between jobs, and not lose sight of the plot. Fortunately, on the telly comes Bryan Forbes' rambling Victorian all-star romp, a film everyone over thirty has seen at least five times (source: 2001 UK census). Your schedule should run something like this.

Montage of dying old buffers – prepare joint.
Sir Ralph Richardson walks free from crashed train – peel spuds.
Wilfrid Lawson harangues Cicely Courtneidge – top and tail parsnips.
Peter Sellers coughs up a furball – in with the Yorkshire.
Michael Caine finally becomes too wet to watch any further – stick the peas on.
Cast converge on cemetery – pour self large Bristol Cream.

JAMES HAYTER

JAMES HAYTER

BUMBLING AND MUMBLING

It's the lot of most character actors to find eventual fame in the medium that probably means the least to them. By the time James Hayter had served a single term as the short-lived, toupee wearing replacement for Mr Grainger in *Are You Being Served?* on television, he already had the best of a hundred film credits, stretching back five decades, under his very Dickensian belt.

Hayter's first film appearance was in an adaptation of a Basil Dean thriller – not a rare species in the 1930s – crime melodrama *Sensation* (1936), where he appeared alongside the likes of notorious hellraisers Athene Seyler, Henry Oscar and Felix Aylmer. Hayter is fittingly down, down, down the bill of players whose names are lost to posterity. However, he soon powered up the list to within striking distance of Paul Robeson for his next film, *Big Fella* (1937). In that pleasingly antiquated effort, wherein the law enlist the help of Robeson, as opposed to their later habit of harassing him into the ground (or trying to), James appears well above an uncredited Margaret Rutherford as a nanny, presumably with cheek and jowl aquiver.

After that it was a never-ending cornucopia of work for the booming boy. Hayter deployed his trademark bluster and port-and-stilton looks to great effect in all manner of famous works. Radar biopic *School for Secrets* (1946) with Ralph Richardson gave him scope to shout at recruits and go red (or at least redder) in the face. *The October Man* (1947) allowed him to eye the suspicious John Mills and inevitably draw every wrong conclusion available. *Nicholas Nickleby* (1947) provided a first crack at the broad Dickensian cartoon figures he was to make something of a speciality. There was even an appearance with talisman of the 1930s British film industry, George Formby, in *Come On, George!* (1939). The best of this early boom time for Hayter was undoubtedly *Vice Versa* (1948), the firstest and bestest film adapation of the old father-son switcheroo, directed by a juvenile Peter Ustinov and also starring James Robertson Justice, still smarting from his experiences fighting for the uncool side in the Spanish Civil War.

However, those Dickensian clowns made Hayter more than just a face. The likes of *Nickleby, Oliver!* (1968) and especially *The Pickwick Papers* (1952) made him a face with a name that nobody could remember, too. His well-stuffed frontage and rosy visage lent themselves nicely to the sort of game pie-scoffing idiots with which Dickens liked to populate his less harrowing works, and Hayter did well claiming the lead role, and his name above the title for once, in *Pickwick*.

There were also other period pieces to keep him in gout for many years beyond. *Tom Brown's Schooldays* (1951), *Flesh & Blood* (1951), *Beau Brummell* (1954) and Egyptian curio *Land of the Pharaohs* (1955), again with James Robertson Justice, though in slightly different surroundings, the tatty public school of *Vice Versa* replaced by, of all things, the Great Pyramid. At least no one can ever say casting directors in the 1950s lacked imagination.

After that bizarre episode it became slightly more formulaic, but there was still room for the odd memorable appearance, including The Memory Man in the Kenneth More version of *The 39 Steps* (1959) and the strange but compelling *The Horror of Frankenstein* (1970), with Ralph Bates as the Baron and Hayter the Bailiff, wondering what's going on up at the 'ol' caaarsul'.

The lure of television then became too strong for a man in need of a hefty pension. After the odd guest appearance on long-running favourites such as *Doctor Finlay's casebook* as a miller, in which he accidentally poisoned locals with less than perfect flour – diabolical ingenuity! – he progressed to *Are You Being Served?* Eventually Mr Kipling cakes, or whatever arms combine ultimately owned it, insisted he leave that job and continue with his voiceovers for their ads, with only a measly 300% increase in his fee to show for it. So it was sayonara Grace Brothers with minimal hesitation. Still, for an almost forgotten name James Hayter has graced and enhanced some of the best films made in Britain. And it has to be said, he did have some exceedingly good takes.

THE ESSENTIAL DISASTER FILM

JUGGERNAUT (1974)

Forget *The Poseidon Adventure* (1972). Forget *The Towering Inferno* (1974). Try to dimly recall William Shatner's colliding train epic *Disaster on the Coastliner* (1979). Then forget it again. In the much-maligned realm of the disaster movie, one film effortlessly demolishes all its peers, in super-slow motion from eight different angles. And surprisingly for a genre so typically Hollywood, it's British.

Omar Sharif captains luxury cruise ship the *Britannic* from Southampton to New York. Yes, it's Omar Sharif, but that's where the glamour trail ends. Sharif commands a slate-grey hunk of Clydeside engineering across even greyer seas under greyer-still skies. No priests or actresses are among this ship's passengers; it's a lower middle class, recession-hit purgatory before the inferno.

All is shiftless, fruit machine-playing British reticence until brash US mayor Clifton 'Live and Let Die' James starts asking difficult questions. Eventually it comes out: a rogue explosives expert called Juggernaut has festooned the *Britannic* with eight superbombs, primed to explode before dawn in lieu of a ransom. Grizzled bomb disposal expert Richard Harris is dispatched to the boat. Onshore, detective Anthony Hopkins, whose family is aboard, rounds up the usual suspects for leads.

All fairly unremarkable; there's certainly no disaster movie revolution in *Juggernaut*. Countless hoary old cliches of the genre are duly observed: Harris as the maverick hero, rakishly smoking an outsize Sherlock Holmes briar – while defusing a bomb; the hard-boiled 'buddy' banter between Harris and number two David Hemmings ('I'll bring you back some dry toast, Charlie!'); passengers and crew, thrown together in disaster, getting to 'Really Know Each Other'; and a final red wire/blue wire cliffhanger that would have the staunchest Andy McNab fan chuckling at its corniness if it wasn't so brilliantly handled.

Doing most of the handling is Richard Lester, a long way from his amiably daft Beatles features here. Or is he? The rather dry, downbeat and unexpectedly realistic world that housed the zany antics of *A Hard Day's Night* is pushed to the foreground here, with help from Alan Plater on dialogue duty.

Any potential glamour in the derring-do is relentlessly uncut with subtle touches. Harris is first seen in a provincial town hall, defusing a home-made device housed in a Rover biscuit assortment tin. The various arms-related boffins Hopkins tracks down are convincingly dishevelled: the jailed bomber who refuses to grass, figuring he's only got another 'seven years to go, with a bit of luck and a decent Home Secretary', and Michael Hordern's disgraced former civil servant, reduced to working the electronic scoreboard at a dog track ('there's always work for a skilled pair of hands'). Even the tense moment of

Juggernaut's first call to the shipping line owner is undercut by having said magnate in the middle of giving breakfast to his three kids.

Best of all, there's Roy Kinnear's perfect turn as the ship's entertainments officer, who has a bad enough time of it at the start, trying to inject fun into windswept games of quoits and peppering the bingo calling with blue jokes to glumly echoing silence, then ends up, after Sharif's solemn announcement of the situation to the passengers, trying to generate enthusiasm over that evening's fancy dress ball. And what a ball that turns out to be. 'A night to remember!' claims Kinnear bleakly, after running through psychotically cheery, whisky-fuelled renditions of *Roll Out the Barrel* and *The Lambeth Walk*, again to a total vacuum of response ('Sod you all, then!').

However, *Juggernaut* is not just a sardonic pastiche of the disaster genre. It still believes in its story enough to be a thoroughly gripping thriller in its own right. The bomb squad's fraught trip from plane to ship in a storm is properly hair-raising. The scene where Harris and Sharif drink solemnly to 'the insanity of governments and the poor simple sods who pick up the pieces' is a cliche, but an effective one for all that. And Hopkins' dilemma – the shipping line wants to pay the ransom and get it over with, but he must side with the government, who won't allow it – is a well-judged downplaying of the old 'that's my wife up there!' chestnut.

For the climax, where most films would open out into huge (and unconvincing) panoramas of crumbling dams and flaming scaffolding, *Juggernaut* closes in on the microscopic inner workings of the booby-trapped bombs, and replaces the standard suspenseful musical score with claustrophobic silence. Never mind Shelley Winters' swimming medal or Steve McQueen's fireman's uniform with the word 'chest' helpfully written on his chest, the only trappings you really need to generate nailbiting thrills are a pair of pliers and a pipe. Now that's blockbusting on a budget.

ROY KINNEAR

OH, PLEASE YOURSELVES, THEN

There's a very British facial expression that starts off with a hearty laugh. Then, at some point mid-chuckle, signs of a slow, sad realisation that all's perhaps not so funny begin to creep in. At the exact moment this sense of impending gloom meets the outgoing hilarity halfway, the queasy half-grin on the subject's face is that very British expression. Since gathering despondency is just as much a part of British comedy as shiny avuncularity, this hybrid expression crops up in many a British comedy film, and no one mastered it quite like Roy Kinnear.

Wigan-born Kinnear graduated to the stage via a brief stint at RADA and Joan Littlewood's Theatre Workshop in Stratford, London. Tiny film parts began to amass, as tiny film parts will, with Roy standing in the background of Powell and Pressburger's contemporary version of *Die Fledermaus*, the Vienna-set *Oh, Rosalinda!!* (1955), Sellers–Loren romp *The Millionairess* (1960) and delinquent cockney courtroom caper *The Boys* (1962 – Judge Felix Aylmer presiding). More Stepney struggling was to be had in *Sparrows Can't Sing* (1962), a Joan Littlewood production from a script by no less than Stephen 'Blakey' Lewis, with Roy cast in a more substantial part as brother to Barbara Windsor's AWOL young wife of absentee merchant seaman James Booth.

Kinnear was simultaneously planting his ample girth foursquare in the nation's living rooms every Friday night, as a founding member of the satirical rep company gathered round David Frost in *That Was the Week That Was* (1963), so it's hardly surprising Roy's character parts in the cinema got a boost: a junior member of Eric Sykes' wretched family in *Heaven's Above!* (1963); teaming up with Booth again in Ken Russell's all-the-swinging-trimmings sexcom *French Dressing* (1964), as a pair of randy no-marks in a seaside backwater trying to bag a French film star; a Beatles-ignorant laboratory assistant to Victor Spinetti's mad professor in *Help!* (1965); training gladiators in *A Funny Thing Happened on the Way to the Forum* (1966); and turning in a vintage bit of expressive mime in Eric Idle-penned silent street sweeper comedy *Albert Carter, QOSO* (1968). All this among starring roles in various TV sitcoms meant a busy 1960s for Kinnear to say the least.

A role in sour satire *How I Won the War* (1967) ramped up the gloomier end of the Kinnear persona, as did a second overcast Richard Lester comedy, *The Bed-Sitting Room* (1969). Kinnear's relationship with Lester, begun on the set of *Help!*, led to both his finest role – the increasingly desperate Social Director Curtain on board the doomed cruise ship in *Juggernaut* (1974) – and his most famous – the hearty Planchet in *The Three Musketeers* (1973) and its back-to-back sequel. Thereafter the mould was set, and his roles fell into two categories: ones tailor made for him – coarse industrial tycoon Henry Salt in *Willy Wonka and the Chocolate Factory* (1971), coarse mate of Alf Garnett in *The Alf Garnett Saga* (1972) and coarse porn magnate Benny U. Murdoch in *Eskimo Nell* (1975) – and those challengingly against type – Prince Regent in Barbra Streisand rom-com *On a Clear Day You Can See Forever* (1970) and the Bishop of Paris in *Barry McKenzie Holds His Own* (1974). Kinnear ran with anything he was given, ending up with one of the most varied CVs of any British actor, while still commanding that ready recognition in audiences.

Although work increasingly consisted of bowler-hatted council baddies in Children's Film Foundation productions and bumbling crooks and Ingerlish coppers in Disney films, his untimely death on the set of belated sequel *The Return of the Musketeers* (1989) robbed cinema of a brilliant, unassuming and often very subtle performer. And no one did *that* expression quite the same ever again.

TEN ICONS OF THE CHILDREN'S FILM FOUNDATION

From 1951 to 1987, the Children's Film Foundation turned out mini-masterpieces of prepubescent crime-solving on an almost monthly basis. Stars as diverse as Phil Collins and Keith Chegwin, Gary Kemp and Matthew Wright cut their teeth on its rigid dramatic formula - a formula consisting of perms and combs of these essential elements.

1. A RED-FACED, BOWLER HATTED AUTHORITY FIGURE GETTING HIS COMEUPPANCE

As far as the Foundation was concerned, those in power are seldom up to any good (exceptions are the police, who are always helpful but tend to turn up too late). Ronnie Barker in *A Ghost of a Chance* (1978), David Lodge's corrupt councillor in *Cup Fever* (1965) and countless others had their pomposity pricked by spirited youths. Comeuppances generally represented by said authority figure slipping in a puddle and falling on his arse.

2. A STIFF, STARCHY SCHOOLTEACHER WHO JUST DOESN'T GET IT

As perennial as those dastardly councillors, anyone in gown and elbow patches is grist to the Foundation's revolutionary manifesto. Many an adventure was held up by pesky demands for homework and detention, but the most impressive of all was Jeff Rawle's apoplectic history master 'Sniffy' Kemp, forever putting the kybosh on the time-travelling fun of *A Hitch in Time* (1978).

3. A BUNGLING HENCHMAN

Every criminal mastermind in CFF films somehow felt obliged to employ a clueless sidekick whose stupidity allows the kids to foil his dastardly schemes and make good by teatime. Roy Kinnear in *High Rise Donkey* (1980), Bernard Cribbins in *Night Ferry* (1977) and Bill Maynard in *Sky Pirates* (1977) are archetypal criminal dunderheads.

4. A HEALTHY OUTDOOR ACTIVITY

Anti-authority they may have been, but it was still an odd boy who didn't like sport in the world of CFF. Football aside, there was cricket in *Egghead's Robot* (1970), cart racing in *Go,*

Kart, Go! (1964) with Dennis Waterman, skiing in *Avalanche* (1969), scrambling in, er… *Scramble* (1969) and athletics in *Sammy's Super T-Shirt* (1978), albeit illegally helped by the titular tiger-print garment. By 1984, the kids were allowed to participate in such rebellious activities as forming a ska band (*Pop Pirates*), as long as they foiled some record-copying villains along the way.

5. A KINDLY RAG AND BONE MAN

The middle-aged may be untrustworthy councillors to a man, and young men are inevitably hoodlums and petty crooks, but old people are, of course, always on the side of the kids and rag-and-bone men more so than anyone else, for some reason. Wilfrid Brambell, funnily enough, majored in these roles in *The Salvage Gang* (1958) and *High Rise Donkey*. Sadly, he was not on hand for *A Horse Called Jester* (1979), in which a knee-high Sadie Frost saved a tinker's flea-bitten nag from the knacker's yard.

6. A KINDLY BUT INEVITABLY RATHER TATTY FANTASTICAL FRIEND

Wonders were performed on microbudgets to bring to life such magical creations as: Electro-Nic, the ski-wearing electrical educator in Michael Powell's *The Boy Who Turned Yellow* (1972); a Battersea-bound Yeti saved by William Hartnell in *Zoo Robbery* (1973); the titular giant rabbit in *Mr Horatio Knibbles* (1971); *Glitterball* (1977), a ball-bearing from space, no less; and *Kadoyng* (1972), the environmentally-sound alien who saves a small village from motorway obliteration. Speaking of which…

7. THE ENVIRONMENT, BEING SAVED

Your bog-standard CFF kids have little time for those who would defile our endangered wildlife, as *The Peregrine Hunters* (1977), *The Last Rhino* (1961) and, er… *Calamity the Cow* (1967) make plain. Elsewhere pollution was the enemy, in whimsical man-seal fantasy *Mr Selkie* (1979) and *The Battle of Billy's Pond* (1976) or even nuclear meltdown in quarrybound Welsh nailbiter *One Hour to Zero* (1976). Failing that, a bit of National Trust conservation is always good for a laugh: the kids saved John Pertwee's branch line in *Runaway Railway* (1965), and of course the crumbling dwelling place of loveable old ghosts Jimmy Edwards, Patricia Hayes and Graham Stark was rescued from bowler-hatted demolition in *A Ghost of a Chance*.

8. SUPER POWERS CONFERRED BY MUNDANE OBJECT OR OCCURRENCE

Providing wish-fulfilment for many a child, and an easy way of getting out of 'scrapes' to boot: super strength conferred by t-shirt (*Sammy's Super T-Shirt*); invisibility conferred by a pair of plimsolls in *Paganini Strikes Again* (1973); invisibility conferred by ingestion of 'chemical chunks' in *Where's Johnny?* (1974); and, perhaps most desperate of all, clairvoyance conferred by a bump on the head in *What's Next?* (1974).

9. A DAFFY BUT LOVEABLE PROFESSOR WITH AN UNRELIABLE INVENTION

The kind which, naturally, adventures could start from, such as a time machine, invented by Patrick Troughton in *A Hitch in Time* and John Bluthal in *The Flying Sorcerer* (1973), a robot in *Egghead's Robot*, a teleporter in *Junket 89* (1970), a sky bike in, er… *The Sky Bike* (1967) and superglue in *Hoverbug* (1969). They don't have to be old: David Spooner invented a 'goal repeller' in *Blinker's Spy Spotter* (1972) and, improbably, Keith Chegwin cloned his sister in *The Troublesome Double* (1967).

10. A BOY WITH HALF A PLASTIC FOOTBALL ON HIS HEAD

As modelled by Plastic Head in gang war drama *Terry on the Fence* (1985). Never quite took off the way it might have.

OFF THE RAILS

Talent is a wayward beast, never more so than in the creatively nebulous world of film directors and stars. The vast amounts of time, effort and personnel needed to turn even the most straightforward idea into several hundred yards of sprocketed celluloid, afford creative types ample opportunity to get out of their depth, up a creative gum tree, or just act on extremely bad advice, creating an end product that no sane person could have cooked up on their own. Sometimes they can go very wrong indeed.

Films of this sort are not all miserable flops, by any means. Neither are they all lost masterpieces. But some are well worth celebrating as true one-offs, and all are fascinating misfires in some way, proving that when the Hollywood conveyor belt buckles, the results are often more spectacular than a whole year's worth of boringly efficient productivity.

THE TROUBLE WITH HARRY (1955) – derailing: Alfred Hitchcock

A trend that seems to run through a lot of these films is of the talent behind them taking what they normally do and extending it just that little bit too far. Going beyond the bounds of decency-as-was, Hitchcock took his trademark black humour and shoved it into the foreground, with this whimsical tale of a body discovered in the woods, and various folk's reactions to it. It was decried as tasteless in its day, but its main drawback – as with so much 'dark' comedy – is the sheer plodding dullness of the thing, especially when compared with Hitch's suspense-chafing best. *Arsenic and Old Lace* it ain't. It's barely even *Weekend at Bernie's II*. Unfortunately, Hitch's customary cameo is about as enthralling as the rest of the film. Just sort of idly walking along in the background? Make an effort, Alf!

SKIDOO (1968) – derailing: Otto Preminger

The late 1960s had a mind-expanding effect on Hollywood. Even Otto Preminger, director of such sober fare as *Anatomy of a Murder* (1959), found himself 'turned on' for this weirdo masterpiece. The story is fairly innocuous: mob boss Groucho Marx gets Jackie Gleason out of retirement to rub out incarcerated gangster Mickey Rooney. Things are, however, rather complicated by pretty much every character tripping on LSD at some point in the film. The result is a jaw-dropping mish-mash of acid-addled visions (tap-dancing dustbins) and dialogue ('I see mathematics!'), which is all the more incongruous as the majority of the cast are well into middle age. Preminger, still ordering script rewrites when the project was halfway through filming, lets himself go – in all senses. By the time Harry Nilsson brings proceedings to a close by scat-singing the end credits, the cinema audience is firmly divided between those who absolutely love this misbegotten mess, and those who are already on the bus home. As Sammy Davis Jr put it in the film's slightly panicky publicity: 'Anyone who don't like that don't like chicken on a Sunday!'

CANDY (1968) – derailing: Richard Burton
...and Marlon Brando, and Walter Matthau, and Charles Aznavour, and James Coburn... All the big names involved in this ludicrous adaptation of Terry Southern's highly suspect sex satire could be said to be losing it with this one. Burton, as comedy Byronic poet MacPhisto, with permanently windswept hair (even indoors), takes the piss out of his famous gravelly voice with a silly mock lecture, gets driven about by Sugar Ray Robinson and ends up shagging a life-size toy doll. Walter Matthau is a stock 'crazed general' flying about in a special plane and suffering from premature ejaculation. James Coburn is a bearded surgeon conducting a triumphantly bloody operation. Ringo Starr plays a revolutionary Mexican gardener who shags the 'heroine' over a pool table. Charles Aznavour plays a demented acrobatic hunchback who shags the 'heroine' over a knackered piano. 'Best' of all, Marlon Brando plays a levitating Indian guru. No-one, as you may have guessed, is coming out of this looking very good, except perhaps the cast and crew of the other Southern film adaptation *The Magic Christian*, which is a masterpiece of coherent narrative and razor-sharp satire by comparison.

LONDON (1971) – derailing: Orson Welles
Perhaps Welles is not a character who was ever firmly on the rails in the first place, but this peripatetic metropolitan sketch show is an oddball late-period project that stands apart even from all his other oddball late-period projects. Welles hooked up with the nascent *Goodies* to make a rag-bag of sketches called *Orson's Bag*, which was then re-hashed a couple of years later as *London*, but was still never properly finished. The most famous section involves Tim Brooke-Taylor as a bowler-hatted reporter in perpetual search of Carnaby Street, bumping into assorted Welles characters – flower seller, Norman Evans-style old crone, Jimmy Edwards-esque bobby, slightly dodgy Chinese strip club proprietor, even a Morris dancer – in a fantastic Dick Emery-style tour de force. He even performs Bill Oddie's *One Man Band* song. Other bits and pieces are more fragmentary: a beautifully shot scene in a cobwebbed gentleman's club, with Welles as all four crusty members, has no soundtrack. Even in slivers, it knocks his *Don Quixote* project into a cocked hat.

NEW YORK, NEW YORK (1977) – derailing: Martin Scorsese
So good they re-edited it twice. Martin Scorsese manfully attempted to revive the golden age of the Hollywood musical with a knockabout tale of actress Liza Minnelli and sax player Robert De Niro's torrid romance in the swing era. Big production numbers and bigger sets jarred somewhat with the prevailing economic thriftiness of the times. The cast's improvised method acting jarred with the rigid musical structure. De Niro started turning into Travis Bickle. Minnelli, shooting on the same stages that Judy Garland once hoofed over, started turning into her mum. The cast-of-thousands opening scene is brilliant, but it's all downhill from there. Scorsese fudged the romantic ending. Audiences fancied it not. The film barely covered its $14 million costs. Still, great theme song, eh?

OFF THE RAILS

1941 (1979) – derailing: Steven Spielberg

Post-*Jaws* and *Close Encounters*, Steven Spielberg emerged fresh from having 'Wunderkind' installed as a middle name to tackle a genre for which he'd hitherto exhibited little affinity – the ensemble slapstick comedy. Thus an all-star knockabout romp amid the onset of post-Pearl Harbor war hysteria was dragged kicking and screaming – literally screaming – into being. Spielberg equated 'loud' with 'funny', and strung endless set-pieces (Ferris wheel collapsing, tank running amok in paint factory) together with film-buffy in-jokes (slightly smug parodies of *Dr Strangelove* and *Jaws*). Punters took one look at this queasy blend of *Tora! Tora! Tora!* and *Animal House* and kept well out of it. Costing a whopping $35 million, it nevertheless managed to claw its way back into profit some time during the 1990s. Still, things could have been worse – at one point during production, according to Spielberg, he considered reworking the whole thing as a musical.

HONKY TONK FREEWAY (1981) – derailing: John Schlesinger

1977: producer Don Boyd, driving through America to get to the set of horse opera *International Velvet*, casts his eye at the suburban sprawl that throngs the freeway and gets an idea for a film: a low-budget comedy set in the gas-guzzling deep south milieu, which could be filmed – literally – off the back of a lorry. Boyd takes his idea to EMI. They like the script. Their plans for it, however, prove more grandiose, involving over 100 speaking parts, a dozen locations, gigantic sets built by master Italian craftsmen, a whole Florida town painted pink, a specially-constructed two-mile length of freeway and an elephant on water-skis. Director John Schlesinger turns in a three-hour epic. All concerned think it's rather good. American preview audiences don't share that opinion. *Heaven's Gate* is invoked in the boardroom. The attempt by British filmmakers to beat the Americans at their own game takes barely a tenth of its estimated $24 million budget. Schlesinger moves quietly back into TV work, and EMI vow 'never again'...

INCHON (1981) – derailing: Sir Laurence Olivier

Whether or not the Reverend Sun Myung Moon was told by Jesus to fund an epic retelling of this pivotal moment in the Korean War is a moot point. Whoever told Laurence Olivier to accept the lead role as General MacArthur, wearing truly bizarre prosthetic make-up and getting paid in briefcases full of cash flown to the film set by helicopter, must have been working for the other side. The film looks fine, but with acres of long, expository speeches by main characters telling other main characters what they must surely already know, it's a crashing two-and-a-half-hour bore. Meteorological destruction of outdoor sets and language barriers among the crew ensured that the price inflated well beyond what was visible on screen. The Moonies saw a return of about – yes – one-tenth of their $46 million outlay, scuppering the Rev's plans for a billion-dollar series of Biblical epics. So it wasn't all bad news.

LEONARD PART 6 (1987) – derailing: Bill Cosby

Incoming Columbia studio head David Puttnam inherited this headache from his predecessor. Bill Cosby, a major presence on the studio's board and official spokesman of Columbia-owning Coke at the time, was rewarded for his service with this putrefying spy comedy. The plot, such as it is, has that ageing clairvoyant woman off of *The Matrix* as a psychotic vegetarian Bond villain, on a mission to attack good, honest meat-eating folk with mind-controlled fauna and the aid of a team of henchmen dressed as wildlife. Cosby is a former secret agent who has retired to open a meatcentric restaurant, but is coaxed back into action by Joe Don Baker. A trout is ordered to attack someone, and starts looking at a copy of Playboy instead. A gang of frogs push a car off a pier and drown a CIA man. Joe Don Baker gets attacked by a rabbit. People hit their heads on low-slung objects, with a comedy noise dubbed on. And then they do it again. Through all this, Cosby does four things of note: puffs along to a Jane Fonda workout video, does a spot of ballet, snogs Tom Courtenay and rides on the back of an ostrich. When he isn't doing this, he's generally just standing about looking knackered. Oh, and supping heartily from a bottle of Coke, in some totally shameless product placement. The best you can say is that, where that year's other big Columbia all-star flop *Ishtar* was merely tediously bad, this is driven by some manic energy – the energy of wanton stupidity, crassness and total humourlessness, admittedly, but energy nonetheless.

JB MAHON: A MAN FOR ALL SEASONS

JB MAHON: A MAN FOR ALL SEASONS

In the uncertain and expensive world of film, if you're not right at the top of the tree, it makes financial sense to keep your options open. No-one understood this more than Jackson Barrett 'Barry' Mahon, former WWII Spitfire ace and *Stalag Luft* escapee (rumour has it he was partly the inspiration for Steve McQueen's Cooler King in *The Great Escape*) who moved into Hollywood, flying stunt planes for Errol Flynn, and later set up on his own, producing cheapo films of two varieties.

The first kind was the 'nudie cutie', those queasily winsome topless montages given the thinnest of plots and, in Mahon's case, fantastically coy titles. In fact, it's unlikely the contents could have provided much more enjoyment for the average sweatshirted, all-American, drive-in teenage boy than the titles of such efforts as *1,000 Shapes of a Female* (1963), a supposed study of the artist/model relationship, and braless cookery romp *International Smorgas-Broad* (1965).

Then, after a final spate of nudie releases in 1968 (including *Forbidden Flesh: as Seen from a Hayloft in the Hills* and *The Diary of Knockers McCalla*) Mahon relocated from seedy New York to sunny Florida and set about tackling the very opposite end of the cinematic catalogue, taking on Disney with a series of Day-Glo children's fantasy matinees with art direction that made *H.R. Pufnstuf* look like *Brideshead Revisited*.

He began with the first American adaptation of L Frank Baum's books since Judy Garland clicked her heels thirty years before, with *The Wonderful Land of Oz* (1969). Combining the weirder of Baum's notions (a flying sofa with attached moose head called The Gump) with an ultra-cheap, all-cardboard approach to set and costume design, lit harshly from wherever Mahon could find space for his meagre lighting rig. It's a retina-scorching primary school play from the avant garde's deepest nightmares.

1970s *Thumbelina* and *Jack and the Beanstalk* continued the lurid claustrophobia, with occasional outdoor relief filmed at the Pirate World amusement park. Mahon also made a brief, but crucially late, diversion into intentional psychedelia with titillating hippie finger-wagger *The Love Cult* (1970) and cautionary, crash-zoom-happy LSD parable *Musical Mutiny* (1970), capturing a performance from *Iron Butterfly* at, yes, Pirate World. Mahon then moved into the administrative side of Hollywood, but not before re-releasing *Thumbelina*, padded out with a bit of queasily seasonal footage, as *Santa and the Ice-Cream Bunny* (1972). He's unlikely to ever receive a posthumous AFI honour, but for embodying the resourcefulness, tenacity and gumption demanded by the cutthroat world of bottom drawer filmmaking, a certain groggy respect is due.

RAY BROOKS

MR NARROW SLACKS

A chance meeting in a London pub in the summer of 1965 encapsulates the moment that 1960s British cinema began to take off. Ray Brooks, in St James for an audition for a Walt Disney live action adventure being shot in England (*The Fighting Prince of Donegal* or *The Legend of Dick Turpin*, or some such long-forgotten period swashbuckling), stops by a pub on the way. Enter David Hemmings, fresh from the auditions and looking beat. No chance, he tells Ray. Everyone who's available in the Isles is up for the part. Big names such as John Hurt. Queues round the block. Hopeless. A despondent Brooks decides not to bother. Talk turns to the small-time British films they've been involved in lately. Hemmings has been doing something impenetrable called *Blowup*. Brooks has just come off a micro-budget comedy, *The Knack*. Well, you have to take work where you find it, don't you?

Falling into legendary films was easier in those cottage industry days. When Brooks took time off filming BBC play *Girl on a Roof* (1961) to get married, the Beeb lent him a suit. Try even getting that on expenses now. The landscape was ripe for a young actor to explore. First big screen stop for Brooks was *Play It Cool* (1962), a British rock 'n' roll vehicle for *Billy Fury*, helmed by no less than Michael Winner, as part of Fury's fictional backing group *The Satellites*. Ray achieved higher pop billing in *Some People* (1962), as part of a fledgling Bristolian rock band (along with Hemmings) who rehearsed in a church hall with sympathetic choirmaster Kenneth Griffith's consent, and Brooks belted out *Little Richard* standards on the organ. This was youthful rebellion with a freshly scrubbed face – the whole film was little more than a plug for the Duke of Edinburgh Award Scheme.

After a stint in *Coronation Street* as one Norman Phillips, Brooks landed a part in Richard Lester's aforementioned cheapo New Wave swinging comedy *The Knack… and How to Get It* (1965). As Tolen, the suave, leather-gloved Boy with the Knack, he's held in awe by clumsy schoolteacher housemate Michael Crawford for his singular way with the birds. When deceptively mousy Rita Tushingham turns up, a three-way standoff ensues, interspersed with wry asides and Atomic Age interior design tips from Irish weirdo Donal Donnelly. While Crawford capers, Brooks is sinisterly slick, rearranging his pompadour, taking a belt to Tush in a weird lion taming game, and uttering the immortal line 'I can't get involved with raping girls today!' Amid tricky camerawork and vox pop editing, he still manages to leave a big impression.

More swinging was to be had in the Beeb's great teleplay *Cathy, Come Home* (1966), Michael Bentine's short silent paean to London *The Sandwich Man* (1966) and fighting an underground resistance in the slightly better of the two much-reviled Amicus *Dr Who* films *Daleks: Invasion Earth 2150 AD* (1966). Then, after a big screen hiatus, Brooks fell in with no-budget horror supremo Pete Walker, and became an occasional member of his repertory company.

Former stand-up comic Walker has an uneasy reputation as king of the tattier end of the British horror market, but some of his films stand up to scrutiny beyond the breasts-and-ketchup basics. *The Flesh and Blood Show* (1972) is one of them. Brooks is the director of a troupe of young actors (including Jenny Hanley and Robin Askwith) engaged by a mysterious agent to rehearse a murder mystery in a derelict end-of-the-pier theatre. Members of the troupe start getting mysteriously bumped off. As Brooks observes in the films' typical workmanlike dialogue, 'somebody's having us on and I don't like it!' That somebody is aggrieved ageing actor Patrick Barr, taking prudish but grisly revenge on the 'new generation' of thesps, all 'sex-crazed, evil and obscene young jackanapes'. Other Walker roles were less satisfying: a photographer in execrable spy spoof *Tiffany Jones* (1973) and the standard 'concerned boyfriend who rings the police' in *House of Whipcord* (1974), either a searing indictment on the sadistic hypocrisy of right-wing Puritanism, or any old excuse to show scantily-clad blondes being slapped about, depending on your point of view.

Big breaks in telly such as *Big Deal* – and, of course, *King Rollo* – led to a seemingly permanent retirement from the fleapits after *Whipcord*. But the days when Ray Brooks had a foot in both camps, and could hop from having a half in the Rovers Return to kidnapping Rita Tushingham on a moped, or narrate *Mr Benn* by day and be covered in Kensington Gore by night, were rare times indeed.

TONY TENSER

SAVIOUR OF BRITISH FILM

The story of Tony Tenser is the story of a sizeable chunk of the British film industry. Not the respectable, heritage-stuffed, award-winning chunk, but the much larger but less-celebrated chunk that went after bums-on-seats rather than statuettes-on-sideboards or fingers-on-chins.

After a tyro stint as publicity man for Miracle Films (originating, among other things, the term 'sex kitten' for Brigitte Bardot), Tenser hooked up with Soho strip club owner Michael Klinger to open a private cinema club on Old Compton Street, which eventually begat Compton Films, a production partnership that started as they meant to go on by financing 'nudie cutie' *Naked as Nature Intended* (1961), something of a legend in the era of pre-permissive cinema-going with its cheekily coy depiction of a St Alban's nudist colony.

Before long, such quaint forms of sexploitation made way for stronger stuff. A tabloid story about a girls' school sex fad inspired *The Yellow Teddybears* (1963), a product of single-minded director Robert Hartford-Davies and exploitation scribes *sans pareil* Donald and Derek Ford. This unholy trinity were also responsible for *The Black Torment* (1964), an eighteenth century paranoia thriller the lagging production schedule of which Tenser characteristically sorted out by walking onto the set and tearing a random handful of pages out of the script.

Compton had a brush with greatness when Roman Polanski arrived on their doorstep, looking for funding. The result was *Cul-de-Sac* (1966) and the brilliant Catherine Deneuve crack-up psychodrama *Repulsion* (1965), remembered by Tenser primarily for the logistics of marshalling the toilet breaks of the many actors contributing to the famous 'wall of groping hands' set-piece. On more solidly swinging ground, *The Pleasure Girls* (1965) enveloped Carol Cleveland in the fast-moving world of the London flatshare, coming up against epoch-personifying characters such as the Jag-obsessed Peter 'E'-Type.

Something close to mainstream respectability was dangerously close at hand when the Arthur Conan Doyle Estate approached Tenser for a new Sherlock Holmes flick. Fortunately, anything so boring as a straight film was out of the question. With almost textbook exploitative aplomb, Tenser set the sleuth against Jack the Ripper in *A Study In Terror* (1965), complete with all the trad Ripper clichés – footsteps in the fog, the ominous Gladstone bag and, yes, Babs Windsor as one of the screaming victims.

In what would nowadays be classed as a post-modern move, Compton purchased the famous Windmill Theatre, converted it to a cinema and created a promo 'expose', *Secrets of a Windmill Girl* (1966), to show in it. But the film's glamour-to-gutter travails of Pauline Collins were of course created solely with a bum–seat interface in mind. But by now Compton was struggling with ill-fated projects like *The Projected Man* (1967), a crib from *The Fly* in which teleportation experiments turn a scientist into a shapeless monster, suffered from on-set kerfuffles, and it shows. Another flopping curio was *Wonderwall* (1968), in which a shabby old professor obsessively spies on Jane Birkin's swinging pad next door via holes drilled into the wall, all to a sitar-drenched George Harrison soundtrack.

So Tenser split from Compton, and with a £5000 bank loan set up on his own as Tony Tenser Films Ltd (swiftly changed to the more modest Tigon British Films) starting off with a tempting blend of imported Japanese impotence comedies and home-grown fluff such as swinging sex fantasy cheapo *Mini Weekend* (1967). So far bog standard, but paydirt was hit when young director Michael Reeves was employed to make *The Sorcerers* (1967). Ageing hypnotist Boris Karloff is pressured by nasty wife Catherine 'Whisky Galore!' Lacey into controlling the mind of young turk Ian Ogilvy for a spot of vicarious rejuvenation. This fairly routine B-flick idea is transformed by Reeves into a thoroughly bleak nightmare. The sorcerers' lair is a drab south London bedsit and the laboratory equipment seemingly cobbled together from school physics labs; this along with oppressive editing makes the 'possession' sequences genuinely uncomfortable to sit through.

All this was just a warm-up, though, for *Witchfinder General* (1968), a beautifully atmospheric piece of historical horror with eponymous brooding charlatan Matthew Hopkins (Vincent Price), together with nasty sidekick Robert Russell, making their way through Civil War-era Essex, burning and deflowering gullible townsfolk as they go, until roundhead Ian Ogilvy catches up with them. Reeves' intention was to make a completely realistic film of the period, and it's masterfully crafted stuff throughout. Price's performance is a joint career-best with his campier turn in *Theatre of Blood*. Sadly, Reeves died of an antidepressant overdose the following February, and what could have been an amazing career (beginning with Poe adaptation *The Oblong Box*) was cut cruelly short.

These two films alone would have cemented Tigon's reputation as the third greatest British horror film company after Hammer and Amicus, but there was more: *The Blood Beast Terror* (1968), which saw Robert Flemyng injecting human foetuses with African moth serum in his oak-panelled, bell jar-stuffed laboratory, to produce bloodsucking giant moth-girl Wanda Ventham ('Her schizo-frantic embraces making corpses of her lovers!'); Brush-daft rural shocker *The Beast in the Cellar* (1970), with Dame Flora Robson and Beryl Reid combining teatime tittle-tattle with disposing of the victims of the titular underfloor psychopath; a sequel to *Witchfinder*, of (very tenuous) sorts, the campy, virgin-baiting *Blood On Satan's Claw* (1971); Hammer-like knock-off *The Creeping Flesh* (1973), in which Peter Cushing, as a stereotypical waistcoat-and-quizzical-eyebrow Victorian scientist, and his dodgy asylum-owning brother Christopher Lee inject the former's daughter with a dodgy rejuvenating serum taken from an old skeleton; a fair-enough film of old BBC science intrigue chestnut *Doomwatch* (1972); Price–Lee–Cushing acid bath triple-header *Scream and Scream Again* (1969); raincoat-tempting Vicki '*Allo 'Allo*' Michelle showcase *Virgin Witch* (1972); plus several gems from the megaphone of Pete Walker.

The 'saucy' end of the business was kept up too, via pseudo-worthy projects such as a slipshod film of Kenneth Tynan's blockbusting paean to the revolutionary power of the untrammelled nork *Oh! Calcutta!* (1972) and largely made-up 'national sex survey' *Love in Our Time* (1968), produced by Elkan Allan, better known as the mastermind behind pop telly extravaganza *Ready, Steady, Go!* Rather less auspicious, but arguably a lot more fun, were Charles-Hawtrey-meets-nipple-tassels sci-fi romp *Zeta One* (1969) and joyous portmanteau comedy *The Magnificent Seven Deadly Sins* (1971), in which Bruce Forsyth scours London's sewers for a missing ten bob, Galton and Simpson turn in a masterful 'war of the motoring organisations' skit and Spike Milligan stars in a demented silent film in the name of sloth ('I'd love to save you, but I can't let go of my walnuts!').

After 1974, which saw him put money into Spike Milligan's *The Great McGonagall* and executive produce Pete Walker's *Frightmare*, Tenser wound down his film commitments, and Tigon sat out the rest of the decade distributing other people's soft porn flicks. Still, his mercenary tactics can lay a fair claim to having kept British independent filmmaking alive through its darkest years. As the man said, 'I'd rather be ashamed of a film that was making money than proud of a film that was losing it.'

RITA TUSHINGHAM

THE GIRL WITH THE CHINESE EYEBROWS

The Americans had Audrey Hepburn. Well, we had her first, but appearances such as her one-liner in *Laughter in Paradise* (1951), saying 'anyone fancy a ciggy?' aren't technically the stuff of legend. However, by the time Tony Richardson was preparing *A Taste of Honey* (1961) for production, La Hepburn was Americanised enough to have her participation in the film come with a series of weighty Hollywood star's conditions. The story, a naturalistic adaptation of Shelagh Delaney's experimental play was too bleak, he was told. Single girl living in penury with her mum gets up the duff by a black sailor – we can't have Aud doing that! The 'happy' ending they came up with was a miscarriage, cheerfully sidestepping the hot racial potato. Richardson wisely took his screenplay elsewhere, to a Liverpool rep company where La Tush was plucked out and flung wide-eyed, and even wider-mouthed, at the screen.

Wide-eyed but far from innocent, Tushingham went beyond the Hepburn cuterama model in *The Leather Boys* (1964), marrying a biker and losing him to no less than Dudley Sutton, and as a gigglingly wicked convent school rebel (as indeed she used to be in real life) in *Girl with Green Eyes* (1962). The Modness continued with the only slightly more conventional Bethnal Green melodrama *A Place to Go* (1963), where she fell for would-be fag factory robber Mike 'Come Outside' Sarne.

Then in swanned *The Knack* (1965), and all bets were off. Another play adaptation, but taken in the opposite direction by Richard Lester, amping up the slapstick, cross-cutting and telly references, and with Rita's initially mousy London ingénue moving from cowed innocence to strident cockiness in short order, operatically shouting 'Rape!' to alert the local populace ('Not today, thank you!') to Ray Brooks's titular slithy predatory technique. In stark contrast to that shoestring effort, Rita took a fortnight out to appear in a film costing over thirty times *The Knack's* budget, playing the mysterious girl who listens – wide, eyed, natch – to the story of Alec Guinness's life at the top and tail ends of *Dr Zhivago* (1965).

Meanwhile, things moved quickly in Swinging London, and the Mod era of London films she'd helped usher in with *Honey* was now turning sour, so she ushered it back out again with Lynn Redgrave in the delightfully daft Carnaby Street cataclysm *Smashing Time* (1967). On a more mainstream note, the trend of European heist comedies started by *Topkapi* (1964) – and continued with *How to Steal a Million* (1966), starring Audrey H – called at Tush's door in 1968 in the form of *Diamonds for Breakfast*, in which swinging Russian boutique owner Marcello Mastroianni enlists an all-girl gang of crooks (including Rita's oddball safecracker) to nick the Imperial diamonds. As a result, Tushingham's autopilot kook's turn gets lost among a muddle of ancestral ghosts and Mastroianni's strangulated singing.

Even period drama swung in those days. Merchant–Ivory production *The Guru* (1969) sent Tushingham to India as cohort of Michael York's sitar instruction-hungry pop star, the superbly named Tom Pickle. Then she was pregnant again, carrying the last hope of post-nuclear humanity as bewildered daughter to Arthur Lowe and Mona Washbourne in peripatetic parable *The Bed-Sitting Room* (1969).

She had clearly demonstrated that there was more to her than the shy girl down to London from Liverpool finding it hard to fit in with the trendy scene, but this is what she was once more offered, in 1972 of all years, playing a ridiculously neurotic outsider befriending a dangerous serial killer in Hammer's 'love story' *Straight on Till Morning*. Thereafter the Brits didn't seem to know what to do with her and she toured Europe and Canada for a fine enough body of work, but one with none of the revolutionary zeal she exhibited in those half a dozen classics of the 1960s, a time when the eyes definitely had it.

THE ESSENTIAL MASSIVELY COMPLICATED SPY THRILLER

THE KREMLIN LETTER (1970)

When ideas for films are pitched to studios by various waiters and retired office workers, which inevitably feature characters very like themselves in prominent roles, they are required at the outset to present the premise of the proposed film in a line or so. If it cannot be summed up in such a concise precis, the theory goes, it'll never work. Quite how John Huston managed to sell the men in the Lear jets on *The Kremlin Letter* is a bit of a mystery, for reduced to one line the best anyone could do would be, 'Mercenary spies are paid to recover dangerous letter from the Soviet Union in the most convoluted and complicated way possible'. Not a line that would have resulted in handshakes over lattes too speedily, but complicated and convoluted *The Kremlin Letter* most certainly is.

Nevertheless, wordy dialogue and intricate plot were Huston staples. His first film, *The Maltese Falcon* (1941), is a minefield of red herrings, cross-talk and stylised patter that's incredibly difficult to follow. Only familiarity and the genius of Humphrey Bogart's and Sidney Greenstreet's delivery make it commonly decipherable. It's still criticised as 'too wordy', which is like complaining that *Lawrence of Arabia* (1962) is 'too visual.' *The Kremlin Letter* is a film very much in this vein. Although there are a frightening number of locations, from illicit discos in Moscow to laboratories in Siberia, from the New York Zoo to brothels in Mexico, they are fleeting glimpses used more to illustrate the reams of exposition than anything else. But while some films are complicated for the sake of it such as *The Usual Suspects* (1995), or for which their complexity is the motivation for the film itself such as in *Memento* (2000) – which really ought to have reintroduced the old practice of having an interval so the audience could confer – the labyrinthine nature of the plot of *The Kremlin Letter* is necessary simply because the attempt at portraying the world of espionage at all accurately requires it.

For this tale of spies and spying in the Cold War is a universe away from the cosy security of the world of James Bond, where the goodies are the freedom-loving democracies of the West and the baddies are everyone else. The spies of Huston's tale are greedy, amoral and dismissive of ideology or nationality. Their creed is money and their allegiance is to the highest bidder. In this instance the troops – George Sanders, Nigel Green, Barbara Parkins, Dean Jagger, David Kossoff, Richard Boone and Patrick O'Neill – are being paid their share of a million dollars divvied up according to 'the usual rules' (whoever is alive at the end gets a share) to recover a letter threatening that the USA will back up the Soviet Union in any war with China. To this end the gang take possession of a flat in Moscow and begin their mission after the obligatory lengthy discussions in America.

The teeth of the opposition are represented by Max von Sydow as the secret service chief attempting to foil the plans of the spies and Orson Welles as the Kremlin security watchdog more involved with his own plans and working more angles than a triangle salesman. Again, the common perception here of a united front of resistance to interlopers within the Evil Empire is blown asunder as the incredibly juvenile and blond von Sydow is thwarted and cajoled all along the line by Welles, giving one of his finest performances, whose character does all he can to undermine his subordinate and indeed to eventually replace him with one of the invading spies.

Beyond dispelling notions of intergovernmental relations and the role of the secret services in both open and closed societies, what *The Kremlin Letter* also gives a unique insight into are the sorts of fun and diversion available in late 1960s Moscow. Bibi Andersson as the wife of von Sydow's character, herself a secret agent, is first encountered in a brilliantly tawdry disco that could easily be the similarly tatty dance hall in *Get Carter* (1971) for example. Nigel Green's character Whore is put in charge of ferreting around in the world's of narcotics and prostitution, not traditionally thought to be popular leisure pursuits in the re-Stalinised USSR of Brezhnev, and Warlock, the codename used for George Sanders' character, is set loose on a particularly specialised brief, described to him in a manner that might now be labelled as 'delightfully non-PC', of 'art and homos'. All told they paint a picture of a Moscow quite different from the potato-brewing and bread-queuing grey masses pining for democracy and the American way which was most likely to be peddled in western films of the period, or even now. The Moscow of *The Kremlin Letter* seems no worse than anywhere else in fact – unless you get caught up in secret intrigue that is, in which case, like almost all of the spies in the film, you will end up dead.

Another aspect of the film which is quite unlike any other in its genre is the extraordinary conclusion to the story. There is a conclusion but no resolution since the letter of the title is not recovered, the characters hardly make it home and the big baddie, Orson Welles being typically big in every sense, comes out best over all. Nigel Green's character just vanishes at some stage, reported by the fantastically tawdry pimp Madame Sophie to have been taken away by von Sydow. George Sanders leaps from the balcony of the apartment to save himself from interrogation, the red yarn from the bedsocks he was knitting for his young 'friend' rolling off him like knitted blood. Eventually, even von Sydow succumbs and at the end only O'Neill and Boone are left as the survivors of a plot that is unravelling right up until, literally, the final shot.

The relative anonymity of the film, which is a real credit to the Huston canon, is most likely down to a combination of its complexity and sheer pessimism. It takes several viewings to unravel precisely what is going on and the way the story winds up can hardly be called anything like a happy ending. In fact, it can't be called a happy ending at all. What *The Kremlin Letter* does is to dare the audience to stop paying attention. Quite different from a film that just makes no sense, it makes sense if you watch it really very closely and listen very, very hard. If you don't get it first time round then don't blame the director, screenwriter or stars, just try harder next time.

PETER BULL

UNMISTAKABLE BULL WHATEVER THE REQUIREMENT

Some actors pride themselves on their abilities to alter their appearance in both sound and vision in a display of chameleon-like versatility that is often regarded as the epitome of 'the craft'. The likes of Daniel Day Lewis will spend anything up to a year crying in a social security office in Govan in order to play the part of a sociopathic dole bludger in a donkey jacket and wellies convincingly. On the other hand, some actors don't. Peter Bull was never anything other than Peter Bull in any of the parts he played on film, even when he really ought not to have been.

In his first role as 'A Country Fellow', a quintessentially Bullish part, in *As You Like It* (1936) he was Peter Bull. As the defence lawyer in wartime melodrama *Dead Man's Shoes* (1940) he was Peter Bull. In *Scrooge* (1951) as one of the businessman in the exchange, patting his hefty stomach and talking of lunch, he was very much Peter Bull. Even in *The African Queen* (1951) as a German naval captain he was never anything but Peter Bull. There has hardly ever been another actor who hid himself so little behind the roles he played whether deliberately or otherwise. When critics level accusations at the likes of Sean Connery and Arnold Schwarzenegger that they only ever play themselves, they forget that none of them come close to Bull in that respect.

That is far from being a bad thing. For when an actor is not a leading player they have to grab on to whatever they have to ensure that they stay in work. In Bull's case it is was his extraordinary face and singularly historic countenance. Like a visitor from the seventeenth century he stared out of from the screen with that remarkable visage, like a contemptuous and permanently perplexed bulldog. For some reason however his features, although verging on the grotesque in the purely artistic sense of the word, seemed to suit the depiction of awful women far more than that of ordinary men. If there was ever an actor who was better suited to playing Lewis Carroll's pepper-spraying Duchess, as Bull did in *Alice's Adventures in Wonderland* (1972) then they kept it a very good secret. Indeed, Bull's last film role was another befuddled but grand old lady. As Queen Anne in Graham Chapman's *Yellowbeard* (1983) Bull was one of the few actors to emerge from that palaver with reputation intact. This is partly because he had screentime in which it wouldn't be possible to hard-boil egg but also because he was so good, depicting the old girl as a confused but regal old galleon, scorned by the cognoscenti but still in charge.

Bull's most famous film role was that of the Soviet Ambassador in *Doctor Strangelove* (1964), hotly expressing outrage at the perfidy of the Americans while coolly photographing the Big Board on the sly. Warning of the terrors of the doomsday shroud in one breath he dropped to a level of petulance after the manner of a narked schoolboy when challenged by George C Scott in the next. It is a brilliantly nuanced performance that is so much more interesting to watch than Sellers' own one-chord depiction of the US President. However, little credit ever gets thrown Bull's way simply because his own curiously Russian features – and he had played a Russian once before in *Knight Without Armour* (1937) – make him so identifiable. Credibility as an actor, at least on film, was never going to be his strong suit, though by the time he was happy to take the appearance money for *Rosie Dixon – Night Nurse* (1978) that could scarcely have been an issue.

It takes a lot of courage for actors to play themselves on screen and most don't like to expose themselves even in a publicity interview, sometimes going to the extent of George Segal, who confessed to creating a character who appears on chat shows, which he can then play in order to keep himself hidden. Segal chose the character of an irritating banjo-playing has-been – a character that he startlingly realised. However, the evidence of the various volumes of Bull's own excellent autobiography, not to mention his seminal work on teddy bears, 'Bear With Me', convince that on screen as well as off, Bull did as Bull was.

INCONGRUOUS CASTING

Casting is an odd business. One of the favourite games that cinema 'insiders' like to play is throwing about alternative cast lists for films. The likes of George Raft as Rick in *Casablanca* (1942) and Tom Selleck as Indiana Jones in *Raiders Of The Lost Ark* (1981) are often bandied about to prove film-buff credentials. The film with the most permutations, however, always seems to be *Jaws* (1975). Alternate casting here ranges from Sterling Hayden as Robert Shaw to Robert Redford as Richard Dreyfus and Jon Voight as Roy Scheider. Typically, fans of the film throw their hands up in horror, as if the actors eventually chosen to play the parts had it scribbled on their birth certificates, and even considering any other competent actors for the parts is akin to signing Reg Varney, Bob Grant and Stephen Lewis to crew the *Orca*. Anyone with a pulse and the ability to point themselves at a camera was considered for *Jaws* if you were to believe these people. Other actors considered for the parts of Quint, Brodie and Hooper are said to include Lee Marvin, Charlton Heston, Jan Michael Vincent, Harrison Ford, James Robertson Justice, Robin Askwith, Peter Butterworth, Marianne Stone and Henry Hall on the piano.

After alternative casting comes miscasting. The most famous example is the selection by Cubby Broccoli and Harry Saltzman of Australian swimmer George Lazenby to take over as James Bond for *On Her Majesty's Secret Service* (1969). As before, this choice is seen as being on a par with casting Jimmy Krankie as King Lear, but Lazenby was fine and suffered only from having to follow Sean Connery.

After miscasting comes an area as fascinating as it is undiscussed: incongruous casting. These are decisions made by casting directors obviously about to retire, which lead to audiences in the dark mouthing their astonishment in unison at whoever has just wandered into shot. Some actors managed to make an entire career out of this, especially Charles Hawtrey, whose increasingly demented performances in the *Carry On*s always managed to single him out of even that supremely mixed bag of casting delights. Other, rather less extreme examples include the following.

Ludovic Kennedy in *HEAVEN'S ABOVE!* (1963)

The Goodies knew that actors cannot play newsreaders convincingly, as they have a tendency to emote over the less fortunate bulletins in an attempt to land a regular spot at the Old Vic. Proper newspersons don't do this, which is why the lads preferred to rope in the likes of Corbett Woodall and Michael Barratt to lend an air of reality and gravitas to their maniacal proceedings. Dashed clever chaps that they were, legendary film producing partners the Boulting Brothers knew this too, so when they needed to lend a bit of Radio Newsreel realism to the scenes of ever deepening crisis in this brilliant but often overlooked entry in the Peter Sellers canon, the man their civilised attention alighted upon was now-veteran, then-ludicrously-junior-looking newshound Ludo Kennedy, who steps into a very

INCONGRUOUS CASTING

British riot (people shouting 'Boo!' and the odd policeman's helmet being knocked off) to ask Sellers' character, a vicar providing groceries free of charge as an act of charity, just what he's up to. Now, this may seem like a sensible thing to do (hire Ludo that is, not give away shopping for nothing) but it's impossible to maintain any form of suspension of belief when you immediately lean forward in your chair to yelp, 'Bloody hell! It's Ludovic Kennedy!' and it's a taxi for the casting director.

Malcolm Muggeridge in *I'M ALL RIGHT, JACK* (1959)

The Boultings had a bit of a thing for using the popular media types of their day for early doors media-crossover zeitgeist cobblers. Towards the end of this justly famous satire on industrial relations, again starring Sellers the Great, a television debate is staged in which all the lead characters take part – Dennis Price for the baddies and Sellers for the goodies. What was required to make the whole thing ooze with realism was a chairman who could add some gravitas and intellectual weight to the proceedings. No one did that better at the time, and indeed for some time to come, than Malcolm Muggeridge. Muggers had already appeared in *Heaven's Above* in character as a cleric, capitalising on his famous connections with religion (in the 1950s and 1960s the Pope and Archbishop of Canterbury were not really players compared with Mal) so he was no stranger to the Boulting set up. However, when he appears on screen as the studio cameras move in on him sat among the nervous and twitching lead characters, it's impossible not to once again turn to someone – the cat even – and say, 'Blimey, look! There's that Malcolm Muggeridge!' Muggeridge conducts the play within a play in a massively patronising and pompous manner, proving at least that he received little direction, as he is obviously playing himself. So when the whole set-up collapses into chaos it's a little joy in itself to see the old git flailing about in panic, just one extra little bonus in an already great film.

Patricia Hayes in *WILLOW* (1988)

Willow demonstrates George Lucas' post-*Star Wars* 'difficult second album' period nicely. A mostly pleasing but overwhelmingly daft effort directed by Ron Howard, with Lucas as producer, this was a doomed attempt to reopen the book on fantasy films. Doomed because if the mighty *Dragonslayer* (1981) couldn't do it, this had no chance. Still, it has some pleasing moments as the eponymous character, short Lucas favourite Warwick Davies, tries to get a baby prophesied to hold the key to the downfall of an evil queen to a powerful sorceress to facilitate the… well, you get the picture. What's astonishing here isn't anything to do with the story or the action or the effects or anything like that, but the sorceress herself. Quite what possessed Howard to cast elderly British character actor Patricia Hayes, famous for nearly forty years to this point for playing drunk bag ladies and hopeless comedy charwomen, as the mystical and magical Fin Raziel is anybody's guess. Not that anyone should complain, as Hayes is as brilliant as she always was. But her appearance in the film, having been transformed from a crow through a series of other animalistic permutations before finalising on *Edna, the Inebriate Woman*, does rather grind everything to a halt. For in 1981 Pat Hayes was Alf Garnett's annoying cousin Min, not a female wizard charged with the elemental powers of nature. Perhaps it's a case of casting that's just too good? Whatever the reason, the rest of the film is spent wondering how it happened. Which is at least better than wondering why the film was made at all.

Rikki Fulton in *GORKY PARK* (1983)

So you're a director with an adaptation of a major book set in the Soviet Union with a screenplay by a major script writer (Dennis Potter) and a brace of Hollywood stars lined up (Lee Marvin and William Hurt) but you need an actor to play the ruthless and sadistic KGB major who acts as the face of a shadowy Kremlin conspiracy. Who you gonna call? Well, if you're Michael Apted the answer is legendary Scottish pantomime dame Rikki Fulton. Fulton himself never understood why he was cast in this unusually serious role, though he was no stranger to films. The same year saw the release of Bill Forsyth's rather more whimsical *Local Hero* (1983), but in that Fulton was playing a comedy scientist, grumbling about not getting support from Burt Lancaster for his plan to melt the polar ice caps while he played in his water tank, and not a psychopathic secret policeman. Still, he's very good at it; the same force that allowed him to spend a lifetime facing down Abanazar did not go to waste in the snows of Russia. Odd as his casting undoubtedly is, it certainly paid off for the longevity of the film as a whole, since his involvement in it is about the only thing that anyone can ever bring to mind of the escapade.

Hugh Griffith in *BEN-HUR* (1959)

This really is the granddaddy of all incongruous casting decisions. No one will ever know what the hell William Wyler, or whichever of his little wizards were responsible here, was thinking when they put in the call to the valleys to rope drink-sodden Welsh character actor Griffith into his mammoth spectacular biblical epic in Cinemascope (so big only the biggest of the big religions could be responsible for it). At some point however, someone must have said, 'Gee! You know who'd be swell as Sheik Ilderim, the fierce but fair nomadic chieftain of a proud desert race? That Welsh guy with the eyebrows!' Not that Griffith wasn't any good, he was brilliant, and his work is so resonant that when George Lucas came to 'homage' the chariot race in *The Phantom Menace* (1999) Griffith's part is almost entirely mimicked by CGI Hugh wannabe Watto (voice of Harry's son Andrew Secombe, Welsh casting conspiracy fans). So baffled were the Academy they gave Hugh an Oscar for his portrayal, and Wyler one for picking him. Try to imagine, if you can, Brian Blessed as the lead in *Edward Scissorhands* (1990). Or Julie T Wallace in *Roman Holiday* (1953). That's the level of incongruity we're working on here.

…For when a plain roller caption just won't do.

TRY SINGING IT

Orson Welles may have inaugurated spoken film credits with *Citizen Kane* (1941), but the legendary *Skidoo* (1968) went one step further and had them scat-sung by Harry Nilsson ('the film was directed by - ska-ba-dooo-ooo - Ot-to Pre-min-geeeer...') But they were way behind Danny Kaye, who introduced *The Court Jester* (1956) with an entire song and dance routine perfectly synchronised with the opening titles, and promising: 'of plot, we've got a lot!'

SAY CHEESE!

Why have a mere list of names rolling up the screen when you can film the filmmakers? That was the thinking for both Lionel Jeffries' marvellous children's ghost story *The Amazing Mr Blunden* (1972) and less marvellous undertaking sitcom spin-off *That's Your Funeral* (1972), with everyone from stars to clapper loaders waving cheerfully to the stalls in true *Hi-De-Hi* 'you have been watching' style.

LEAVE 'EM GUESSING

It became a cliché within seconds of its first deployment, but the cheeky addition of a question mark after the words 'THE END', preferably accompanied by a comedy musical sting, did well for the original feature-length *Batman* (1966) and all manner of daft old sci-fi such as force field stupidity *4D Man* (1959). Ironically enough, for both films that really was the end.

FOOLED YA!

This extremely odd late-period John Houston mystery *The List of Adrian Messenger* (1963), with George C Scott and Kirk Douglas investigating the titular roster of recently-assassinated individuals, ends with Kirk (playing a Master of Disguise) physically stopping the end credits before revealing several famous 'cameos' that appeared in the course of the film (legend has it the stars in question weren't actually present for the film proper at all) and various extra-curricular roles Douglas himself took on - all revealed in time-honoured Kenny Everett tradition by ripping off latex noses and chins and delivering a cheeky 'it was me all the time!' wink to the camera.

YOINK!

In *If It's Tuesday, This Must be Belgium* (1969), Ian McShane wooed Suzanne Pleshette aboard a whistlestop coach tour of European landmarks in a fluffily comic parody of cinema travelogues, but Aubrey Morris stole the film as, appropriately enough, an amiable old kleptomaniac. Fitting, then, that the picture ended with Morris half-inching the film's 'THE END' placard, for what nefarious purpose only he knew.

HUGH GRIFFITH

HUGH GRIFFITH

MUCH MORE THAN JUST A PAIR OF EYEBROWS

How an actor as extraordinarily distinctive as Hugh Griffith can pass into the hinterland of obscurity is a genuine enigma. But for all his recognisable traits, the fiery eyes – like those of some mystical Welsh prophet descended from the mountains to deliver of the word, though he'd probably have forgotten what that word might be by the time he got down – the bristling badger eyebrows, the hawkish nose and solid, almost squat figure, his legend has cooled and not many can, or care to bring him to mind these days. Most likely they would mix his name up with the other creditable cinematic Griffiths: Derek, Kenneth or Richard. But Hugh's legend deserves to be rekindled, if only for the sheer weight of quality films he was involved with.

Difficult as it is to believe, considering his extraordinary appearance, he began his working life as a bank clerk and even when he got his first part in films, an uncredited appearance in comedy drama *Neutral Port* (1940), starring a bizarre mix of broad Glaswegian comedian Will Fyffe, world beating stooge Wally Patch and actual proper glamorous film star Phyllis Calvert, it wasn't really happening for Hugh and another part didn't follow for the next seven years.

His agent had the, perhaps reasonable, excuse that a major world conflict had taken place in the intervening period but at least when Griffith got going, he got going good. Dark Alistair Sim comedy *London Belongs to Me* (1948) is one of the very best of its period and *Kind Hearts and Coronets* (1949), *Laughter In Paradise* (1951) and *The Titfield Thunderbolt* (1953) are all justifiably famous.

An appearance in the splendid Boulting adaptation of Kinglsey Amis' *Lucky Jim* (1957) added to his credibility but whether or not that gained for Hugh his selection to play the fruity and distinctly un-Welsh Sheikh Ilderim in *Ben-Hur* (1959) is difficult to say. Perhaps the braying students of the provincial university of the former created a suitably chaotic atmosphere for the casting directors of the latter so that they found themselves easily able to imagine Hugh among the roaring crowds of the Circus Maximus. Whatever the logic, should there have been any, he played the part with his usual bristling gusto and bagged an Oscar in the process – an incredible, well-deserved and baffling achievement by any actor.

The Academy hadn't done with Hugh yet though and he received another nomination for his portrayal of the intemperate, flash tempered and goggle-eyed Squire Western in *Tom Jones* (1963). He didn't win though, and it seems ironic that he should have bagged a statuette for a role so out of character as Sheikh Ilderim, yet missed out on one for what was essentially an extended cameo as Western. Such are awards.

There was still more quality work to come from under that brow, however, with *How To Steal a Million* (1966) and *Oliver!* (1968), as the brilliantly drink suffused magistrate, and then the winning duo of *The Abominable Dr Phibes* (1971) and *Dr Phibes Rises Again* (1972) as well as the slightly more sober *Luther* (1973), supporting Stacey Keach playing the titular Teutonic God-botherer.

Hugh's last few films count as an extremely mixed bunch. In *The Last Remake of Beau Geste* (1977) he was back on the bench again as a judge in that superlative piece of manic flummery from Marty Feldman before settling comfortably into a brilliantly B-list cast including Derek Deadman, Brian Croucher, Davey Kaye and Bruce Boa in *A Nightingale Sang in Berkeley Square* (1979) for what was a small but creditable appearance in a small but creditable film. Sadly, his nigh on last real film part was in the atrocious *The Hound of the Baskervilles* (1978), a protracted exercise in demonstrating how unfunny Peter Cook, Dudley Moore and even Kenneth Williams could be if a useless director – in this case the particularly clueless Paul Morrissey – really tried hard at it. Not a fitting end to an otherwise spectacular career.

Hugh Griffith may not be the name most readily upon the lips of the film-going public, but his is still a face that guarantees a pleasant afternoon in with a film matinee – an unexpected yet satisfying treat, like finding a box of chocolates with one orange crème too many. For the naysayers, he still has that Oscar to wave at them unsteadily from his whisky-laced cloud.

THE ESSENTIAL HORROR COMEDY

THEATRE OF BLOOD (1973)

Horror comedy is never an easy gig. The two genres are mutually exclusive at best, and at worst actively pull against each other. Add to that the fact horror films have, from *Bride of Frankenstein* onwards, exhibited a healthy knowledge of their own daftness anyway, so the task of the horror parodist becomes Herculean.

Theatre of Blood, a prime cut of United Artists folderol, is well up to the challenge. That grand master of borderline self-parody, Vincent Price, is Edward Lionheart, a classical actor of the declamatory old school miffed at constant desultory notices and the incursion by trendy 'Method' types on what he sees as his turf. Eddie sets out to off the eight members of the London Critics' Circle who've served up his most crushing reviews. Being a Bardhead, he themes each death after an on-stage coil-shuffling from each of the Shakespeare plays he's been slagged off for being shite in, making it up when the plot doesn't quite fit his purposes.

This leads to some memorable vignettes indeed. Robert Morley choking on his own poodles and Arthur Lowe's severed head are the most famous, but there's also the brilliant death-by-perm for Coral Browne, Dennis Price being dragged behind a horse, Ian Hendry facing an ocular dagger mechanism straight out of *The Perils of Penelope Pitstop*, and the, er… singular spectacle of Price in a white suit humping away at Diana Dors before Jack Hawkins bursts in and strangles her.

However, it's more than a series of Sellotaped-together bumpings-off, as Eddie's tragic backstory gradually revealed, and there's a nicely gruesome technique of using the body (or bits thereof) of the previous victim to hound the remaining nerks.

It was reputedly Vinny's favourite of all his films, and it's not hard to see why: a green light for unrestrained fruitiness, umpteen costume changes, bizarre make-up, action scenes aplenty, a suicide, the chance to electrocute his future wife while impersonating Princess Margaret's hairdresser, assorted camply wonky European accents and eight separate Shakespeare recitals. Handed the opportunity of a lifetime, Price inevitably runs riot, but as well as providing fantastic entertainment all along the line, his singular ability to make the ham look convincing as a ham, and not just an actor's hammy idea of a ham, helps the club-footed logic of the baroque serial killer film no end.

The rest of the cast bulges with notables. Diana Rigg is Eddie's daughter-cum-partner-in-crime. On their trail are the regulation blundering plods, senior detective Milo O'Shea (silver-haired, bluff, one step behind but doesn't like it pointed out) and dogged sergeant Eric Sykes. The critics vary from the shamefully underused (Michael Hordern and Arthur Lowe) to the brilliantly overdone (Harry Andrews and Robert Morley), and a well-judged 'main victim' performance from the always-reliable Ian Hendry. Then there's Joan Hickson being repeatedly injected in the arse, Madeline Smith as a secretary, and Stanley 'Bungle off *Rainbow*' Bates reviving a drowned Price with a Mazola bottle half-full of meths.

Blood takes place in real 1970s London, in and around real landmarks, with real knackered old police Ford Zephyrs to boot. Consequently, it all looks grand. Director Douglas Hickox pulls off enough fantastic little moments to put Kubrick worshippers in the 'Eight Idols or Less' queue. Thrill as Michael Hordern is vertically stabbed against a sheet of polythene! Marvel at the incredibly complex horse-in-a-make-up-mirror shot! Swoon as the camera follows Price's *Hamlet* recital from balcony to balcony! And stare open-mouthed at the use of wide-angle lenses in general, coming to a head when Hendry faces off with Vince in a trampoline-boosted fencing tournament. No other horror film – no other film, come to that – varies so wildly in tone.

Anthony Greville-Bell's script perfectly balances on the point of self-parody, yet it's serious enough within its own daft world to deliver some genuinely chilling goods – Hordern's violent death in particular is not easily expunged from the memory. This is how to do horror parody: first, take horror itself seriously, then let daftness reign as you extrapolate a warped version of it, but make sure you turn the seriousness back up when it comes to the characters. Camp Lionheart may be, but he's clearly deadly serious.

Besides, you have to love a film that credits a 'Meths-Drinker Choreographer'.

ERIC SYKES

ERIC SYKES

IN SEARCH OF MALTHOUSE PASSAGE

He's a Comedy Hero with a legacy spanning six decades. For the best part of two of those he wrote and starred in one of the most original and brilliant sitcoms in television history. Despite incipient deafness, he improvised a fresh show every night for years on end with Jimmy Edwards across five continents. He 'never swore or did anything suggestive'. He is a freeman of the City of London and, more importantly, Eric Sykes' film career is as singular as they come.

Sykes got his first proper feature role, as (to all intents and purposes) did Peter Sellers and Tony Hancock, in corny old 'film crew on army base' farce *Orders Are Orders* (1954), playing a fairly minor military role as Tony Hancock's mugging band conductor. Sid James' bizarrely accented American director took centre stage. Even more minor was his role in Max Bygraves' 'golden age of rep' musical *Charley Moon* (1956), as a punter who gets beaten up when he won't keep quiet during Max's act.

Sykes crossed paths with Spike Milligan in *Invasion Quartet* (1961), as a Nazi bandleader getting slowly but inevitably tangled up in a fishing net. A breakthrough of sorts came – or at least seemed to – when Sykes copped his first lead role, as inept salesman Herbert Harris in *Village Of Daughters* (1962), a quaint little comedy set in a Sicilian village bereft of young males, who mistake his bumbling merchant for a foreign envoy arriving to select a bride for a rich ex-pat. The Edinburgh premiere convinced Sykes he wasn't leading man material. 'Some people actually enjoyed it', he recalled, 'but they are either now dead or in a mental home'. More success was to be had in *Kill Or Cure* (1962) as the psychotic fitness trainer at Dennis Price's health farm, giving private eye Terry-Thomas a memorable medical ('We'll start you off with parsnip pulp and carrot juice, before gradually working you up to grass salad!').

In 1963 Sykes clocked up his first stone-cold classic, playing the scruffy squatter husband of the equally scruffy Irene Handl, both heads of the numerous, down-at-heel Smith family given shelter by Sellers' idealistic vicar in *Heavens Above!* *The Bargee* (1964). This is a forgotten oddity in which randy narrow boat owners Harry H Corbett and Ronnie Barker cruise the canals in search of crumpet, finding instead an assortment of English eccentrics, none more doolally than Sykes' oddball skipper, convinced he's the reincarnation of Lord Nelson. Bond spoof *The Liquidator* (1965) cast Sykes against type as a ruthless hit man, hired to off defecting spies on behalf of secret service colonel Trevor Howard.

The blockbusters arrived with *Those Magnificent Men in Their Flying Machines* (1965), the first and best of those all-star 1960s Eurocomedies, with Sykes having the time of his life as put-upon stooge to Terry-Thomas' caddish pilot. Eric's golfing chum Douglas Bader judged it 'A masterpiece. I've seen it seven times!' The sequel, *Monte Carlo or Bust* (1969), was less fun. Second-string Boultings payroll romp *Rotten to the Core* (1965) saw Sykes cast as a bumbling detective on the trail of a gang of criminals led by Anton Rodgers in various disguises, a role seemingly modelled for Peter Sellers. Also intended for Peter was Lionel Jeffries' part as a mild-mannered reluctant spy in Galton and Simpson's *The Spy With the Cold Nose* (1966), getting moderate laughs out of various Bondesque situations with Eric as – what else? – a bumbling sidekick.

While knocking around with Sellers, Sykes suggested a homage to the good old silent days of simple physical, intricately-choreographed, one-camera, one-take comedy. Sellers avidly agreed, and the pair dreamt up a Laurel and Hardy-style scenario with themselves as two hapless brown-coated workmen. *The Plank* (1967) was born. Buoyant, Sykes went off to think about practicalities such as funding, when Sellers rang and announced shooting was due to start in three weeks. Never one to sit about when there was a new toy to play with, he'd gone straight to Bernard Delfont offering the film as a package, with his star leverage guaranteeing the green light. Then, days before shooting, disaster: Blake Edwards offered Sellers the lead role in *The Party*. Suddenly all bets were off, and so was Sellers, to Hollywood, leaving Sykes to draft in Tommy Cooper as alternative partner in chaos. Despite never having acted before in his life, Tom, full of the confidence that comes from being the rising talent *du jour*, took to the role with gusto – as did Sykes behind the camera. Despite being fresh to the directing game, Eric implemented an on-the-hoof filmmaking method. Not a word was written down. You can't write physical comedy, posited Sykes, therefore the best place for the shots to be worked out was in the director's head – 'writing with the camera' as he called it. And it worked. Looking at *The Plank* today, it's clear this sort of thing can only be done properly when writer, director and actor are singing from the same hymn sheet, although in this case all three are the same person and there is no sheet. The atmosphere on set was joyful, with the many guest stars all too keen to do a bit of old-fashioned physical clowning (for example, Jimmy Edwards' timeless bicycally challenged bobby).

For a change of pace, Sykes was scooted off to Spain as the comedy Ingerlish butler in oddball western *Shalako* (1968). On return Sykes threw himself into more silent shorts, with two more successes: *It's Your Move* (1969) was more or less *The Plank II*, with Sykes, Cooper and Edwards all reprising their roles for the house-moving of newlyweds Richard Briers and Sylvia Syms whereas *Rhubarb* (1969) was less derivative and miles better – all dialogue replaced with the titular muttering crowd cliché.

Sykes turned in his best film cameo as the dogged Sergeant Dogge in *Theatre Of Blood* (1973), but sought further directorial kicks. *If You Go Down In The Woods Today* (1981), his first and only feature-length directing job, boasted a fine cast, including Robin Bailey, Roy Kinnear and Fulton MacKay, but at eighty-odd minutes the 'Agatha Christie gone mad' gags didn't prove enough to sustain the length, proving that Sykes' singular film-making method was best kept short.

At least his tiny role in *Absolute Beginners* (1986) manning an amusement arcade was easily overlooked amidst greater lapses of dignity such as David Bowie's 'Transatlantic man' and Lionel Blair's slimy record producer. With his last directorial stint – ill-fated Scandinavian-set comedy *The Big Freeze* (1993) – behind him, Sykes looked set to retreat into the book and chat-show circuit, but surprised everyone by turning in the performance of a lifetime as Tuttle, the decrepit gardener in otherwise ho-hum revisionist horror *The Others* (2001), being the best thing in it by a country mile. You can't keep a good man down.

THE ESSENTIAL
COMEDY TROUPE FILM

HORSE FEATHERS (1932)

The first thing that strikes you about *Horse Feathers*, the fourth Marx Brothers feature, is what they haven't bothered with. In those days, feature length comedy films felt obliged to envelop the 'comedy' aspect with various 'serious' bits of business: half-baked jewel thief plots, chorus lines, feeble romantic interludes and the like. Almost as if in apology for the rude intrusions, the comedy was smothered by second-rate drama.

With *Horse Feathers*, however, things go completely in the other direction. No one in authority gets more than a snout round the door. Stiff and starchy professors dance about to Groucho's songs. The two football heavies Harpo and Chico are sent to kidnap are never going to keep the pair detained for long when they can pull the old 'sawing a hole in the floor' routine not once, but twice. The plot is at the mercy of the stars, not the other way round. It is a testament to this unique state of affairs that you have to keep reminding yourself *Horse Feathers* is three-quarters of a century old. A film that did this today would label itself 'postmodern' and spend two hours patting itself on the back for being so clever. *Horse Feathers* just gets on with it.

The set-up is high concept indeed - Groucho is Quincy Adams Wagstaff, newly-inaugurated Dean of Huxley College. A lesser, newer comedy would have a lengthy, tiresomely logical preamble explaining how this unlikely event came to pass, perhaps with a tedious montage sequence, and maybe the odd joke if anyone round the table remembers. Here, Groucho's straight into proceedings after a minute, shaving during his enrolment, holding a mock auction and turning a series of puns into the best Marx song, the oddly hybrid *I'm Against It/I Always Get My Man*. Then we're taken to a speakeasy for passwords, drinks and general chaos. You won't find a better opening reel in any comedy film of the past or the future.

The rest of the film is a mess. The endless tours and rewrites that would mark the best of the MGM pictures were not in Paramount's budget. Sets were hastily improvised or nicked from other productions, and the cameramen were never allowed enough time to work out where Groucho and co. were going to be next, hence all the aimless pans and weird cut-offs. Scenes fade out without a decent punchline, and sometimes with no punchline at all. A seal appears out of nowhere. *Gone With the Wind* this ain't.

There is love interest, though. Thelma Todd is Connie Bailey, the college widow (basically a mature woman who lives in the college grounds in order to shag assorted students – how did *that* get past the censors?) She's wooed by the Brothers in turn, but none of them, save possibly Zeppo, are really that bothered about her. Chico butters her up by teaching her his pistol-fingered piano-hammering technique. This standard 'musical interlude' is exploded when Groucho looms into the foreground and advises 'I've got to stay here, but there's no reason why you folks shouldn't go out into the lobby until this thing blows over!'

Groucho mugs to camera and confuses and insults anyone who dares play it remotely straight. Chico takes the stereotyped 'idiot/immigrant' role and carries it so far off into the realms of oblique dimness he starts to look almost bright. Harpo blunders effortlessly in and out as if he were part of some silent film from a decade before that the projectionist spliced into this picture by accident. This winning spirit – Groucho attacking the film with ahead-of-his-time cynicism, Harpo gleefully running rings around it in antiquated silence and Chico proudly refusing to understand any of it – is infectious enough to let them get away with murder.

Which they so often do. The 'swordfish' password routine is one of the most quoted bits of verbal business in cinema history, yet it's full of eye-rolling rubbish. 'What do you take for a haddock?' 'Sometimes aspirin, sometimes I take a Calomel.' 'Say, I'd walk a mile for a Calomel!' 'You mean chocolate Calomel!' Calomel was a vomit-inducing medicine made from mercury and 'I'd walk a mile for a Camel' was a fag-ad slogan. Neither has seen much action since the war, so there you have an exchange that needs to be comprehensively researched before it can even be dismissed as woefully unfunny, yet it doesn't matter in the slightest. Talk about audience goodwill!

'And that reminds me of a story that's so dirty I'm ashamed to think of it myself!'

THE OTHER BROTHERS

By the mid 1930s, the Marx Brothers were firmly ensconced at the top of the Hollywood pecking order. So what if you were a film producer anxious for some copycat sibling vaudeville troupe action, yet couldn't get the real McCoy? You could always call...

THE RITZ BROTHERS

Best described as a low-rent Marx knock-off, this trio of less-inspired comedy dancers was wooed by several studios. To modern scholars it may seem a mystery as to why, but at the time they were boffo B.O. on a par with Groucho, despite their *piece de resistance* being a routine where they, er... eat a really big sandwich. They're cited as a major influence by Mel Brooks, which is something. Their finest hour came in *The Three Musketeers* (1939) as foils to Don Ameche's D'Artagnan, plucking fowl, singing a merry ode to the joys of chicken soup, and doing an admittedly very impressively choreographed acrobatic dance number. Unfortunately, Harry, Jimmy and Al didn't have properly defined comic personalities like the Marxes. In long shots they look pretty much all the same. The joke told against them back in the day was that the funny one was 'the middle one'. Still, they kept themselves busy enough, so you might have had to try...

THE RIO BROTHERS

Frank, Jim and Larry Rio were a high-wire act contemporary with W.C. Fields, but they made a modest incursion into movies via a Marx-ian comedy, mime and song route. Their big moment came as comic relief in Mexican musical *Casa Manana* (1951), pretending to walk in slow motion. Maybe you were better off with...

THE WIERE BROTHERS

Musical mittel-Europeans Harry, Herbert and Sylvester were bigger on TV than in the cinema, though they did provide much-needed relief in rubbish Elvis-goes-to-swinging-London film *Double Trouble* (1967), alongside Norman Rossington and Chips Rafferty. Their finest hour, though, was in *Road to Rio* (1947), fifth in the long-running Crosby/Hope screwball series, as a trio of itinerant Brazilian troubadours, whom Bing and Bob naturally corral into being their backing band. The gag here was the same one used in an episode of *Father Ted*. As the Wieres speak Portuguese only, to avoid the scam being blown, Crosby teaches each brother one English phrase each, to parrot whenever any question is asked - 'You're telling me!', 'This is murder!' and, most famously, 'You're in the groove, Jackson!' Cue much mirth when the wrong brother says the wrong thing at the wrong time.

On second thoughts, maybe Zeppo's got a window in his diary after all…

BRITISH INDEPENDENT FILM COMPANIES: A CHEAT'S GUIDE

The British film industry in the old days was rather like wrestling in the old days. In the blue corner, you had the big fellers. The Rank Organisation, the British offshoots of the American studios, and that multi-headed beast, Associated-British-Anglo-Amalgamated-Elstree-EMI-Thorn-Cannon-Westinghouse, or whatever it ended up being called. In the red corner, however, were a score of plucky independent production companies, often consisting of nothing more than a bloke sat at a desk in a damp Wardour Street loft apartment waiting for the Trimphone to ring. Quite often, these companies went for niche markets, specialising in one particular type of film. So much so that film buffs of a certain age and girth can nonchalantly flick a fag at the telly during a film about Ida Lupino's cousin buying a horse from Bob Monkhouse and blithely chant 'Ah yes, a typical Incorporated Woking Studios production!' To help you join those fellows' exalted ranks, here's a cut-out-'n'-peep crib sheet to help determine the parentage of any old British independent film, based on its key traits and elements. Happy buffing!

BRITISH INDEPENDENT FILM COMPANIES: A CHEAT'S GUIDE

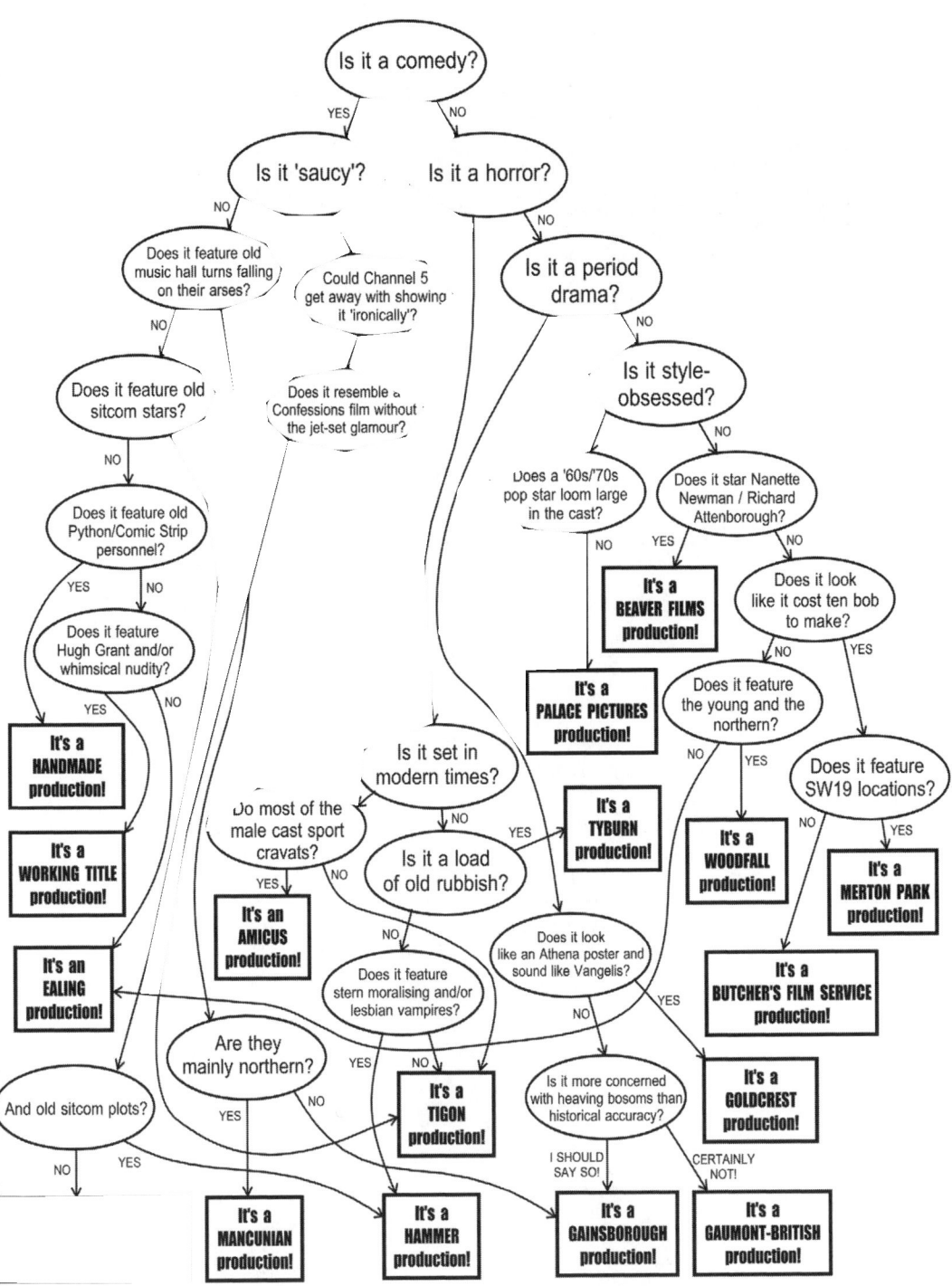

DERYCK GUYLER

DERYCK GUYLER

PLEASINGLY ANNOYED FOR THIRTY YEARS

Deryck Guyler belonged to that cadre of stars, like Madonna, or Cher, or Schnorbitz, who became famous for appearing on screen with one name. As 'Corky', the grumpy and inane police constable in sitcom *Sykes*, Guyler cemented his place in the affections of the nation as a gruff, stubborn and forever frowning character, always on hand to add a dash of pedantry into whatever situation he was placed. In the many, many years prior to his gaining a formidable pension on which he eventually retired to Australia, Guyler had taken part in, and enhanced, a formidable array of films all of which needed someone to come and look irate, but in a nice way.

Filmmakers knew how to capitalise on Guyler's abilities from the very beginning. In his first screen appearance, *A Day to Remember* (1953), he sets up his type good and early as Angry Man In Ferry Queue, a role that he was to play – with various changes of situation – for years to come. From there he went straight into Ralph Thomas' *Mad About Men* (1954) as a suitably irate editor, fulminating in the company of a top class cast including Margaret Rutherford and Irene Handl.

Thereafter it was into that equivalent of a 1960s cinematic celestial conjunction, *It's Trad, Dad!* (1962), alongside what seems like every other British character actor of the period. A happily silly tale of popular singing star of the day *Helen Shapiro* and her fight to convert her small town to the delights of Trad jazz in the teeth of vigorous opposition from suitably stuffed shirts who 'just don't get it', the likes of Arthur Mullard, Hugh Lloyd and Derek Nimmo tussle with the joys of modern rhythm music as represented by *Del Shannon, Gene Vincent, Kenny Ball* and *Terry Lightfoot* (both *avec Jazzmen*). The words 'Daddio' and 'square' are much employed. Deryck himself doesn't appear in vision but instead provides the narration, taking advantage of what Eric Sykes called his 'magnificent voice'. Deep and rumbly, with a tell-tale hint of frustration always trembling on the edge, Guyler's vocal stylings were indeed a definite asset.

Two professions seem to have provided something of a motif for Deryck's career: doctors and policemen. Perhaps it's the austere physical presence, a living embodiment of the teacher in *The Bash Street Kids*, coupled with the fruity vowels, that suggested Establishment to so many (though for the necessary sympathy for his characters on the audience's part, the additional adjective 'twit' was never too far off). Whatever the fiendishly clever motivation, he stepped into the blue serge for *A Hard Day's Night* (1964), *The Big Job* (1965) and *Barry McKenzie Holds His Own* (1974) then behind the stethoscope for *The Fast Lady* (1962), *Nurse On Wheels* (1963) and *Carry On Doctor* (1967) In addition to those come the quasi-authoritarian figures of a park keeper in *No Sex Please, We're British* (1973) and a station master in *Smokescreen* (1964). If there was anyone less suited to the role of authority it was probably Guyler, but it just shows what an imposing voice and stern glasses can do for a man.

Sadly, the sharp downturn in demand for cinematic starched collars and truncheon-wielding cretins in the late 1960s, when society went swinging off into the era of anti-authoritarian class rebellion (or something) meant Deryck's natural constituency dried up a little. His last proper film role was in Disney's *One of Our Dinosaurs Is Missing* (1975), though it was a blink-and-miss effort, and not even in a lab' coat. Thankfully, he'd already found a far more welcoming home on television. In addition to the aforementioned *Sykes*, he gained further notoriety as former Desert Rat and current pain the arse, janitor Norman Potter in *Please, Sir*, a role he recreated in the spin-off film of the same name in 1971.

After that not much was seen of Guyler, although he lived to a ripe age in retirement, where it has to be hoped he spent much time criticising the powers that be Down Under in the vein of Angry Man In Post Office Queue.

189

CHRISTMAS FILMS

Generally speaking, films are not terribly seasonal. Summer blockbusters can be about almost anything and the people who give any real consideration to the time-period of a film are generally the sort who write furious letters about the wrong number of tunic buttons on jumpers in films about Waterloo and similar. The only exceptions to this rule come at Christmas, when suddenly everyone hankers for a bit of idealised tinsel on the screen, probably to take their minds off the bloody awful time they're actually having.

Unfortunately, the successful Christmas film is something of a lost art. *The Santa Clause* (1994) and its increasingly appalling sequels don't really hit the spot, and although *Scrooged* (1998) has an excellent first half hour, it goes seriously wrong towards the end, even managing to subsume the brilliant Bill Murray. Only Robert Mitchum, effortlessly great as the television network president insistent on the advertising potential of cats, escapes with his image actually enhanced. *Scrooged* demonstrates how incredibly hard it is to strike the right balance between homely, whimsical fun and severe, unacceptable schmaltz.

Most original efforts tend to tip into the latter camp, going heavy on the redemption of some old jake who typically has a lifetime of wandering/boozing/exploiting/not washing excused on his return by his long-abandoned family simply because 'it's Christmas'. In *A Hobo's Christmas* (1987) Barnard Hughes shuns his regular trampish company (played by William Hickey, the actor most likely to have seen millennium celebrations first time round) in order to rediscover some family he couldn't be fagged paying any attention to for twenty years. It all turns out well with the old codger welcomed back into the bosom of the family, presumably after washing. Well, it's Christmas, after all.

Another schmaltz-ridden effort, *One Magic Christmas* (1985) made by Disney (who else?), focuses on the quivery-voiced Mary Steenbergen being reawakened to 'the true spirit of Christmas' by an angel called Gideon, played by the distinctly non-angelic looking Harry Dean Stanton. A supreme example of miscasting, Stanton looks as if he's actually the Angel of Death, just covering for the cuddly angel who had a cold and couldn't make it.

Next up, and trying to corner the market in Christmas repeats in a ploy as cynical as it is hopeless, comes the Salkind brothers' abysmal *Santa Claus: the Movie* (1985). As charmless as it could possibly be, this godawful parade of relentlessly jolly old toot is an embarrassment to everyone who took part in it. It's doubly painful for involving Dudley Moore, neck deep in his desperate 'will work for food' late period. It has no redeeming features other than, possibly, John Lithgow's eye-rolling turn as the toy-making baddie. Lithgow must have taken one look at what was going on around him and realised the only way to get anything more than a 'don't call us' card from every studio in town was to ham it up atrociously. Everyone watching ought to be grateful for something to at least divert their eyes from the horrors elsewhere. It's a film that makes *Santa Claus Conquers the Martians* (1964) seem Dickensian by comparison.

CHRISTMAS FILMS

As a result of all this tat, most thinking people tend towards more traditional stories for their Christmas fayre, and that normally means an adaptation of *A Christmas Carol*. At Yuletide telly companies indulge the middle classes in this little peccadillo and provide one or other of the canon for their sherry-sipping pleasure, but the hairs on the Pringles can stand on end if the wrong one is trotted out. The best one is the Alistair Sim one. Directed by Brian Desmond Hurst, *Scrooge* (1951) is quite superb. A film can truly be said to be brilliant when it replaces the original text as the source of future adaptations, and this has done just that. Sim is the living embodiment of the Phiz cartoons that adorned the Dickens book on its release. Every one of the tableaux recreated, from the stock exchange with its well-stuffed denizen Peter Bull, to the filthy hawker's shop presided over by Miles Malleson in fantastically odious form, is magnificent. The whole is as close to perfect as it is possible to get; each following production works in its shadow, but they try and try again.

Scrooge (1970), with Albert Finney, adds songs and a certain amount of dance to the mix, but Bert wasn't really up to it then. Rex Harrison, who turned it down, would have been much better, if only because it would have been so much easier to imagine him as a miserable old bastard. Nowadays, Bert would be fantastic, but this one remains a bit of a pale imitation of its illustrious predecessor. Nearer the mark is *A Christmas Carol* (1984) with George C Scott as Ebenezer. Scott manages to make the switch between nasty git and bumptious old geezer especially well, and comes second to Sim in the Scrooge stakes on the basis of that. The rest of the cast is excellent too, particularly the magnificent Edward Woodward (always underrated despite being one of the best film actors of all time) as the Ghost of Christmas Past. No chuckling jolly simpleton this ghost, Woodward's version looks as likely to beat Scrooge to death with a turkey leg for being a sod as to offer him a chance at salvation. Given half a chance he looks more likely to kick tiny Tim's crutch away and tell him to bloody well get on with it and stop moaning. It's a performance to relish.

There have been dozens of other versions, including one starring Reginald Owen. The Bloody Reginald Owen one, as it's most often referred to, doesn't really benefit from the presence of the eventual Admiral Boom as the title character. Reg seemingly couldn't do much more than he did as that nautical character in *Mary Poppins* (1964), so when he plays Scrooge in *A Christmas Carol* (1938) he goes from incredibly shouty bad man to incredibly shouty good man without any visible metamorphosis, and it takes the presence of snow and jingly music in the foreground to apprise the viewer of any significant change. This is the version screened when the world has been very, very bad all year. *The Muppet Christmas Carol* (1992), meanwhile, is so excellent even Michael Caine fails to put a downer on it. Caine actually manages to get Scrooge's character across extremely well, and when he joins in the big finale number at the end it proves to be a welcome addition, unlike Finney's warblings at the end of his outing. The Muppets of course are brilliant and really, after Sim, this is as good as it gets Scrooge-wise.

Not all Christmas films revolve around Dickens and alkies. The most famous and well regarded of the non-traditional stories is *It's A Wonderful Life* (1946). Hugely popular now, this almost finished off director Frank Capra's career since at the time not many people cared for a tale of suicidal despair and financial ruin. They could get that, as the old saying goes, at home. But a mixture of nostalgia for 'I Like Ike'-era smalltown America, mixed with a copyright mistake that allowed it to be shown on an eternal loop on US cable telly, meant the masses were battered into submission, and it has become well loved. It deserves the accolade. *It's A Wonderful Life* is a quite brilliant film that demonstrates perfectly how to tread the high wire of sentimentality. James Stewart as George Bailey Jr is far from what you might call a nice guy. Like Patrick Duffy in *Dallas* he has his hands on a fine set of Principles, but manages to cover all that with a pleasing layer of self-obsession. George doesn't want to be in Bedford Falls at all and by Jove, he makes sure everyone knows it. While everyone else with a brain and a feeling heart would realise that his daft uncle didn't lose that plot-revolving $8 000, George can't help but go off on one and call the old duffer for all he can think of. Then, when faced with ruin, does George stand up and take it on the chin? He certainly does not. He goes off into the night crying like a big girl resolved to take the coward's way out.

In short, George is human and not a bit like some contrived movie character that would pull himself together and go to pieces like a man. At the first sign of trouble his granite chin begins to quiver and he snaps at his kids who are, to be fair, bloody annoying. So when something good finally happens to George, no less a thing than divine intervention, it happens not to an idealised version of what a person should be but more what most people actually are: a bit weak, a bit hopeless and a bit useless. This is the basis of the film's appeal. What also sets it apart is the fact that when the schmaltz comes, and it comes in an Irwin Allen-scale tidal wave, right at the very last available moment. The first rumblings are heard amongst the words, 'Zuzu's petals!' and it builds from there until the last words of the film, 'Attaboy Clarence!' If by this point you are not in a blubbering mess on the floor then you must be dead and should be heading for the light rather than watching pictures.

The next most famous 'Made in USA' Christmas treat is *Miracle On 34th Street* (1947) which, for the time it was made, took cutesy-poo shtick to dangerous new places. Based on the premise that Kris Kringle, played by cosy Edmund Gwenn, is the real Santa Claus and not just some department store schnook, it promises to be a proper festival carnival of a treat but falls at the final fence. A bizarre and completely illogical court case fills it out to no great effect. However, people seem to enjoy it, most likely because it makes it appear that anyone could beat a rap in court by presenting a load of letters addressed to someone else that no one has even bothered to open, which is indeed a comforting thought.

THE TEN BEST YEARS FOR CHRISTMAS DAY FILMS ON BRITISH TV

1971: *AROUND THE WORLD IN 80 DAYS* (ITV)
David Niven canters elegantly around the globe in the company of every famous person ever. Good from the excellent animated stop-watch-with-legs titles to the final Reform Club harrumph.

1974: *THOSE MAGNIFICENT MEN IN THEIR FLYING MACHINES* (ITV)
Ludicrous spectacle, great fun and the best excuse to get Willie Rushton, Eric Sykes and Terry-Thomas on screen at Christmas yet devised.

1975: *THE WIZARD OF OZ, BUTCH CASSIDY AND THE SUNDANCE KID* (BBC One)
The former remains the undefeated champion in the family film stakes, with the latter ensuring that Mums get to sigh over Redford and Newman, and Dads get to chortle over horseshit.

1979: *GOLDFINGER, THE THREE MUSKETEERS* (ITV)
In the days before Bond was desperately tired, Sean Connery on Christmas Day was a sure-fire winner. The follow-on of Michael York, Oliver Reed and, more importantly, Roy Kinnear ensured those York Fruits went down in good company.

1979: *THE GNOME MOBILE, THE STING* (BBC One)
Pleasingly daft Disney live action caper with Walter Brennan and those kids from Mary Poppins. Then every Dad's favourite film - official - with Redford and Newman fast becoming the Morecambe and Wise of the Christmas film world.

1983: *SUPERMAN, THE REVENGE OF THE PINK PANTHER* (ITV)
Excellent pap for the big day. Thrills and spills in the original Reeve/Brando/Hackman comic book edition followed by child-friendly fart with Peter Sellers at his Franglais best.

1984: *MARY POPPINS, SOME LIKE IT HOT* (BBC One)
Perfect family film followed by perfect comedy film. What more is there to say?

1989: *CROCODILE DUNDEE, CLOCKWISE* (BBC One)
Not seasonal, but nicely silly and inoffensive in the first instance, then superb home grown roustabout nonsense with John Cleese in that rarest of birds on a Christmas Day, a British film.

1992: *INDIANA JONES AND THE LAST CRUSADE, SHIRLEY VALENTINE* (BBC One)
Last entry in the world's most successful B-movie trilogy has Sean Connery joining Harrison Ford to ensure even the Queen would have set the video. Then massively, and rightly, successful feel-good, life-affirming fantasy with Pauline Collins talking Turkish in Greece, making every Mum in the land forget what a crap day she's just had.

1994: *MARY POPPINS, SLEEPING BEAUTY* (ITV)
Another throw for Julie and another Disney entry so festive it practically sparkles. What else would anyone have wanted to be doing other than watching these films on the telly?

MARGARET RUTHERFORD

ALL DOTTY ROLES CONSIDERED – OWN BICYCLE

Interesting family, Margaret Rutherford's. In her own words, 'Cousin Tony [Benn] would have made a fine actor but he chose to join the Labour Party instead'. Rather less happily, the young Margaret finding out about her dad – convicted of the murder of his father, found criminally insane and incarcerated in Broadmoor – was the seed for the slightly melancholy air that hung round the gallery of outspoken but often lonely eccentrics she played on stage and screen.

A second-to-none stage career grew out of her first speaking part at the Old Vic Theatre School: Fairy with Long Nose in *Harlequin Jack Horner and the Enchanted Pie*. First on screen, however, was a part in *Dusty Ermine* (1936), as a gangster's moll in her mid-forties, beating a detective over the head with a lead-filled umbrella. When it came to marking out her cinematic territory, Margs didn't hang about.

She was by all accounts a natural on screen – un-selfconscious, with excellent diction and a rapidly growing range of facial tics for those all-important reaction shots. In *The Demi-Paradise* (1943) Laurence Olivier told her 'I've been in films for four years now, and I'm just getting the knack'. Rutherford, though, was born with it. *The Yellow Canary* (1943) saw her unafraid to improvise during a shot, aiming a convincingly violent kick at the ankles of a Nazi officer.

The stage, still her main career, crossed over with the big screen version of *Blithe Spirit* (1945), giving millions the chance to see Rutherford's peerless take on the ethereally batty medium Madame Arcati, replete with chatty parrot and cucumber sandwiches 'to keep up my ectoplasmic strength'. Every bit as great, in a less orchestrated way, was her girls' school headmistress battling with Alistair Sim's boys in finely wrought 'when schools collide' comedy *The Happiest Days of Your Life* (1950).

Rutherford nursed fishy old Glynis Johns in the much-copied modern mermaid frolic *Miranda* (1948), eschewing the offer of a stunt double when duty called and plunging fully-clothed into a lake. Bizarrely, prudish US censors had a problem with the unmarried Johns revealing her tail (manufactured by Dunlop) to the camera. 'It's a wonder they didn't make her wear bloomers', pondered Margs.

Then came another stage-screen crossover, with the celebrated film of *The Importance of Being Ernest* (1952), playing Miss Prism to Edith Evans' iconic Lady Bracknell, and not coming off too badly in the process, 'handbaaaaaaag' notwithstanding. *Innocents in Paris* (1953) allowed her to flex her contractual muscles, with the first insertion of a clause, to be repeated anon until her final films, that husband Stringer Davis also be found a part. Thus, installed down the cast list, he could then join her on the French location for a canny second honeymoon.

A string of eccentric turns supporting comics of the day, including Frankie Howerd in *The Runaway Bus* (1954) and Norman Wisdom in a couple of his drab efforts, saw her move into the phase of her career lesser actors would call 'parody yourself and think of the money', but Rutherford never gave less than the whole Dame. Whether as a dotty old dear who inherits a brothel and gin palace in *Aunt Clara* (1954) or a dotty old dear who owns a pet shop and can talk to animals by breathing up their noses in *An Alligator Named Daisy* (1955), there was no on-screen hint she was sleepwalking through the role, even if she was.

Then came the big time, as she overcame her aversion to crime subjects by taking on Miss Marple in the Agatha Christie adaptation *Murder She Said* (1951). This initiated a string of films in which she won over the books' initially sceptical author. 'Gusto' was the watchword for her performances as never before. Admittedly, she wasn't actually riding that horse in *Murder at the Gallop* (1963), but that is her indulging in some spirited swordplay in *Murder Ahoy* (1964). During the series run, Rutherford became Britain's highest-paid actress. Rutherford was also an essential part of the trio of decrepit fleapit staff in peerless Basil Dearden comedy *The Smallest Show on Earth* (1957) as the mad box-office woman to Peter Sellers' projectionist. She deputised as the Duchess of Grand Fenwick in the underrated space-bound sequel *The Mouse on the Moon* (1963), nailing the air of ditzy olde worlde authority bang on, and hobnobbing gleefully with invited astronauts at the film's Cape Canaveral premiere.

Any or all of these parts could have commanded an award, but she had to wait for being the best thing by far in turgid Burton–Taylor airport lounge drama *The VIPs* (1963), as the pill-popping Duchess of Brighton ('I'm flying already!') before the Academy honoured her. Thenceforth, a new wave of respectability was afforded her by Hollywood. There was nothing like a Dame for Charles 'Charlie' Chaplin, who cast her as a bed-ridden loon surrounded by stuffed animals in turgid misfire *A Countess from Hong Kong* (1967), or Orson Welles, graciously giving her name-above-title billing in his rather better Shakespeare reimagining *Chimes at Midnight* (1965).

While filming the Terry-Thomas farce *Arabella* (1967) in Italy, she slipped and broke her hip in the hotel; this was the first of a series of falls that tragically put paid to any more acting roles. The best the stick-bound Dame could muster after that was a voice-over in less-than-enthralling cartoon saga *The Wacky World of Mother Goose* (1967) – an ignominious full-stop on any CV, but positively tragic on one as lustrous as hers. Still, the phrase 'a good innings' was never more apt than here, and as lifelong friend Robert Morley observed, 'She was for a long time the safest box-office bet in the business, and she knew it, the dear old bird'.

THE ESSENTIAL SWINGING 'SIXTIES FILM

SMASHING TIME (1967)

Towards the end of the 1960s, many films took it upon themselves to pastiche, satirise or otherwise put the boot into the increasingly self-absorbed remnants of London's 'swinging' culture, but none did it with as much panache, cheek and messy abandon as *Smashing Time*. Scripted by monocular jazz surrealist George Melly while he was writing *Revolt Into Style*, his definitive look at the 'selling out' of pop culture, it takes many of the sharp insights of that book, wraps them up in a pleasingly corny 'Northern girls come good' fairy-tale, and adds a liberal dollop of pie-based slapstick.

Tall, flame-haired, trend-obsessed Yvonne (Lynne Redgrave) and mousy, pragmatic Brenda (Rita Tushingham) arrive on the train from Oop North, desperate to grab a piece of the swinging world of pop, glamour and 'six foot circular beds with black sheets' which Yvonne has read avidly about in *MiniTrends* magazine. Promptly getting their money nicked, they find themselves unable to pay for bread-'n'-scrape in Arthur Mullard's greasy spoon, so Brenda is left to wash up while Yvonne capers blithely through Carnaby Street, singing a delightfully tuneless ode to the pop epicentre ('*Carnaby Street!/Carnaby Street!/ Carnaby-arnaby-Carnaby Street!*') whereupon she's promptly chatted up by moustachioed fashion photographer Michael York – and so begins the girls' string of random associations with the hip and happening.

York sets Yvonne up via an *Evening Standard* fashion shoot, mocking her provincial gaucheness as 'The Girl Who got it Wrong'. Brenda embroils the cafe's patrons (including *Corrie*'s Eddie Yates) in a sauce/paint/liquid manure fight. Bonzos-affiliated artist 'Professor' Bruce Lacey appears as a mad sculptor exhibiting skeletal robots designed to destroy all their owners' other *objets d'art* ('The end of civilization in your sixty-foot, L-shaped drawing room!'). Irene Handl is the youth-mistrusting owner of an antique fur shop ('Come in 'ere, them young Mods, asking for animal paws, then while yer back's turned a nice bit o'skunk vanishes up their knickers!'). Lascivious toff Ian Carmichael picks up Yvonne in a nightclub and takes her back to his plush bachelor pad with nookie in mind, to her consternation ('Going the whole way is really square and out of touch. Besides, I never 'ave.'). Anna Quayle employs Brenda in her boutique, Too Much (which uses a hearse as delivery van), only to sack her after she treats the place as a proper shop rather than a hip hang-out ('She made us all buy something before we parked our botties!').

Finally luck comes their way as their Grudge Street lodgings are demolished in the name of *Candid Camera*-like TV programme *You Can't Help Laughing*, presented by Peter Jones as a patronising, oleaginous hybrid of Bob Monkhouse, Hughie Green and David Frost ('He's got a lovely speaking voice you know, and he sounds very nice when he isn't pretending to be common!'). The girls get 10 000 pounds for their trouble, and immediately invest it in getting famous. Under York's wing, Brenda becomes a model and the face of Direct Action perfume, posing in a cynical TV ad intercut with riot footage. Yvonne is marketed by pop impresario Jeremy '*Allo Allo*' Lloyd as a sub-Lulu singer ('Psychedelic, but not turned on. Friendly, unspoilt... and a virgin') with wall-of-sound-backed hit *I'm Still So Young* ('I can't sing, but I'm young/Can't do a thing, but I'm young/I'm a fool/But I'm cool...'). Now mutual enemies, the girls live the high life of 'pacy' split-level apartments, doorstep deliveries of Johnnie Walker and meeting the Bishop of Runcorn. Eventually things come to a head in a party at the top of the Post Office Tower ('the scene with the built-in trip!'), when Brenda sets the controls from 'slow' to 'very fast', and blows the whole town's circuits, before the pair make up and head back Northwards.

Redgrave and La Tush are, quite simply, made for their roles. Awed by the in-crowd, but still able to fight back with volleys of ultrasonically high-pitched, 100 mph banter when the occasion demands, they're more rounded victim-heroes than you'll find in many a more serious 'London's a bit of a bummer' drama. They are simultaneously naive and more clued-up than their southern hosts, as is the script, using the timeless devices of saucy put-downs and all-out slapstick to deflate the scene's self-regarding pomposity. While the cafe patrons heartily join in with the messy mayhem, the uptight clientele of Sweeney Todd's Eating House (a dessert-only version of an East End pie shop, with the waitresses dressed as Victorian strumpets) can only stand rigid, trying deperately to look cool as a volley of flans hits their solemn fizzogs. It's the sight and sound of the real spirit of the 1960s – the unabashed, classless, energetic spirit – triumphing over the self-conscious, snobbish and conservative clique it had become by the decade's end. And all with the skillful facial deployment of a large gooseberry syllabub tart. What a fabulous, knockout scene!

FOUR FAB FICTIONAL BANDS

THE PUDDLIANS

During his peripatetic paranoid wanders as *The President's Analyst* (1967), James Coburn bumped into a quartet of loveable, wisecracking, drug-addled Scouse moptops ('Blue ice cubes? How degenerate!') who, naturally, turn out to be Canadian secret servicemen in disguise.

TOOMORROW

In the 1970 film of the same name, Roy Dotrice is a centuries-old alien stranded on earth who seeks out the titular band of art students, headed by Olivia Newton-John, in their Chelsea squat, for the crazy new brand of amplifier they've invented, which could - somehow - save the universe. Sci-fi hippyness alternates with earthbound student politics in a very 1970s way, punctuated by songs such as *Happiness Valley* and *Spaceport*.

BILLY BEETHOVEN

Rock band in daffy 'musical Carry On' *Three for All* (1974), comprising *Rainbow*'s Graham Bonnet, Robert Lindsay, Paul Nicholas and Christopher *'Adventures of a Private Eye'* Neil and managed by one Jet Bone (Richard Beckinsale). The band tour the Costa Del Sol, followed by girlfriends of three of them (including Adrienne Posta) and the mother of the other (Diana Dors), who meet up with the usual assortment of Brit character actors while The *Beethoven* belt out numbers such as *Don't Drink the Water*.

THE FABULOUS STAINS

'We don't put out!' In *Ladies and Gentlemen, the Fabulous Stains* (1981), Diane Lane gets bored touring with identikit pop band *The Looters* (backed by Ray Winstone, Paul Simonon and the quiet half of *The Sex Pistols*), and enlists her cousins (including Laura Dern) to form the eponymous riot grrrl trio, who go from lo-fi success to commercialised sell-out stardom in a grainy tale which sits squarely in the rather broad middle ground somewhere between *This is Spinal Tap*, *Jubilee* and the Children's Film Foundation's *Pop Pirates*.

LYNN REDGRAVE

THE GIRL WHO GOT IT WRONG

Despite being a fully paid-up member of what's still the number one acting dynasty in the British Isles, Lynn Redgrave, tall, red-haired, angular and, in her own words, initially a 'horrible ugly bulk' on screen, was destined to play cinema's misfits and oddballs.

A brief tavern role in *Tom Jones* (1963) led to her first pairing with Rita Tushingham in the Edna O'Brien adaptation *Girl with Green Eyes* (1964), playing the vivaciously chatty best chum of Tush's sensitive girl in love with an ageing Peter Finch. The gawky-yet-lively role fitted Lynn like a slightly laddered elbow-length silk glove, and after big sis Vanessa pulled out at the last minute, Columbia cast her in her name-making role, the eponymous 'lost puppy' in *Georgy Girl* (1966).

Georgy Girl is many things – swinging parable, valuable visual record of the King's Road and Maida Vale in the mid-1960s and important reminder of title song lyricist Jim 'Carry On' Dale's musical acumen – but best of all it serves as deft comparison between old-school class snobbery (caddish toff James Mason assuming that Lynn, his butler's daughter, is there for the taking) and that of the emergent 'beautiful people', as personified by Charlotte Rampling, Lynn's icily cool but emotionally immature flatmate. Thanks to a quality Peter Nichols script, Georgy's inevitable emergence as the 'better person' of the trio comes as a brave slap in the face for the superficial prejudices of the time, and not the treacly 'just be yourself' homily it could easily have become. Nearly $14 million grossed worldwide was the result, and Lynn just missed out on an Oscar that year, as did Vanessa for *Morgan*.

Could such early success lead to gawkily vivacious typecasting? A small role as a virgin in a play-within-a-film in the James Mason spy flick *A Deadly Affair* (1966), followed by that magisterial variation on the Tush pairing of …*Green Eyes* in *Smashing Time* (1967), seemed to point to 'yes', great though the latter was. Equally virginal was a role she was literally born to play – Rachel Kempson's daughter – being fought over by Private Hywel Bennett and Sergeant Nigel Davenport in Malay war saucecom *The Virgin Soldiers* (1969). The frankly odd Tennessee Williams adaptation *Last of the Mobile Hotshots* (1969) had Redgrave again involved with an ageing aristo (this time James Coburn in a wedding dress). The roles were becoming as claustrophobic as that film's steamy Mississippi mansion.

As usual, it was comedy to the rescue. *Every Little Crook and Nanny* (1972) may be as riotous as its title, but Redgrave stood out as the feisty etiquette school marm who kidnaps mob boss Victor Mature's son. Rather funnier was her chastity belt-clad cameo in the Danny Kaye pastiche segment of Woody Allen's *Everything You Always Wanted to Know About Sex* (1972). Slightly loftier of brow was the film of Peter Nichols' state-of-the-hospitals satire *The National Health* (1973).

The brow came crashing down with *The Happy Hooker* (1975), the fictionalised (and ruthlessly sanitised) true story of a Dutch immigrant's rise to the position of New York's premier brothel madam. Whatever traces of comic gold lay in that less than tantalising premise were not struck here, although the sight of Lynn pedalling frantically between clients on a bicycle has a certain semi-innocent charm.

Wider seams of laughter were around the corner, thankfully, strip-mined by pre-*Airplane!* disaster spoof *The Big Bus* (1976). As one of the stereotyped passengers on the ill-fated inaugural voyage of the titular New York–Denver nuclear-powered coach, she has as much of a whale of a time with her role as nymphomaniac, phallus-obsessed fashion designer as the rest of the cast. It may lack *Airplane!*'s snappy surrealism, but the forced atmosphere of *Airport*-style hysterical gravitas is played pitch perfect.

Both TV and the stage occupied Lynn's career for a good while after that – save questionable titles such as *Disco Beaver from Outer Space* (1978) – until a recent resurgence in well-received stuff such as *Peter Pan* (2003). However, the characters of her early years, the walking masses of contradictions – statuesque but shy, awkward yet fiery, virginal yet saucy – are a fine legacy in themselves.

GLAMFLIXX!

British pop in the early 1970s is a tale of two brothers. There's the older, more studious, kid - let's call him Prog - holed up in a josstick haze, donning 'cans', owlishly perusing fantastic artwork and dreaming of elven hordes, robot armadillos and spaceships powered by song. Then there's his grotty, snotty little brother, can of Top Deck in one hand and ticket to the Roxy in the other, grabbing his donkey jacket on the way out of the house for a raucous evening of stomping boots, easy birds and pints that think they're quarts.

Though they share the same bedroom, they're worlds apart: one grapples with elaborate time signatures, the other with nothing more high-falutin' than his own belt loops. Who'd have thought, then, that it would be the little bro' – Glam, of course – who'd make the greater impression on celluloid? This was indeed so, as the early 1970s played host to the short but coruscating heyday of the glam rock feature.

What appeals nowadays, when one of these extinct creatures is briefly resurrected for a wet Sunday afternoon on regional telly, is the yawning chasm between what glam sought to represent: rocket-powered, dynamic future-pop performed by beautiful, star-spangled creatures the like of which the Earth had never seen, and the cash-strapped reality: four ex-roofing contractors from Netherton in Satinex jumpsuits sweating through umpteen reverb-saturated variations on *Johnny B Goode*.

To be fair to the lads, there was always a big element of self-awareness to the glam scene. While *T Rex* regarded themselves with *Panorama* seriousness, the likes of *Mud* and *Slade* were as down-to-Earth as late-period *Skylab*, larking through their careers with a carefree 'We're only here for the leer' swagger. Such characters were never going to write *Tommy*-style rock operas. The unapologetic lack of ambition of most of the glam showcase films adds even more to their tarnished charm, with a glorious, in-for-a-penny grimace looming out from the often po-faced annals of rock-related cinema, while putting the 'fist' into 'sophistication'. Long may they rock on.

BORN TO BOOGIE (1972)

Although glam is normally only associated with the word 'Fab' in ice-lolly terms, it owes its cinematic existence, at least in part, to *The Beatles*. Marc Bolan's valedictory showcase kick-started the glam film bandwagon, and it has the mop-top stamp all over it. It's an Apple Corp. production, directed and produced by Ringo, with the original pop pixie doing numbers, looking pseudo-mystical and generally arsing about in the grounds of John Lennon's mansion, joined by a worryingly hirsute Ringo, Elton John and Geoffrey 'Catweazle' Bayldon for a number of shambolically vague *Magical Mystery Tour*-type sketches. This ethereal element didn't, as we shall see, translate to the rest of the genre.

GLAMFLIXX!

TAKE ME HIGH (1973)
Cliff Richard moved his film career on from the days of Una Stubbs and *Summer Holiday* with this wondrously frothy confection, which went all the way back to the 'hey, let the kids groove' ethos of the old 1950s rock 'n' roll films, by way of a promotional puff for a freshly Bull Ringed-up Birmingham. Cliff plays narrow boat-dwelling fast-food entrepreneur Tim Matthews, who invents the Brumburger, markets it to tremendous success (and the chagrin of staunch socialist George Cole), sings a song about it and then, for reasons best known to himself, gets into a mini-hovercraft chase on the Gas Street canals, before triumphing over staid old Britain with his youthful winning ways. It is, you may have guessed, fantastic.

THAT'LL BE THE DAY (1973)
It's not really a glam film, since *That'll* is set in the 1950s, but it does come from David Puttnam's Goodtimes Enterprises, who did plenty of good work in this field, and there's another cameo from Ringo Starr, as dodgem car attendant and mentor to David Essex's wannabe rock star. There's also Billy Fury as Stormy Tempest, Keith Moon as, er... Keith Moon, Robert Lindsay, Vivian Stanshall and Karl Howman among the names to look for, all set against a bleak Isle of Wight landscape, with woodbines and squalid caravan sex adding to the Byrite-budget grimness.

STARDUST (1974)
The Essex saga continued into the early 1960s, with Dave now the lead in *The Stray Cats*, a Beatlesesque band on the way up - namely Paul 'Kneetremble Johnny' Nicholas, Dave Edmunds, Karl Howman on keyboards and Keith Moon, again, on drums. This time Adam Faith is the suave manager/older brother type, and the 'romping' takes place in a proper hotel room, although, winningly, the tabloids of the time abounded with tales of David refusing to take his kecks off during filming. Elsewhere Larry Hagman fights for screen time with Marty Wilde, Peter Duncan and Michael Elphick, and one of the main 'themes' of these films – that the music industry's a right bugger – is laid out in no uncertain terms.

REMEMBER ME THIS WAY (1974)
The first film made by GTO records, under the aegis of one Ron Inkpen, who would produce a couple of real stormers before the genre fizzled out. This, however, wasn't one of them, being part live concert footage of Gary Glitter at the Rainbow Theatre, part half-arsed backstage 'portrait of the artist' vanity cobblers, and part Netto version of *The Beatles'* 'Help', with its perfunctory plot about a mysterious far-right group out to assassinate Mr Do You Wanna Touch Me. Never has a film's title accumulated so much sad irony.

FLAME (1975)
Slade were the Daddies of the glam scene (just as *Mud* were the HP), so it's only fitting that their sole cinematic foray lords it over the rest. Noddy and the boys work their way up from the pubs (as Iron Rod) to fame as the titular *Flame*, under the wing of cynical plugger Tom Conti. As with *Take Me High*, the Midlands provide the backdrop, though this being another Goodtimes production, it's far from tourist board fodder. Yep, it's all seedy stuff

under the foil-toppered surface, as their crooked former manager sends the boys round to sort Conti out. Tensions flare and the lads object to their cynical commoditisation ('I'm not a bloody fish finger!') and crazed Sladettes smash up a venue as a helpless Emperor Rosko looks on. But there's a nice line in sarky dialogue, comedy aplenty with Dave Hill and Don Powell buying a new car, the band's trademark 'Hair by Robert Dyas' anti-glamour, and Tommy Vance as one Ricky Storm. Plus there's *Slade*'s best ever song – fact – 'How Does It Feel', on a bulging soundtrack. Perfect, innit?

SIDE BY SIDE (1975)
Not to be outdone, the GTO label turned out this classic old school rock film, in which the young(er) Cliff Richard or Acker Bilk wouldn't look out of place. It's a no-nonsense tale of two rival club owners, old fashioned Terry-Thomas and slightly more turned-on Billy Boyle. The latter enlists Barry Humphries (with hideous greasy Richard III hair) to book some glam acts for his venue, among them *Hello*, *Stephanie de Sykes* and the immortal *Fox*, whose performance of 'Imagine Me, Imagine You' (shame it wasn't 'S-S-S-Single Bed') is the undoubted highlight.

NEVER TOO YOUNG TO ROCK (1975)
The third entry in the glam film's *annus mirrorballis* was this delirious GTO/Inkpen sci-fi oddity with a plot premise to make *Side by Side* look like *Crime and Punishment*. In a hazily defined near future, with pop music outlawed, Peter 'Dennis off *Please Sir!*' Denyer converts an ice cream van into a 'group detector van', enlists curmudgeonly old silver band fan Mr Rockbottom (Freddie Jones) to drive it and generally grumble, and goes out into the British countryside to, er… find some bands. What he comes up with is *Mud* starting a food fight in Sheila Steafel's transport cafe, Bob Kerr's *Whoopee Band* arsing about in an old house, the *Rubettes* doing 'Sugar Baby Love' on the back of a lorry, and best of all, a pre-*Tiswas* Sally James. While not holding a candle to *Flame*'s magisterial closing rendition of 'Far, Far Away', the final song's a belter, too – an ensemble performance in a knackered ballroom of the specially written anthem which neatly sums up the determinedly inoffensive ethos of the GTO films in six and a half words - 'Bless My Soul, It's Rock 'n' Roll'.

CONFESSIONS OF A POP PERFORMER (1975)
Not much happened in the cinema after glam's miracle year. Marc Bolan went into telly, David Bowie became a 'Proper Actor' (kind of), and the only film that sneaked in under the wire before Bill Grundy momentously decided to have an extra scotch before work was this second entry in the moneyspinning Askwith backside showcase, boasting Jill Gascoigne, that sainted pretend band, the 'mean as Jack the Ripper' *Kipper* ('I fink the ol' joanna comes in 'ere!') and brick-subtle *Opportunity Knocks* parody Star Knockers. But the very existence of this breastspotting pastiche spelt the end of the glam film, if not (quite) glam itself, as disco films moved in to seduce the SRB-gulping public. But that's another story.

MINIATURE HEROES

Filling the gaps between 'proper' films in the most delightful ways.

BRITISH TRANSPORT FILMS

Growing out of railway nationalisation, this purveyor of short road and rail documentaries showed more creativity than you might at first think. John Betjeman, John Schlesinger and Michael Redgrave lent their talents to such mesmeric wonders as *I Am a Litter Basket*, *Let's Go to Birmingham* and melodic inter-city paean *Overture One-Two-Five*. Slightly more prosaic were the likes of *Southampton into the Seventies* and *The Channel Tunnel Project 1973-1975* and, at the bottom of the lyrical league table, *Mechanical Rail Creep Adjuster*. Perhaps the most vividly recalled film, however, was the decidedly unlovely *Robbie*, the notorious tale of a foolhardy young boy faffing about on a railway line, and getting his feet gruesomely removed for his trouble. *Robbie* toured school halls up and down the land, with a stern BR representative holding a Q&A afterwards. 'He won't be playing football again!'

SPEECHLESS WHIMSY

The 1960s heralded a renaissance in British silent – or at least, largely dialogue-free – comedy shorts. Eric Sykes was to make the genre his own with *The Plank* (1967) *et al.*, but Dormar Productions got there first with snug ensemble building site whimsy *A Home of Your Own* (1964), starring stonemason Bernard Cribbins and cement mixer Ronnie Barker among many others, and French holiday Tati homage *San Ferry Ann* (1965). A more swinging slice of slapstick came when Judy Huxtable sought two-wheeled love in groovy Hampstead in *Les Bicyclettes de Belsize* (1968), to an Englebert Humperdinck soundtrack.

BUTCHER'S FILMS

Butcher's Film Service grew from a nineteenth century magic lantern manufacturer into one of the most prolific producers of short, 'quota quickie' programme fillers. *Paul Temple* crime dramas alternated with *International Circus Review* and music hall vehicles for Frank Randle, George Formby, Billy Cotton and the like. Most famously, there were the no-nonsense, no-frills, no-money filler thrillers of the 1950s and 1960s that can still be found lurking in the small hours on television today. Often derided for their shoddiness, they nevertheless helped a good many nascent talents get a foothold both in front of and behind the camera, in particular providing straight acting roles for the unlikely likes of Frank Muir, Peter Glaze and Jackie Collins.

PETE SMITH SPECIALTIES

Chirpy New Yorker Pete Smith produced and narrated over a hundred and ten minute slices of 'infotainment' during the 1940s and 1950s, blending stock footage of people doing the Lindy Hop on top of a flagpole with slapstick scenes of blokes in hats accidentally sitting on light bulbs, all held together with his trademark gee-whiz patter. ('Ouch! That's gotta hurt! Well, g'bye now!') See also the *Joe McDoakes* series of mock instructional films starring George 'George Jetson' O'Hanlon as the titular hapless everyman.

GEOFFREY BAYLDON

GEOFFREY BAYLDON

THE CRAZY OLD DUFFER'S CRAZY OLD DUFFER

Another of the elite cadre of British character players for whom the word 'ubiquitous' is perhaps the most extreme understatement since Neville Chamberlain eventually confessed that he found Hitler a bit on the rum side, Geoffrey Bayldon, has appeared in every capacity from top of the bill star to blink-and-you'll-miss-him bit parter. In *Tales From the Crypt* (1972) for example, Bayldon is splendid as the Crypt Keeper, linking together the segments of that excellent portmanteau with the air of creepy shabbiness that he has been perfecting since his first appearance in *The Stranger Left No Card* (1952). Yet he is as likely to be seen in a fleeting glimpse as, for example, the wireless operator in *A Night to Remember* (1958) .

However, Bayldon is no one-trick faintly disturbing fairground carousel pony. For every distinctly creepy horror such as *Frankenstein Must Be Destroyed* (1969), there are a clutch of comedies such as *Steptoe and Son Ride Again* (1973) or *Porridge* (1979), a gaggle of period dramas along the lines of *Becket* (1964) or *55 Days at Peking* (1963) or even bizarrely miscellaneous ephemera such as non-Sellers Franglais odyssey *Inspector Clouseau* (1968), diabolical HandMade low ebb *Bullshot* (1983) or the frankly stupid self-indulgent cobblers *Gawain and the Green Knight* (1973).

Horror is what Geoffrey became synonymous with though, probably because of the likes of *Asylum* (1972) and other choice portmanteau from the segmented shocker masters Amicus, who were also responsible for the aforementioned *Tales From the Crypt* as well as *The House That Dripped Blood* (1970) and their last gasp venture, *The Monster Club* (1980). Bayldon's skill is to mix his olde worlde courtesy with a clipped pronunciation that makes John Gielgud sound like Bobcat Goldthwaite, then use that to lure in the viewer to a true sense of security before the big reveal that all is not as it seems. The very best type of antique period horror works on the reversals that come from the audience being trapped in what they think is a comfortable situation by distinctly uncomfortable people. Bayldon, with his initial impression of being a cosy grandad, is well placed to set that trap.

The rest of the Bayldon canon confirms that his abilities make him suited to all those genres and more. *Casino Royale* (1967), for one, made good use of his knack for portraying the pleasingly dotty professor type as he attempted to fill the role of Q in that supremely maniacal and entertaining Bond alternative. That alternative being that it was actually funny and interesting. Clearly, one of the several dozen directors involved in *Royale* at the time picked on Geoffrey as a practical substitute for Desmond Llewelyn, but in truth Bayldon's version was far better than the 'official' Q until the latter reached the age of about seventy, when his contempt and frustration with Bond became endearing and funny instead of just annoying.

In later years Bayldon, whose most recent film role was in Charles Dance's *Ladies in Lavender* (2004), has been cast more and more as the shambolic relic of a more gallant and educated time. Whether that is in TS Eliot biopic *Tom & Viv* (1994) or in the slightly less intellectual (but only slightly) *Asterix in Amerika* (1994) for which he provided the voice for the druid Getafix, the dotty old loon end of his repertoire is what is still in demand now. Television provides most of the Bayldon crust these days but that is mostly because of the vapidity of casting directors who don't know that by simply placing him in the mere vicinity of the camera they can raise the tone of their production exponentially. If Geoffrey Bayldon can't get much film work in the twenty-first century then it is because the levels of culture and taste have dipped dramatically. He is as good as he ever was and probably better.

AUTEURS:
A BLUFFER'S GUIDE

The cinema is all good fun, but when discussions across dinner tables and alehouse bars turn to film directors, you have to watch what you say. One wrong remark about Kubrick's *mise-en-scene* and you'll find yourself laughed out of the door. To help you in such daunting situations, there follows a glossary of what to say about the big directorial names in conversation and print. Use it wisely.

ANDERSON, Lindsay
The socialist Eisenstein. Had a rough time of it at school, by all accounts. 'The introverts always scream the loudest'. 'Not true! A swift roundhouse to the lower abdomen and Brian Blessed can drown out a 737!' 'A delightful piece of whimsy! Though ironically just the sort of thing the serious-minded Mr Anderson would have had little time for'.

ATTENBOROUGH, Lord Richard
An institution. Always 'the indefatigable Sir Dickie'. The professional's professional. Never approaches the cinematic wicket at half-cock, however small the job. Only a lifetime of helming big budget epics with a cast of thousands could have given him the wherewithal to convince so utterly as the avuncular dinosaur farmer in Jurassic Park. No need to explain why. When reviewing an old film of his for *The Guardian* Guide, always affect to be amazed that he was ever less than sixty years old.

BERGMAN, Ingmar
Always 'the sombre Swede'. More people have filmed humorous sketches parodying *The Seventh Seal* than have actually seen the original.

BURTON, Tim
The spindly small-town elf who made Goth respectable. The Obergruppenführer of odd. 'When he was a little boy, the circus left to join him!' The Billy Smart of the big screen. 'Does that make Jack Nicholson his Charlie Cairoli?' 'It's a thought, certainly'.

CAMERON, James
Mention his 'unmatched on-set generalship'. The De Mille *de nos jours*. He may not know one end of a camera from the other, but when he submerges Kate Winslet in a thousand gallons of saline solution, she stays submerged.

AUTEURS: A BLUFFER'S GUIDE

CARPENTER, John
The no-budget polymath. Never happier than when directing a high-octane action sequence with one hand and simultaneously playing the score on a battered old Korg with the other.

COPPOLA, Francis Ford
Always 'the bearded colossus of the sprawling American saga'. The director's director. In a wry article for *The Guardian Guide*, speculate on the relative financial and environmental costs of *Apocalypse Now* and the Vietnam war itself. 'At least Vietnam had a relatively tidy ending!' In an article on film sequels, always mention that *The Godfather Part II* showed that a sequel can improve on its progenitor. In an article on film trilogies, always 'draw a discreet veil' over *The Godfather Part III*.

CORMAN, Roger
The budget behemoth. Personally oversaw more than 2000 motion pictures from 1960 to 1965 alone, on an average budget of fifty dollars apiece. All but six are unwatchable garbage, but the achievement stands. Every great American director of the subsequent generation learned their craft filming ten nude beach stock car horror films back-to-back in five days under his aegis.

CRONENBERG, David
The Dauphin of decomposition. Make reference to his 'Freudian use of prosthetics'. Can't adapt books for toffee. His catalogue of aesthetic obsessions is best seen in the film *eXistenZ*, or alternatively by paying a visit to London's famous Trocadero centre. 'Are you suggesting his primary aesthetic obsession is a large group of sullen French teenage boys?' 'Steady on there, squire!'

FELLINI, Federico
Always 'the Master'. 'Fellini's *La Dolce Vita* marks the consummation of his "mature" style. Gone are the self-conscious neo-realist artifices, to make way for unforced allegory, intelligent social observation and a truly passionate discourse on the decadence of postwar Roman high society. At least that's what they tell me. I was too busy staring at the knockers on that smashing Swedish bird'.

FORBES, Brian
In a wry article for *The Guardian Guide*, make mocking references to Nescafe adverts.

FORD, John
Always 'the Master'. He painted the broad canvas of the American west with the meticulous brush of personal dignity. 'Of course, the awe-inspiring Monument Valley scenery is every bit as much a character in his films as John Wayne himself'. No-one knows what any of this means.

TV CREAM'S ANATOMY OF CINEMA

HITCHCOCK, Alfred

Always 'the Master'. His influence remains so all-pervasive in modern cinema it is perfectly possible to write a wry article about his oeuvre for *The Guardian Guide* without having watched a single one of his films all the way through. The director's director. It's not often remarked that out of his many cameo appearances in his own films, two-thirds were entirely accidental.

JARMAN, Derek

Scourge of the establishment. Would think nothing of making a Pig Latin musical in which Michelangelo is transported to twentieth century Bermondsey starring Bill Grundy, Christopher Biggins and *Adam Ant*. His films may not be to everyone's taste, but they provide an invaluable record of the fluctuating weight of the young Toyah Willcox. Without him, the fledgling Channel Four would have had to close down at ten o'clock on many an occasion. In a debate on censorship, lighten the tone by mentioning the 'half-mast Harold' in *Sebastiane*.

JORDAN, Neil

The controversial Irish firebrand. Roguish male punters should allude to the lasting impression made by an adolescent encounter with *Danielle Dax* in her scanties. More people have filmed humorous sketches parodying The *Crying Game* than have actually seen the original.

KUBRICK, Stanley

Always 'that bearded recluse, the shy, indefatigable Stanley Kubrick'. Perennially mistreated by his countrymen, he sought refuge from the Hollywood machine in rural England, travelling everywhere by milk float in case of terrorist attack. Only the French truly understand him.

LEAN, David

Always 'the Master'. Would think nothing of spending a fortnight on getting a three-second seascape shot just so. More fond of trains than he was of actors. 'After six months in the desert with Peter O'Toole, I can't say I'm surprised!'

LYNCH, David

The wing-commander of weird. Never happier than when filming scenes of oxygen-fuelled rape, thuggish violence and steamy lesbo-dwarf sex, yet is physically unable to say rude words out loud. Sleeps in a canoe with his top button done up.

PASOLINI, Pier Paolo

He knew better than anyone the dark, perverted heart beating at the centre of the Catholic church. Mention that, despite the contents of the 'customers' other purchases' lists on Amazon, *The 120 Days of Sodom* is an extremely moral film.

AUTEURS: A BLUFFER'S GUIDE

PECKINPAH, Sam

The viceroy of viscera. In a wry article for *The Guardian Guide*, point out that *The Wild Bunch* actually contains far less blood-letting than *Born Free*. In a debate on censorship, refer to *Straw Dogs* as 'that malevolent meisterwork' and declare the bleak Cornish landscapes to be by far the most disturbing element of the picture.

RAIMI, Sam

The sultan of splatter. In a review of his latest blockbuster, be sure to mention how far he's come since the days of nailing a camera to a plank in the woods.

REINER, Rob

In a review of *This Is Spinal Tap*, refer to it as if it were a genuine documentary, and *Spinal Tap* a real band. No one will have thought of doing this before.

ROEG, Nicholas

The insider's outsider. In a wry article for *The Guardian Guide*, either liken his editing technique to a food processor, or make a joke about Anita Pallenberg and a bottle of Matey

RUSSELL, Ken

The visual symphonist. Scourge of the establishment. His louche biopics of classical composers may have failed to impress the general public, critics and music lovers alike, but you have to admire the way he keeps making them. Only Melvyn Bragg truly understands him.

SCHLESINGER, John

During rehearsals for *Marathon Man*, to acquire the appropriate look of dishevelment Dustin Hoffman went a fortnight without sleep and hired a brace of Teamsters to beat him up with assorted plumbing. Upon his arrival at the studio, Larry Olivier looked him up and down and exclaimed 'Good heavens! I should take a taxi next time if I were you'. Thoroughly crushed by this elegant bon mot, Hoffman went into a six-week sulk that cost the production $2.1 million. 'Anecdotes that priceless are worth every penny!'

SCORSESE, Martin

The streetfighting scholar of the silver screen. As of the year 2007, he had seen every film ever made in the western world twice over.

STONE, Oliver

America's conscience. Shares a ranch with Jane Fonda. In a wry article for the *Daily Telegraph*, always remark that though his films are fundamentally flawed and as politically naive as a Channel Five documentary, they are never less than supremely entertaining slices of wham-bang folderol. Can't do slapstick.

TV CREAM'S ANATOMY OF CINEMA

TRUFFAUT, Francois
The first scholar of Hollywood. His *Cahiers du Cinema* (literally: 'Movie Jotters') raised appreciation of the humble western to the level of Shakespeare, and vice versa.

VERHOVEN, Paul
The gentleman pornographer from the Low Countries. Mention that, despite its overwhelming similarity to a Playstation shoot-'em-up focus-grouped by Norman Tebbit, *Starship Troopers* is an extremely moral film. Retrospectively praise *Showgirls* as a 'schlock masterpiece', but always with the left eyebrow prominently raised.

WATERS, John
The titan of trash. Make a joke about 'Divine' and extra-strong mints. Now, alas, thoroughly absorbed into the mainstream. 'Or is he subverting it from the inside?' 'No.'

WELLES, Orson
Always 'the Master'. Single-handedly revolutionised the cinema with *Citizen Kane*, a film that tops every all-time greatest list but which nobody really likes. 'After that, the only way was downhill, alas.' Couldn't do slapstick. His notorious crispy pancake voice-over tantrums are the stuff of legend, yet on screen you couldn't meet a nicer man.

WINNER, Michael
In a wry article for *The Guardian Guide*, scour the *Death Wish* series for scenes that feature people in restaurants and/or someone running into the back of a new car.

ZEMECKIS, Robert
The joker's joker. It's not often mentioned that *Who Framed Roger Rabbit?* was originally an all-live-action film, and Zemeckis only added the animation at the eleventh hour to detract from Bob Hoskins' bizarre accent. On the merits of *Forrest Gump*, the jury is always 'still out'. 'Cheesy flag-waver for American interventionism or scathing satire of the mentally handicapped?' 'Either way, you can't ignore it!' Actually rather good at doing slapstick.

THE LABOURS OF PUTTNAM

THE LABOURS OF PUTTNAM

In 1986 David Puttnam, *Chariots of Fire* main man and all-round British film grandee, shocked the world by upping sticks to Hollywood to become head of production at Columbia Pictures. Things looked interesting, as Puttnam, a self-confessed 'moral crusader' who thought films should be improving, responsible affairs, went toe-to-toe with the bosses of Columbia's parent company, the Coca-Cola Corporation, who tended to shut their eyes and think of the money. Sure enough, things quickly fell apart. Puttnam made enemies all over Tinseltown, who accused him of snobbery and giving his Brit chums access to studio money via the back door. Inevitably, he jumped ship before he was pushed barely two years later, his choices having lost Columbia $270,000,000, or 4 billion bottles of Coke, to put it in the home team's terms. Still, he got some Oscars out of *The Last Emperor* (1987), and made several other variously notable achievements:

■ Greenlit a version of hoary old father-son body swap comedy *Vice Versa* (1988), without realizing Columbia's sister company Tri-Star had scheduled identically-plotted Dudley Moore vehicle *Like Father, Like Son* the same year. In the end there was no need to worry: both versions bottomed out in their own time.

■ When the studios were all scrambling for their own *Romancing the Stone* knock-off, Puttnam greenlit the supernaturally tinged *Vibes* (1988), with Cyndi Lauper as a – cough – 'Small Medium at Large', thrown together with gawky table-sniffing psychic Jeff Goldblum to form the perfect 'oddball' pair for Peter Falk to enlist in tracking down some long-lost South American mystic pyramid wherein reside awesome supernatural powers. Puttnam is probably alone in harbouring fond memories of *Vibes*, or indeed any memories at all.

■ Greenlit Terry Gilliam's great but wayward fantasy *The Adventures of Baron Munchausen* (1989), the filming of which was beset by language problems, spiralling budgets and heat exhaustion in Rome, thanks to an interminable legal battle with the rights-holders to the original, who fired off endless letters, which on the surface looked like threatening legal documents but turned out to be mostly written like this: 'NOW COME ON...! GET OFF IT, *PUTTNAM!* The fact(s) is (are): COLUMBIA PICTURES... has been *deceptive, evasive, circumventive*, etc., thus maybe cunning - from Columbia's point of view - but not very smart I say... please *Mr Puttnam*... DON'T MAKE ME LAUGH! If anything, THE JOKE IS ON YOU... *NOT ME!' Points of View* were duly alerted.

■ Greenlit *Me and Him* (1989), a talking penis comedy, giving *Variety*'s headline writer the rest of the day off.

■ Did all he could in his power to resist greenlighting Columbia's one sure-fire banker, *Ghostbusters II* (1989), having publicly slagged off Bill Murray at a gala dinner soon after landing the job. As the execs ground him down, he posited a Murray-less sequel, featuring an all-black *Ghostbusters* squad, headed by Bill Cosby. Since Bill Cosby was an even bigger enemy of his, after the fallout from *Leonard Part 6* (1987), this wasn't much of an improvement. The conventional sequel finally went ahead as Dave left the building and, indeed, it's pretty poor, standing up to its older brother in much the same way Bobby Brown's flaccid theme tune does to Ray Parker Jr.'s original bouncy castle of funk. And it only made $100 million, too!

JOAN HICKSON

JOAN HICKSON

DOTTY AND DIABOLICAL IN TURNS...

When an actor becomes so closely identified with a role that the audience can hardly imagine them as anyone else, they have a problem. If they are lucky, like Jeremy Brett or Leo McKern who made the respective roles of Sherlock Holmes and Horace Rumpole their own, it happens reasonably late in life, though that has the singular drawback of obscuring their previous careers. Hardly any showing of *My Fair Lady* (1964) could have gone by in the 1980s without someone in the room remarking of the posh and youthful suitor to Eliza Doolittle, 'Blimey, it's Sherlock Holmes!' Showings of *The Omen* (1977) must have elicited the same response as regards Leo's role in that superior horror as to quite what Rumpole of the Bailey was doing in assisting in the dispatch of the antichrist. Joan Hickson became extremely famous extremely late in life as Miss Jane Marple on television, a role which Agatha Christie herself had said she knew Hickson could play well. If Margaret Rutherford is the quintessential Marple on film, Hickson has that honour on telly but because of that her phenomenal body of work in films is almost forgotten.

Having made an early start in comedy short *Trouble In Store* (1934), not the Norman Wisdom/Margaret Rutherford effort of later years it should be pointed out, Hickson fussed her way through some top class 1930s and 1940s ephemera including *The Man Who Could Work Miracles* (1936), an adaptation of an HG Wells story starring Ralph Richardson which, in common with every other adaptation of an HG Wells story, misses the point and isn't terribly good. Characters with names such as Mrs Pike, from *Don't Take It to Heart* (1944), Emmy from *Love From a Stranger* (1937), Ada from *The Trojan Brothers* (1946) and Mrs Haldane from the irresistibly titled *Celia: the Sinister Affair of Poor Aunt Nora* (1949) comfortably demonstrate that what Joan was doing was to achieve what every character actor with a mortgage wants: a niche that they can happily and skillfully fill over and over again. In her case, that niche was for fussy suburban women, whether in comedy or drama, and she was good at it too.

By the time the 1950s shrugged off the austerity of the war years only to replace them with the austerity of the peace years, Joan was being required to provide a goodly amount of fuss and nonsense in amongst the choice casts roped together for the likes of Mark Twain adaptation *The Million Pound Note* (1953) and Alec Guinness paeon to unfettered capitalism *The Card* (1952) before installing herself in some of the most successful franchises of the day. She made with the disgusted chicken's-bum-with-a-hat-on face in *Doctor In The House* (1954) and *Doctor At Sea* (1955) and *Doctor In Love* (1960) then *Carry On Nurse* (1959) before going on to take part in a further four of that series in increasingly demented and deranged roles, culminating in underwear-obsessed Mrs Dukes in *Carry On Girls* (1973).

Probably the finest example of what Joan Hickson did so well was the role of the perfectly dreadful suburban cretin of a housewife canvassed at two different points during the plot development of *Heaven's Above!* (1953). Both streams of babble end with the brilliantly modish rider, 'I'm sorry but I have my washing machine on, I'm sure you understand. Good bye!' from within a suitably terrible floral cretonne frock. The idea that someone cannot talk at the door because the machine's on a cycle seems daft now but in the early 1950s it must have seemed like the height of materialism and Hickson's character therefore suitably decadent and crass (an impression she manages to reinforce even by just the screamingly middle-class way she closes the door). It might only last a few minutes in screen time but it nicely defines everything that Peter Sellers' pontificatin' parson is railing against. Unsuccessfully, as it transpires.

One of the principal benefits of the sort of character Hickson developed a virtual monopoly over was that it was relatively timeless as a result of her being possessed of the valuable 'Wicker Gene', wherein, like Alan Wicker, she looked precisely the same age in 1940 as she did in 1970. So as she aged she did not outgrow her area of expertise, rather she grew into it. When she was pushing 70, therefore, and *One of Our Dinosaurs is Missing* (1975) or, more disturbingly, *Confessions of a Window Cleaner* (1974) came along she was able to play precisely the same character she had in *Barnacle Bill* (1958); an admirable skill.

Television came to be the place where the great character and supporting actors of the 1930s onwards came to rest and actually earn some corn after they had managed to outlive the very industry they had spent years propping up and indeed defining. Since modern producers seem to consider that character actors are either a cheap alternative to a 'proper' star or simply crowd-scene fodder happy to turn up for a decent lunch and some beer vouchers, the chances that the likes of Hickson will ever re-emerge are pretty minimal. You don't have to be Miss Marple to work that one out but you would have to be Sherlock Holmes to work out what to do about it.

THE ESSENTIAL PSYCHIATRIC ROM-COM

MORGAN: A SUITABLE CASE FOR TREATMENT (1966)

David Mercer was a young writer from Wakefield who, in the days when such a thing was still possible, wrote a play on spec for the BBC and got it produced within a year. His third, *A Suitable Case for Treatment*, very nearly didn't, but for the persuasive efforts of director Don Taylor on producer Elwyn Jones ('OK, boy, you do it, then. And it damn well better be good, or you're for it!').

It nearly lost out because it broke just about every rule in the then still-flimsy TV drama book: cut-aways to old film clips, freeze frames, dream sequences, wildlife footage and, most alien of all, Morgan Delt, a hero who went beyond the usual dramatic boundaries of acceptable eccentricity into out and out schizophrenia. *Rookery Nook* this was not. Three years later, with the zeitgeist finally starting to catch up with the disillusioned character of Morgan, a film version went into production.

During a post-divorce crack-up, the working class Morgan (David Warner) lays siege to his posh ex-wife Leonie (Vanessa Redgrave) and her smarmily hyper-bourgeois art dealer boyfriend Charles Napier (Robert Stephens) from his new home – a car parked outside their front door. Obsessed with gorillas and berated by his old-school socialist mum (Irene Handl) who 'refuses to de-Stalinise', Morgan becomes a mischievous ape, shaving a hammer and sickle into Leonie's dog, pulling a gun on Napier, blowing up Leonie's haughty mother with a smoke bomb, and finally gatecrashing Leonie and Charles's wedding reception in a gorilla suit.

Morgan doesn't go in for ponderous speeches of self-analysis – he acts his anguish out. Shambling about in a baggy Aran sweater, he's a bipolar cross between Peter Cook and Johnny Rotten, maniacally grinning like a cat that's just been made director of United Dairies one moment, howling at the walls with primate rage the next. There's a tidal wave of razor-sharp comic dialogue – Handl reminisces 'Your dad wanted to shoot the royal family, abolish marriage, and put everybody who'd been to a public school in a chain gang. He was an idealist, was your dad'.

In between, Redgrave makes no secret of which suitor she secretly prefers, Bernard Bresslaw turns up as a childlike, infinitely gullible copper for a kerbside lecture on Trotsky, Arthur Mullard plays a wrestler who helps Morgan kidnap Leonie for an abortive wilderness retreat, and Morgan gives his mum a piggyback ride across Highgate cemetery. In short, everything the makers of *Love, Actually* foolishly left out.

Mercer fell out of love with the film version, claiming that director Karel Reisz took his screenplay too far up the zany swinging comedy route. As the Beeb saw fit to evaporate the original play it's impossible to judge now, but while the film may have swapped the original's claustrophobic teleplay black studio limbo for washed-out west London locations, and removed the character of Morgan's new girlfriend to boot, it's hard to imagine original Morgan Ian Hendry besting Warner's brilliant performance. However, '1960sed-up' or not, it still has the trademark Mercer mix of bitterly sardonic humour and lonely, childlike pathos, all the while punching the viewer with love. 'Will you have love between the eyes or in the teeth?'

BERNARD BRESSLAW

BERNARD BRESSLAW

ANY ROLE PLAYED, APPLY BERNIE

When breathless critics eulogise over versatility and range, they tend to head for the comfortable shores of de Niro, Pacino or Dusty Hoffman. The man they should be looking at however, and who they would never touch lest they lose their seat by the fire at the Groucho, is literal and figurative giant of cinema Bernard Bresslaw. Regardless of what or whom he played, Bresslaw gave it his all, and his all was all good. Not for Bernie a plethora of mumbling losers or a slew of farcical gangsters for a 'career.' Bresslaw could stretch in every sense of the word. Fate has not been kind to his memory though, and it's forever as the procession of gormless nerks in the likes of the *Carry Ons* that he's known; but there's so much more to him than that.

Bresslaw's most famous roles were his thirteen entries in Gerald Thomas' comedy series, and the variety of parts he played put his cohorts in the shade. Where Sid James and Kenneth Williams rarely played beyond their type, Bernie didn't have a type other than 'funny'. In *...Cowboy* (1965) he was Little Heap, demented Red Indian chief Charles Hawtrey's sidekick; in *...Screaming* (1966) he was Sockett, the Lurch-esque butler; in *...Khyber* (1968), he was native Burpa chieftain Bungdit Din; and for *...Abroad* (1972), he was hopelessly repressed Brother Bernard.

Never a serious contender for leading status, Bresslaw struggled against being typecast as a gormless giant. His first success was as Private Popeye Popplewell in ludicrously successful sitcom *The Army Game*, a role he recreated for the film spin-off *I Only Arsked* (1958). Between that and *Carry on Cowboy*, his film credits were a decidedly mixed bunch. In *Blood of the Vampire* (1958) he took a bit part way down the bill from the man for whom swivelling eyes were one of the more subtle parts of his canon, Donald Wolfit, before having a crack at star status in *The Ugly Duckling* (1959) as Henry Jekyll, a shy misfit transformed into the suave Teddy Hyde by a secret elixir a full four years before Jerry Lewis did pretty much the same thing in *The Nutty Professor* (1963).

Post-*Cowboy* Bernie found himself in such contemporaneous fare as *Morgan: a Suitable Case for Treatment* (1966) playing a policeman and baffling Hammer sci-fi production *Moon Zero Two* (1969), a space-bound tale of prospecting and mining claims billed as the 'first space Western'. Sadly, the rest of the genre did not follow it out beyond the stratosphere. Then came Gorgo, a monster wrestler roped in to chuck Frankie Howerd (a stunt man in a bad wig) around in front of Patrick Cargill for *Up Pompeii* (1971), and a furious pub landlord who causes the eventual squashing of Harry H Corbett in Terry Gilliam's masterful 'non-Python' Python film *Jabberwocky* (1977).

Bernie launched into the 1980s in grand style with two of the most iconic fantasy films of the decade, *Krull* (1983) and *Hawk the Slayer* (1980). In both, it was the scale of his physical dimensions that bagged him the parts as, respectively, Rell the Cyclops and Gort the Giant. He brings something to both of them, but *Krull* is by far the best. Rell is a lovely character, powerful in frame but sad, lonely and resigned to a tragic fate, all of which Bresslaw manages to get across, even with the top half of his face covered in latex. Throughout his career he struggled vainly against being an excuse for the props department not to buy stilts. Small actors can get away with anything, since they can either have everyone else stand in a hole, like Alan Ladd, or themselves stand on a box, like Tom Cruise. But big actors inevitably get pointed at roles that call specifically for big people, and are then left to rest in the interim. Bresslaw never stopped working though, probably because he was so good, and the fact that he took such a spread of roles demonstrates that some casting directors were looking for more than just height. They wanted height and funny. Not an easy combination in the peculiarly pygmy world of showbusiness.

Bernard's last role was yet another diversion. He played a rabbi in what was to be his last role on the big screen before his desperately untimely death in 1993 for well-respected indie production *Leon the Pig Farmer* (1993) though his last screen credit was for television in *The Indiana Jones Chronicles* billed as 'Very Big Man'. Up to the very last he was able to show that, regardless of the challenge, give him the lines and he'd turn in a brilliant performance. Now that's a great star.

SERIAL THRILLERS!

They entertained a generation of snot-fuelled youngsters in post-war fleapits, and subsequent generations via the medium of summer holiday telly. They were responsible for shaping the landscape of mainstream Hollywood for decades to come. They routinely saved Earth from destruction in thirteen exciting episodes. They kept the exclamation mark in rude circulatory health through the world's darkest hours. They were the lovely old adventure film serials from the 1930s, 1940s and 1950s. The likes of Columbia (*Superman vs Atom Man, Captain Video: Master of the Stratosphere*), Universal (*Flash Gordon, The Green Hornet, The Phantom Creeps*) and most of all 'poverty row' outfit Republic (with a small mention for plucky Mascot), produced mile upon mile of the sort of transition-wipe-filled, microbudget slam-bang programme filler Lucas and Spielberg spent the best part of two decades trying to resurrect, with massive budgets. But the essential elements of this venerable genre's ramshackle originals, from *Spy Smasher* to *The Masked Marvel*, break down into something like the following.

FRANCHISES!

Many of the early serial successes were purloined from other sources. There are your comic strip spin-offs such as *The Batman, Buck Rogers, Captain America* and *The Green Hornet*. *Zorro* proved popular enough for eight serials, even if some, like *Zorro's Black Whip*, cheated a bit by not actually having Zorro in them at all. Best of them was *Zorro's Fighting Legion*, in which a tribe of Mexican Indians worship a little old boy in a tin hat. Zorro effects several deft escapes, including one from a burning church by swinging through a plate glass window right at the camera, and *that* much-purloined crawling-under-the-stagecoach stunt is performed for neither the first nor the last time. The most famed are surely Universal's three *Flash Gordon* adventures, which set the tone and style of the sci-fi elements in these films until well after the war, despite getting that 'look' from the remnants of 'proper' Universal films such as *Bride of Frankenstein*. Well, except perhaps the demented third installment, *Flash Gordon Conquers the Universe*, which for some reason puts half the cast in Robin Hood outfits.

PLOTS!

As basic as possible, preferably. Because of the serial's episodic structure, the first episode had to feature the set-up – hero encounters bad guy, bad guy nabs hero's girl, sticks hero in pit of snakes, etc. – with the following twelve-or-so episodes consisting of the same thing again and again, plus at least two punch-ups every week between the opposing forces to help chivvy things along. Who could ask for anything more? Even within these production line limitations, the scenarios couldn't help but get weirder and weirder, solely due to the number of them churned out, and the consequent increasing desperation to avoid repetition. Like an ever-mutating adventure story made up by two bickering boys mucking about on a patch of waste ground, the plot gets bored with itself, goes off on some bizarre tangent, sets up an ingenious trap, escapes from it in perfunctory manner, goes back to an earlier idea, stops for a bit of a punch-up, and so, haphazardly, on. Late-period Mascot entry *The Phantom Empire* was perhaps the most bizarre of them all. Gene Autry plays himself, as a singing cowboy with a radio show, who keeps getting captured by the denizens of a Futurist underground city, every week neatly escaping from the Art Deco caverns in time to do his radio show.

EFFECTS!

Howard and Theodore Lydecker are the names to conjure with here. Yes, there was that omnipresent stock footage of a palm tree in a hurricane to signify environmental catastrophe (usually brought about by the antagonist's new secret death ray), and of course Flash's time-honoured rockets with smoke coming out the back. However, for their miniscule budget, there was quite a lot of solid model work going on here. Some of the flying scenes in *Fighting Devil Dogs*, for example, are still pretty good today, and the much-loved tabletop avalanches and volcano eruptions are still top fun for the unjaded eye. Then there were the optical effects, the drawn-on-the-film death rays (best example being The Lightning's zappy ray gun on *Fighting Devil Dogs*). On the minus side, *The Batman* (1943) had, as his Batmobile, a, er… car, with a spare tyre on the back and everything.

DESIGN!

This being the age of Art Deco, or maybe just a little bit after it, sci-fi sets had a streamlined, curlicued look. A fragile, plastery sort of streamlined, curlicued look, but a streamlined, curlicued look nonetheless. This is chronologically halfway between your silent baroque era and the gubbins-festooned 1950s sci-fi heyday, so a little bit of each is what's called for. Elsewhere, labs – sorry, secret labs – were festooned with big bakelite knobs and dials. Costumes were threadbare but various, ranging from the genuinely effective (The Lightning off *Fighting Devil Dogs* had a spiked black helmet and cape combo later half-inched by Darth Vader) to the risibly camp (the denizens of *Phantom Empire's* underground city seem to be wearing campy gear pitched halfway between some modernist ballet costumes and the ever-popular 'Bob Todd in a dress' look); and don't mention *The Batman's* crumpled crepe ears, please.

MUSIC!

Strident scores were the order of the day, many penned by William Lava, who would later be the bane of Seven Arts-period Looney Tunes with his rinky-dink surf guitar. Here, however, he's in full-on overemphatic orchestral mode. No low note is parped when it can be blasted, no doom-laden run of strings left unaccompanied by portentous kettledrums. Perfect.

TV CREAM'S ANATOMY OF CINEMA

TITLES!

Where else will you find such a treasure trove of no-frills, tin-contents-describing cues to kiddie excitement? *Radar Men from the Moon! Flying Disc Man from Mars! Commando Cody: Sky Marshal of the Universe!* And best of all, *Fighting Devil Dogs!* Logical quibbles aside (re: *The Mysterious Dr Satan* – what's so mysterious about a Dr Satan? Isn't he pretty much spelling out his nefarious intentions with every signed prescription?), you just had to watch.

TECHNOLOGY!

In *Flash Gordon*, of course, you had the great Dr Zarkov, forever pulling a new device out of his laboratory just in time for Flash to use it against the advancing Mongo hordes. Needless to say, Flash had no need of a technical manual in order to operate the thing. Hardware in Serial World was made with ease of use to the fore. *The King of the Rocket Men* controlled his hi-tech jet pack with just three knobs – on/off, up/down, and fast/slow. *The Crimson Ghost* had the titular villain – a bloke dressed, for reasons never adequately explained, in ghost-train skull mask and cowl – endlessly going after an electricity-nullifying super weapon called the Cyclotrode: a sewing machine case augmented with bit of twirly tubing and some massive dials on the bottom. In *Fighting Devil Dogs*, The Lightning battled the Marines in a snazzy 'flying wing' aircraft, streamlined to a fault (though still able to do a quick vertical take-off when the need arose). And don't forget those unwieldy gun-toting robots that looked suspiciously like an old tin boiler on legs, as evinced in just about everything from *Undersea Kingdom* to *The Mysterious Dr Satan*.

DIALOGUE!

Emphatic, comic strip balloons by any other name, with a smattering of pseudo-Biblical bombastic syntax thrown in for the baddies – 'There must be some defence against it!' 'We know of none!' 'Then we must find one!' – mostly handled by George Plympton. Not the Pulitzer-winning journalist, the other one who just did this sort of thing.

CRASH!

Where would the serials be without Raymond Bernard, fitness trainer to the stars and, as Crash Corrigan, the meaty presence under many a fur costume as, for example, the Mighty Orangopiod of Mongo in *Flash Gordon: Space Soldiers*, or Bonga the gorilla in *King of Jungleland*. However, he got his big break, sans fake head, as the dashing, fit and mostly topless naval officer in *Undersea Kingdom*, handily also called Crash Corrigan, riding about with an old professor on his 'rocket submarine' (with huge bubbles coming out the back, natch), the requisite stowaway kid and two comedy idiot sailor sidekicks, to mediate in a black-cape-versus-white-cape Atlantean war. When will people learn, eh, Crash? After he retired from films, Crash set up Corriganville, a theme park along the lines of The American Adventure. 'Start the disintegrator!' Also, spare a thought for the perfectly-named Arthur Space, a prolific serial veteran whose oeuvre includes various fistfight-tastic

SERIAL THRILLERS!

bottom-drawer Republic entries such as *Government Agents vs Phantom Legion!*, *Canadian Mounties vs Atomic Invaders!* and *Panther Queen of the Kongo* (sic), where he was an evil scientist scaring folk away from his African diamond mine with giant crayfish, *Scooby Doo*-style. A job of work and no mistake.

CLIFFHANGERS!

A car goes over the cliff. The hero is inside. It smashes onto the rocks below. The end. Gasp! Of course, next week, we see the hero unshackling himself and pegging it out the car just at the last moment (presumably unseen by the first camera). Kids called it cheating, but they still came back for more. Anyway, isn't it more like a third umpire, giving another view on events? A symbol of Republic's thriftiness, that same car went over the same cliff in *King of the Rocket Men*, *King of the Forest Rangers*, *The Crimson Ghost* (twice!) and *Radar Men from the Moon*, to name but four. Other well-worn favourites included the shrinking room, the falling spiked ceiling, piloting a small boat down the ever-narrowing gap between two oncoming larger boats, and any number of burning and exploding buildings housing the bound and gagged protagonist. All immensely satisfying in their innate unsatisfactoriness, as it were.

TEN IMMORTAL SERIAL SPEECHES

1. 'Watch out for those giants! They're dangerous!' – *The Lost City* (Super Serial Productions Inc., 1935)
2. 'This is a court of law, not an optical clinic!' – *Son of Zorro* (Republic, 1947)
3. 'No doubt Vultan will compel the Earth girl to marry him. It is a habit of his.' – *Flash Gordon* (Universal, 1936)
4. 'No wonder my plans never succeed. These wild parties must stop!' – *The Spider Returns* (Columbia, 1941)
5. 'I'm mighty grateful!' 'That's all right, Jack.' 'You know who I am?' 'I should – I'm your twin brother!' 'Alan! But I thought you were killed in that plane crash in France last year!' 'So did everyone, including the news agency I reported for! That's why I became Spy Smasher, to fight the Nazis on their own ground! Now it's time to fight them here! In the United States!' – *Spy Smasher* (Republic, 1942)
6. 'We've been tricked by cleverness!' – *The Crimson Ghost* (Republic, 1946)
7. 'With his vibrator, he could bring the city to its knees!' – *Captain America* (Republic, 1944)
8. 'What you thought was butchery was really a marvellous brain operation!' – *The Galloping Ghost* (Mascot Pictures, 1931)
9. 'She doesn't hear you because she's cracked up. You understand me? Cracked up because you don't have the brains of a moron child!' – *Sky Raiders* (Universal, 1941)
10. Crimson Ghost: 'The Cyclotrode's power is irresistible! Nothing can stop it!' (Duncan Richards shoots Cyclotrode. Cyclotrode stops.) Duncan Richards: 'That stopped it, my ghostly friend!' – *The Crimson Ghost* (Republic, 1946)

GENERAL INDEX

Note: page numbers in **bold** refer to illustrations.

GENERAL INDEX

Chiari, Walter 102
Children's Film Foundation 153, 154–6
Christie, Julie 88
Christmas films 190–3
Churchill, Sarah 69
Clarke-Smith, D.A. 14–15
Cleese, John 43, 45, 78, 193
Cleveland, Carol 164
Coburn, James 131, 158, 199, 201
Cohen, Nat 65
Cole, George 39, 127
Coleman, Dabney 144
Collins, Jackie 205
Collins, Joan 22, 24, **38**, 39–40, 42, **119**, 138
Collins, Pauline 164, 193
Collins, Phil 154
Coltrane, Robbie 79
Compton Films 164
Connery, Neil 132
Connery, Sean 9, 78, 79, 132, 171, 172, 193
Connolly, Billy 78, 135
Connor, Kenneth 4, 29, 75, 97
Connor, Kevin 24
Conrad, Jess 137
Conti, Tom 203–4
Cook, Peter 43, 45, 103, 177
Cooper, George A. 45
Cooper, Tommy 75, 181, 182
Cope, Kenneth 6
Coppola, Francis Ford 209
Corbett, Harry H 5, 64, 71, 181, 219
Corbett, Ronnie 43, 132
Corman, Roger 21, 209
Cornwell, Judy 45
Cosby, Bill 160, 213
Cossins, James 26, 27
Cotton, Billy 205
Courtenay, Tom 160
Courtneidge, Cicely 147
Craig, Michael 23
Crawford, Joan 39
Crawford, Michael 15, 44, 163
Crazy Gang 92–3
credits 175
Cribbins, Bernard 154, 205
Crocker, Barry 103
Cronenberg, David 209
Crosby, Bing 39
Croucher, Brian 177
Crowden, Graham 46
Cruise, Tom 219
Cryer, Barry 137
Currie, Finlay 14, 55

Curry, Tim 63
Curtis, Dan 24
Curtis, Tony 16
Cushing, Peter 22, 23, 24, 39–40, 61–2, 75, 91, **122**, 133, 143, 165
Cuthbertson, Allan 75

Dafoe, Willem 56
Dale, Jim 4, 97, 201
Dance, Charles 207
Daniels, Bebe 69–70
Daniels, Phil 33
Daniels, William 131
Dassin, Jules 128, 129
Davies, Geoffrey 23
Davies, Sammy, Jr 130, 132, 157
Davies, Warwick 173
Davies, Windsor 7
Davis, Bette 39
Davis, Judy 104
Davis, Stringer 195
Dax, Danielle 210
Day, Doris 49, 132
Day Lewis, Daniel 171
de Carlo, Yvonne 55
de la Tour, Frances 62, **118**
De Niro, Robert 158, 219
De Palma, Brian 31, 49
Deadman, Derek 177
Delfont, Bernard 77
Deneuve, Catherine 164
Denyer, Peter 204
Dern, Laura 199
Desmonde, Jerry 94
disaster films 150–1
docudramas 137
documentaries 136–7
Donaldson, Roger 105
Donat, Robert 63
Donen, Stanley 132
Donnelly, Donal 163
Dors, Diana 24, 71, 99, 178
Dotrice, Roy 199
Douglas, Angela 6
Douglas, Jack 9
Douglas, Kirk 16, 59, 62, 175
Dreyfus, Richard 172
Drinkwater, Carol 63
Driver, Betty 94
Du Maurier, Gerald 91
Duncan, Peter 203
Dyall, Valentine 75, 138

Eaton, Shirley 4, 93
Edison, Maxwell 33
Edmunds, Dave 203
Edwards, Jimmy 70, 75, 155, 158, 181, 182
Ege, Julie 16, 45
Eggar, Samantha 61
Ekland, Britt 23
Elliot, Denholm 22, 23, 43, 45, 64, 79
Elphick, Michael 79, 203
Elstree 59, 65, 183
Emery, Dick 95
Emney, Fred 75
Essex, David 64, 203
Evans, Edith 39, 195
Ewell, Tom 35, 36, **114**

Fabulous Stains 199
Faith, Adam 203
Falk, Peter 213
Feldman, Marty 45, 46, 177
Fellini, Federico 41, 42, 209
Field, Sid 68, 94
Fielding, Fenella 5
Fields, WC 141
Finch, Jon 87
Finch, Peter 201
Finley, William 31
Finney, Albert 83, 191
Fisk, Jack 31
Flanagan, Bud 92, 93
Flemyng, Robert 165
Fletcher, Dexter 79
Flynn, Errol 161
Fonda, Jane 127, 138, 160, 211
Fonda, Peter 87
Forbes, Bryan 65, 68, 147, 209
Ford, Harrison 172, 193
Ford, John 209
Formby, Beryl 93–4
Formby, George 91, 93–4, 149, 205
Forsyth, Bruce 41, 165
Frampton, Peter 33
Francis, Freddie 23, 24, 32
Fraser, Bill 16, 70, **74**, 75–6
Fraser, Ronald 45
freebies 17
Freedonia 141
Freeman, Alan 22

GENERAL INDEX

GENERAL INDEX

GENERAL INDEX

Moore, Roger 19
More, Kenneth 39, 63, 97
Morecombe, Eric 75, 96, 145
Morley, Robert **126**, 127, 128, 129, 131, 178, 196
Moronika 141
Morris, Aubrey 175
Morris, Jonathan 25
Morrissey, Paul 177
Morse, Barry 23
Moss, Stirling 132
Mostel, Zero 15
Mower, Patrick 7
Mud 202, 204
Muggeridge, Malcolm 77–8, 173
Muir, Frank 205
Muir, Kenny 5
Mulhare, Edward 132
Mullard, Arthur 23, 145, 189, 197, 216
Murphy, Brian 37
Murphy, Geoff 106
Murray, Barbara 16
Murray, Bill 190, 213
Murray, Chic **134**, 135

Naughton, Charlie 16, 92, 93
Nazis 53, 59
Nedwell, Robin 23
Neil, Christopher 199
Neill, Sam 104, 105
Nervo, Jimmy 92, 93
New Zealand films 101, 105–7
Newley, Anthony 1, 2, 39, 41–2, **111**
Newman, Paul 92, 193
Newton John, Olivia 33, 199
Nicholas, Paul 199, 203
Nicholls, Dandy 71, 75, 132
Nichols, Peter 79, 201
Nicholson, Jack 31, 208
Nightmare on Elm Street rip-offs 53
Nilsson, Harry 32, 157, 175
Nimmo, Derek 91, 189
Niven, David 132, 193
Noone, Peter 30
Norden, Dennis 5, 92
nudists 164

O'Brien, Denis 77, 78, 79–80
O'Brien, Richard 33, 34
O'Connor, Hazel 33, **121**
Oddie, Bill 158
Ogilvy, Ian 24, 164–5
O'Hanlon, George 205
Oliver, Vic 69
Olivier, Laurence 16, 91, 159, 193, 211
O'Neill, Patrick 168, 169
Orchand, Julian 42
Oscar, Henry 149
O'Shea, John 105
O'Shea, Milo 71, 178
O'Shea, Tessie 94
O'Toole, Peter 46, 47, 48, **119**, 132, 210
Owen, Reginald 191

P

Pacino, Al 219
Paddick, Hugh 76
Palance, Jack 22, 40
Palin, Michael 78, 79, 80
Parker, Alan 34
Parker, Cecil 91
Parkins, Barbara 168
Pasolini, Pier Pablo 210
Patch, Wally 96
Peck, Gregory 84–5, **114**
Peckinpah, Sam 210
Penhaligon, Susan 61
Peppard, George 88
Percival, Lance 30, 43
period drama 138
Pertwee, Jon 5, 9, 15, 22, 62, 75, 155
Pettingell, Frank 75
Phillips, Leslie 49
Phoenix, Pat 99
Pierce, Maggie 21
Pitt, Ingrid 15, 19, 22
Plater, Alan 150
Pleasence, Donald 24–5, 26–7, **28**, 29, 61, 102–3
Pleshette, Suzanne 175
Plummer, Christopher 15
Plympton, George 222
Polansky, Roman 76, 164
Pollard, Eric 62
Porter, Nyree Dawn 24

portmanteau 20–5, 39, 138–9, 207
post-apocalyptic films 86–9
Posta, Adrienne 71
Powell, Don 204
Powell, Michael 91, 102
Powell, Robert 23, 104
Preminger, Otto 157
Presley, Elvis 35, 36
Price, Alan 40
Price, Dennis 45, 75, 76, 103, 173, 178, 181
Price, Vincent 21, 22, 24–5, 55, **112**, 164–5, 178, 179
Prince 34
public information films 139
Puddlians 199
Puttnam, David 160, 203, 213

Q

Quayle, Anna 197
Quayle, Anthony 15–16
Queen 11

R

Rafferty, Chips 101, 102
Rafferty, Chris 185
Raft, George 172
Railsback, Steve 47–8
Raimi, Sam 210
Rampling, Charlotte 23, 201
Randle, Frank 97, 99, **99–100**, 205
Rank, J. Arthur 61
Rank Organisation 44, 61–4, 80, 186
Rathbone, Basil 21
Rawle, Jeff 154
Red Triangle films 81
Redford, Robert 172, 193
Redgrave, Lynn **123**, 167, 197, 198, **200**, 201
Redgrave, Michael 20, 21, 67, 205
Redgrave, Vanessa 216
Reece, Brian 97
Reed, Carol 67
Reed, Oliver 37, 193
Reeves, Michael 164–5
Referee, The (1974) 40
Reid, Beryl 37, 68, 165
Reiner, Rob 210
Remick, Lee 84, 85
Richard, Cliff 203, 204

GENERAL INDEX

GENERAL INDEX

FILM INDEX

Note: page numbers in **bold** refer to illustrations.

FILM INDEX

FILM INDEX

FILM INDEX

FILM INDEX

Mad Max: Beyond Thunderdome (1985) 86
Magic Bow, The 68
Magic Christian, The (1969) 45, **124**, 158
Magnificent Seven Deadly Sins, The (1971) 165
Magnificent Two, The (1967) 96
Major Barbara (1941) 91
Malcolm (1986) 104–5
Malice in the Palace (1949) 141
Maltese Falcon, The (1941) 168
Man About the House (1974) 72–3
Man in Grey, The (1943) 67
Man Who Could Work Miracles, The (1936) 215
Man With Two Brains, The (1983) 83
Marathon Man 211
March or Die 59
Marie Antoinette (1938) 127
Mary Poppins (1964) 191, 193
Masquerade (1965) 75, 91
Master of Ballantrae, The (1953) 91
Me and Him (1989) 213
Mr Selkie (1979) 155
Mean Streets 48
Mechanical Rail Creep Adjuster 205
Medusa Touch, The (1978) 59
Meet Mr Lucifer (1953) 75
Melody and Romance (1937) 67
Memento (2000) 168
Memoirs of a Survivor (1981) 88
Merry Widow, The (1934) 141
Midshipman Easy 67
Million Dollar Legs (1932) 141
Million Pound Note, The (1953) 215
Mini Weekend (1967) 164
Mini-Affair, The (1967) 19
Miracle on 34th Street (1947) 192
Miranda (1948) 195
Mission: Impossible 129
Missionary, The (1982) 79
Modesty Blaise (1966) **120**, 131
Mona Lisa (1986) 79
Monster Club, The (1980) 24–5, 207
Monte Carlo or Bust (1969) 181
Montenegro (1981) 81
Moon Zero Two (1969) 219
Morgan: a Suitable Case for Treatment (1966) 83, 216–17, 219
Mouse on the Moon, The (1963) 51, 141, 195

Mouse That Roared, The (1959) 141
Mr Drake's Duck (1951) 9
Mr Horatio Knibbles (1971) 155
Mrs Brown, You've Got a Lovely Daughter (1968) 30
Mummy, The (1959) 91
Muppet Christmas Carol, The (1992) 191
Muppet Movie, The (1979) 59
Murder Ahoy (1964) 195
Murder at the Gallop (1963) 195
Murder at the Windmill (1949) 9
Murder She Said (1951) 195
Musical Mutiny (1970) 161
Mutiny on the Buses (1972) 72
My Brilliant Career (1979) 104
My Fair Lady (1964) 215
Mysterious Dr Satan, The 222

N

Naked as Nature Intended (1961) 164
Napoleon (1927) 49
National Health, The (1973) 201
Neither the Sea nor the Sand (1972) 143
Neutral Port (1940) 177
Never Mind the Quality, Feel the Width (1972) 72
Never Too Young to Rock (1975) 204
New York, New York (1977) 158
Nicholas Nickleby (1947) 149
Night and the City (1950) 9
Night of the Comet (1984) 88
Night Ferry (1977) 154
Night to Remember, A (1958) 207
Night Train to Munich (1940) 67
Night Train to Murder (1983) 96
Night Train to Terror (1985) 25
Nightingale Sang in Berkeley Square, A (1979) 177
Nightwing 83
No Mercy, No Future (1981) 81
No Sex Please, We're British (1973) 189
Nothing But the Best (1964) 43
Nuns On The Run (1990) 79
Nurse on Wheels (1963) 97, 189
Nutty Professor, The (1963) 219

O

O Lucky Man! (1970) 46
October Man, The (1947) 149
Oh, Calcutta (1972) 143, 165
Oh, Rosalinda! (1955) 153
OK Connery (1967) 132
OK Yevtushenko (1968) 130
Okay for Sound (1937) 93
Oliver! (1968) 149, 177
Omega Man, The (1971) 86–7
Omen, The (1976) 83, 84–5, **114**, 215
On the Beach (1959) 86
On the Buses (1971) 72
On a Clear Day You Can see Forever (1970) 153
On Golden Pond (1982) 60
On Her Majesty's Secret Service (1969) 172
Once Upon a Dream (1949) 68
One Hour to Zero (1976) 155
One Magic Christmas (1985) 190
One More Time (1970) 132–3
One of Our Dinosaurs is Missing (1975) 189, 215
Only Two Can Play (1962) 13
Opposite Sex, The (1956) 39
Orders are Orders (1954) 75, 181
Oscar Wilde (1960) 127
Others, The (2001) 182
Ouch! (1968) 9
Our Girl Friday (1953) 39
Out of the Blue (1980) 81
Outback (1971) 102–3
Overlanders, The (1946) 101
Overture One-Two-Five 205
Owd Bob (1938) 67
Oz (1976) 32

P

Paganini Strikes Again (1973) 155
Panther Queen of the Kongo (series) 223
Party, The 181
Passion of the Christ, The (2004) 56
Pastoral Hide-And-Seek (1974) 81
Paul Temple crime dramas 205
Peeping Tom (1960) 145
Percy's Progress 19
Peregrine Hunters, The (1977) 155
Perfect Friday (1970) 83
Peter Pan (2003) 201

FILM INDEX

FILM INDEX

FILM INDEX